Items should be returned on or before the last date shown below. Items not already requested by other borrowers may be renewed in person, in writing or by telephone. To renew, please quote the number on the barcode label. To renew online a PIN is required. This can be requested at your local library.
Renew online @ **www.dublincitypubliclibraries.ie**
Fines charged for overdue items will include postage incurred in recovery. Damage to or loss of items will be charged to the borrower.

**Leabharlanna Poiblí Chathair Bhaile Átha Cliath**
**Dublin City Public Libraries**

Dublin City
Baile Átha Cliath

Raheny Branch Tel: 8315521

| Date Due | Date Due | Date Due |
|---|---|---|
| | | 0 8 JAN 2009 |
| 2 3 APR 2008 | | |
| 2 8 JUN 2010 | | 1 2 DEC 2016 |
| 8 JAN 2019 | | |
| | | - 4 JAN 2017 |
| | | '1 2 JAN 2018 |

# Meetings
## in No Man's
## Land

# Meetings in No Man's Land

Christmas 1914 and Fraternization in the Great War

Marc Ferro, Malcolm Brown, Rémy Cazals, Olaf Mueller

*Translations by* Helen McPhail

Constable & Robinson Ltd
3 The Lanchesters
162 Fulham Palace Road
London W6 9ER
www.constablerobinson.com

First published in the UK by Constable
an imprint of Constable & Robinson Ltd, 2007
Translated from the French: *Frères des Tranchées*, published by
Edition Perrin in 2005.

Copyright Marc Ferro, Malcolm Brown, Rémy Cazals,
Olaf Mueller, 2007

The right of Malcolm Brown, Rémy Cazals, Olaf Mueller and
Marc Ferro to be identified as the authors of this work has been
asserted by them in accordance with the Copyright, Designs and
Patents Act, 1988.

Maps by Christopher Summerville

Translations © Helen McPhail, 2007

A copy of the British Library Cataloguing in Publication Data is
available from the British Library.

ISBN: 978-1-84529-513-4

Printed and bound in the EU

1 3 5 7 9 10 8 6 4 2

# Contents

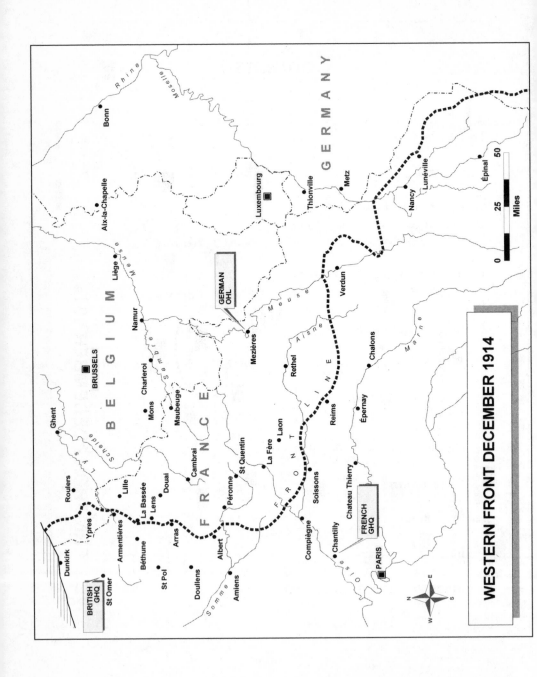

WESTERN FRONT DECEMBER 1914

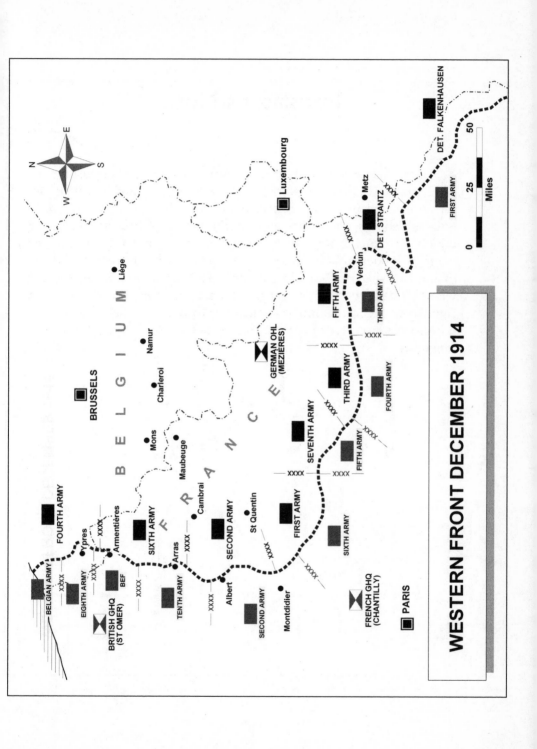

# WESTERN FRONT DECEMBER 1914

# Translator's Note

Military hierarchy is important in the incidents and relationships narrated in these chapters and French military ranks are therefore translated into their British Army equivalents. French army units are shown under their normal number or abbreviation; the initials RI indicate *Regiment d'Infanterie*, or Infantry Regiment, while BCP refers to a battalion of *Chasseurs à Pied*, the equivalent of the British Army's Light Infantry. The *Tirailleurs Sénégalais* were African troops from various French colonies, the *Zouaves* came from Algeria and the *Chasseurs d'Afrique* were light cavalry units formed to serve in Africa. The *Génie* were the French Army's Engineers.

# Introduction

That there was a truce at Christmas on the Western Front in the first winter of the First World War has become increasingly accepted in Great Britain as a historical fact. The episode was given honourable mention in the ground-breaking BBC series *The Great War* shown in the mid-1960s. It was featured briefly but memorably in both the stage and the film versions of *Oh! What a Lovely War*. Subsequently whether through radio and television programmes, newspaper and magazine articles or longer works, the story has slipped across the divide between myth and reality, seizing the imagination of many people in the process. I myself have played a part in putting a shoulder to this wheel, through the BBC Television programme *Peace in No Man's Land*, first transmitted in 1981, which I wrote and directed, and which included the filmed testimony of three former participants, and the book *Christmas Truce*, first published in 1984, of which I was co-author with Shirley Seaton.

Over time, indeed, the subject has aroused such interest that when in December 2006 a four-page anonymous letter describing the truce was put up for sale in a leading London showroom, it was given substantial coverage in the media, provoked a fierce contest at the auction and was finally knocked down for the almost incredible sum of £14,500.

There has been no parallel process, however, in France or Germany. When the original of this present volume was published by Editions Perrin of Paris in 2005, under the title *Frères de Tranchées* (literally *Brothers of the Trenches*), each copy carried a striking wrap bearing the message '*Le Dernier Tabou de 1914*': i.e. 1914's last taboo. The implication was clear; at last the story could be told – or, in France's case, it could now be *admitted*, the sub-text being that there had been something shameful about French soldiers fraternizing with their German opposites while the latter

1

were holding territory not their own, territory constituting part of
*la patrie*, the sacred soil of France. But with the admission there
was a sense of confidence that the event could now be interpreted
in a new light. No longer forgotten, or unacknowledged, as in the
old world of bitter national hostility, it could be revealed to a new
generation in a new Europe as evidence of a step forward in terms
of international understanding and reconciliation.

In Germany, the subject also remained dark for many decades,
until a distinguished journalist and author, Michael Jürgs, raised
the curtain on it with the publication of a book on the subject in
2003. Issued under the imprint of Bertelsmann of Munich and
entitled *Der Kleine Frieden im Grossen Krieg* – perhaps best translated as *The Little Peace in a Big War* – the book produced an
amazing response. Jürgs, whose researches I had the privilege of
assisting in respect of the British participation in the truce, reported
on its impact in glowing terms: 'The reception in Germany was just
overwhelming. The book received wonderful reviews in *Die Zeit*,
the *Faz* and the *Tagesspiegel* and was featured in numerous TV
programmes.' However, the most moving reactions came when the
author went on a ten-day lecture tour during which he found
himself facing, as he put it: 'mixed audiences of young and very old
people. The young ones asked question after question because their
grandfathers and great-grandfathers never talked about the Great
War and of course not about the Christmas Truce (which everybody thought to be UN-GERMAN behaviour), and the old ones
could not hide their tears when I was reading because they had in
their minds the memories of the Second World War and now, old
enough, got the message from my book; that all wars are against
humanity, against dreams, against hope, against the human race no
matter which nation.'

In the wake of such developments, it could be said that the
subject was ripe for further exploitation. This present book,
however, owes its existence not to a spread of interest among
journalists, historians or the media, but to the intuition and vision
of a young French film director, Christian Carion, a native of
northern France, who somehow stumbled across the story which
had taken place more or less on his own doorstep and saw the possibility of making a major film about it.

Previewed at the Cannes Film Festival in May 2005, his effort duly appeared on general release in December that year. But this was not, as it were, a French film with British and German elements thrown in. Its central premise was a scrupulous determination to give equal time to the three nations involved. Thus its script was cleverly devised in three languages and the film appeared in three formats under three different titles; *Joyeux Noel* in French, *Fröliche Weinachten* in German, and *Happy Christmas* in English. It was lavishly and beautifully made, set in an imaginary sector of the Western Front, with a French, a British and a German trench conveniently adjacent around a snow-bound, moonlit No Man's Land. The production deliberately combined elements of history and fantasy so as to leave no doubt as to its genre; this was a feature film, not a documentary. Indeed, in one respect at least, it was almost opera. There are genuine cases of well known opera singers from both sides performing at the front during Christmas 1914 (see Chapter 1, pp. 64–5 and Chapter 2, page 122), but not as here where we had a German tenor and a Swedish soprano, symbolically singing between the lines in the cause of peace, having earlier been shown making love behind the lines presumably in the cause of humanity. The world might be bent on self-destruction but life must go on.

Despite its bold inaccuracies and certain other liberties that had been taken with the story, I admired and approved of the film, though I have to admit it was not a great success in Great Britain; somehow we don't do war in this way. The French, however, were sufficiently proud of it to make it an official entry for an Academy Award. It won no prizes but it was a worthy, honourable and brave production which I shall long remember.

However, Carion did not make his film as best he could and leave it at that. Knowing that he was planning to play freely with the *actualité*, he decided to take what he saw as pre-emptive action. He came forward with the suggestion that a scholarly work telling the true story of Christmas 1914 should appear to coincide with the launch of his film, the book to be written by historians representing the participant nations. He would thus have done his duty to art, while the scholars could balance his work by doing their duty to history.

This is how, in brief, the present work came into existence. Four historians were invited to contribute; two French, including the distinguished Professor Marc Ferro as editor in chief, one German and one British, myself. Each was free to respond to the challenge in his own way and to develop the subject in whatever direction his knowledge and awareness took him. I saw my own role, as the historian from the country where the background to the 1914 truce had been most widely researched, as an opportunity to offer readers for whom the subject was almost totally new a straightforward step-by-step account. The intention was to make it absolutely clear that this almost incredible event really *did* take place, its validity being assured by the written experience, most of it contemporary, of genuine participants. Gratifyingly, this section was put first in the book, partly because it effectively served as an introduction to the subject overall, but mainly because it laid down the basic facts of what was undoubtedly the most significant act of fraternization in the First World War. Additionally, though I could not know this at the time of writing, it confirmed that, with the variations already discussed, Christian Carion's story was basically a true one.

With regard to my continental colleagues in this enterprise, it might perhaps be valuable for a British readership to be offered a brief introduction to their contributions. In Chapter 2, Professor Rémy Cazals offers us a mass of examples of fraternizations on the French front, effectively claiming, the 'last taboo' finally having been lifted, that now the story can really be told, and in abundance. I find myself amazed and moved, as a historian of Verdun, where truces with the enemy, even for the retrieval of the wounded, were rare in the extreme, that there was such a culture of understanding between invaders and invaded in so many areas, the human factor asserting itself against the prevailing patriotic ethos. In Chapter 3, the German scholar Olaf Mueller offers us evidence from a wide range of sources, including material illustrating the experience of the armies of less well known belligerents such as Austria–Hungary and Italy. In Chapter 4, Professor Marc Ferro focuses on the war of the Russian front, with a particular emphasis on the year 1917. He explores the challenging subject of the merging of fraternization and mutiny during a period of military and political collapse. Overall, I believe the virtue of this book is that the concept of fraternization, arguably seen for too long from a British point of view, has now, as it were, gone European, to become a subject of international significance. In brief, it has, rightly I believe, moved into a bigger league.

One effect of this advance is that it is no longer necessary to stay in the shallows of persuading people that, yes, the curious story of the festive season at the front in 1914 might sound bizarre, or crazy, or incredible, but it's not another *Christmas Carol* or a historical leg-pull, it really did take place. There will always be incredulity: there can no longer be doubt. Now we can go even deeper in and discuss the subject at a more mature level, seeing it not as a mere detail but as an essential part of the whole scene. Thus, for example, if we look at the Western Front canvas overall, it is impossible not to be aware that a conflict that began in the relatively innocent days of 1914 ended in the grimmer, harsher days of the all-out assaults of 1918. The concept of enemy in close contact with enemy, which might mean a shaking of hands in 1914, was by this time far more likely to revolve around the mutual thrusting of bayonets. No poem of that later period catches the harsh irony of this sea-change better than the famous *Strange Meeting* by Wilfred Owen in which two enemies recently caught in the destructiveness of mortal combat meet afterwards in the macabre fraternization of death. The poem includes the poignant line 'I am the enemy you killed, my friend.' Perhaps this is its most important one, in that it crystallizes the profound paradox of that chilling, memorable moment.

Lest this seem too great a leap from the earlier year to the later, I have long thought that one of the most moving conversations of Christmas Day 1914 as noted at the time was between two soldiers, a British and a German, who had struck up a genuine friendship during the hours of daylight and who as the darkness closed in sadly made their farewells. One said to the other, echoing a sentiment they both would recognize: 'Tomorrow you fight for your country. I fight for mine. Good luck!' They shook hands and went their separate ways. Might not the dilemma as evoked later by Wilfred Owen have flashed through their minds as they walked away, that either of them might become 'the enemy you killed, my friend'? It is certainly a possibility, and the same thought must have been the 'elephant in the room' during many of the fraternizations described in this book.

A relevant story told in the book *Christmas Truce* is perhaps worth repeating here. In 1914 a young man called Wilbert Berthold Paton Spencer, a former pupil of Dulwich College, volunteered and became a subaltern in the Wiltshire Regiment. His second name gives the game away; his family had German connections. In fact his mother was a German of some distinction, with among her relations the young aristocrat who would shortly become the most famous air ace of the war, Baron Manfred von Richthofen – the so-called 'Red Baron'. The greatest anxiety of Wilbert Spencer was that he might find himself meeting one of his cousins face to face in a charge. Under training at the Royal Military Academy at Sandhurst he made a point of meeting German prisoners held in a compound at nearby Camberley, vowing to meet with them again when the war was over, and subsequently had contact with other Germans briefly while taking part in the Christmas Truce. But the possibility of the 'strange meeting' his family dreaded was forever removed by his early death in the first major action of 1915. Yet the fear was there, and real.

One essential point that should be stressed in this whole context is the fact that, laudable as fraternization might seem in certain circumstances and, perhaps especially, in sentimental retrospect, there is no denying that it was basically an infringement of the established military code. Those who in 1914 argued that the British were in France to confront the enemy, not to sing carols or play football with him, were strictly correct. The point is well made in the book which has been recognised as the classic work on the subject, Tony Ashworth's *Trench Warfare 1914-1918: The Live and Let Live System*, first published in 1980:*

'Truces were usually tacit, but always unofficial and illicit. The agreement between antagonists was unspoken and expressed in certain actions – or non-actions – which were meaningful to front

---

* Macmillan 1980, reissued by Pan Books 2000: for the extract quoted see page 19.

fighters but not always to others. Truces were illegal at all times for they were neither created nor legitimated by authority but explicitly forbidden. The unofficial policy of live and let live was the antithesis of the official [policy of] kill or be killed.'

However, in the rich scriptures of this seminal work, the reader will find numerous competing texts offering examples of the doctrine followed or the doctrine waived. Thus we learn of the high-achieving 8th Division. According to its noted historians Borastan and Bax, whatever 'friendly overtures' were made by the enemy, its troops 'were in no way tempted to abandon [their] customary aggressiveness . . . or abandon their usual practice of making things consistently as uncomfortable as possible for the other side.' Yet Ashworth also has the historians of the 8th Battalion of the Royal West Kent Regiment describing a sector where 'the enemy post was within easy bombing distance of our own, and consequently neither side cared about stirring up strife, as it was apt to become unpleasant for the instigator.'*

These two quotations surely point up one of the essential factors in close encounters, such as those of the Western Front, where opposing forces could virtually see the whites of each other's eyes. Whatever the prevailing theology or the alleged justice of the causes being fought for, there is a powerful instinct for survival at work here, with many if not most of those involved, given the grim alternatives, opting instinctively to live and let live rather than kill and be killed. Julian Grenfell's famous claim in his 1915 poem *Into Battle* that, 'he is dead who will not fight/And who dies fighting has increase' might appeal to some among the *jeunesse dorée*, the gilded youth, of that phase of the war, but the average soldier would much prefer, in the words of a popular catch of the time, that 'the Bells of Hell should go ting-a-ling-a-ling' for anyone other than himself. Fraternization therefore might be, in one sense, shocking and illegal, but seen from another angle it is virtually an integral, indeed arguably a redeeming, element of war.

To revert finally to the 1914 Christmas Truce; the question is

---

* *Trench Warfare 1914-1918*; the two extracts face each other on pages 233 and 232.

often asked as to whether the episode had the slightest chance of bringing hostilities to an end. This subject is discussed at some length in Chapter 1; in spite of this, perhaps there is space here to quote the thoughts of two participants looking at the subject in long retrospect, men moved by the thought of what might have been avoided had the fighting stopped. In 1964, in a BBC radio broadcast, a former Bavarian Captain memorably stated: 'It is wonderful to think that the thought of Bethlehem brought these men together. They heard the voice of 2,000 years back, but the rulers did not hear, and so the war went on for four years, and millions of young men had to die.' A British veteran whom I interviewed about the event in 1981 speculated: 'If the truce had gone on and on, there's no telling what could have happened. It could have meant the end of the war. After all they didn't want war, and we didn't want war and it could have ended up by finishing the war altogether.'

The hard-nosed historian has to comment that there was no chance that the fighting men would be able to put down their weapons where they stood and pronounce the conflict over. Europe's house of cards had fallen and could not be put together again as though nothing had occurred. By this time, moreover, the war had gone global, so that events in one part of one sector of a rapidly expanding conflict were, in the scale of things, of strictly local significance.

Yet the validity of the dream should be respected and the story needs to be told. Fraternization might be against the rules but it can surely be claimed that some of the greatest advances in human history have taken place when the rules are broken.

And this is a book where, for once, this subject is not voices off, but centre stage and, it is hoped, treated with the seriousness it deserves.

Malcolm Brown
March 2007

# The Realities of Fraternization in the First World War

## Marc Ferro

The fighting lasted for more than four full years, from the summer of 1914 until the autumn of 1918. But the debate about the war has continued for more than eighty years. More extensively, indeed, than for the Second World War, which still has secrets to yield. On the eve of this later war, not everyone in our Western democracies was in agreement as to the principal enemy; was it Germany or was it Communism? It took many long months for all doubts to be settled on the legitimacy of the struggle against Nazism. The First World War presented no such difficulty: as it began, everyone thought they knew why they were fighting; by the end, opinion held that the war had been meaningless, that it was 'absurd'.

So it was that, fifty years later, in 1996, at Verdun, veteran French and German combatants shook each other by the hand after a moment's hesitation – and then embraced each other, full of emotion, enemy brothers from a tragedy rare in history . . . Fifty years after the end of the Second World War, did we see Nazis and Jews, Poles as well as Russians and Germans embrace each other in memory of very different nightmares? No, as we all know well. In 1966, the men of Verdun recognized once more feelings from the past, acknowledged and then repressed: the impulse to fraternize with 'the others'.

But how significant was this Great War, and what did it mean? After the initial assertion from each side that their enemy alone was responsible for the conflict came the victors' decision that the losers must bear the burden – or, rather, that Germany alone must be responsible, since the Austro-Hungarian and Ottoman Empires no longer existed. Opprobrium fell afterwards on the politicians as directors of the conflict, except where the horror of the killing could be assigned to military leaders who were incompetent or greedy for glory.

Later, the tragedy lived through by the combatants, the 'victims of History', was acknowledged without debate. After all, until the very end they too had declared war on war and had immediately gone on to kill. To this was added the disruption in their very specific solidarity, while their resentment ripened against their comrades in the rear who were having a good time when they were 'done for'. An abcess so foul that it could secrete the violence that sprang forth in the inter-war years and even more fully during the Second World War. Observation of the progress of this rage between 1914 and 1945 confirmed the link that had developed between the two world wars. As I wrote in the preface to my book *Grande Guerre* in 1969, 'I saw totalitarianism sharpen.' The fall of communism since then has enabled a widespread re-examination of this link.

It still remains difficult, however, to grasp the meaning of such an event as fraternization in a narrow trench where men could hear the breathing and dying of other men opposite and comrades alongside them. In 1914, after several months of marching and counter-marching, soldiers suddenly found themselves immobilized in improvised trenches. From one trench to another, the enemy acquired a face. This enemy was a man like you; at the slightest opportunity he drank, he joked. And soon, between one line and another, after a useless attack, across the invisible frontier came packages of chocolate or cigarettes. It was the same for the French as for the British, the Germans or the Russians. The chapters here by Malcolm Brown, Rémy Cazals and Olaf Mueller throw a clear light on the phenomenon. Christian Carion's recent film *Joyeux Noel* (2005) has added to this understanding.

Now the question can be considered; why have these fraternizations, at Christmas 1914 and later, been so little noticed or commented on, particularly in France? Censorship? Yet the mutinies of 1917 are constantly evoked, at least in anti-militaristic circles. Self-censorship? This was undoubtedly a factor, with letters to the rear not necessarily describing these brief moments except from those who were moved by a militant conscience. As for the reasons for the historians' silence, should these be sought elsewhere?

Only the Russian fraternizations have become widely known. In this case, except for 1914, the movement later became intermingled with mutinies which ended in revolution. These fraternizations were harshly repressed by the military high command, in the name of proper discipline; soldiers understood clearly that this discipline had a counter-revolutionary function and was not merely a requirement for times of actual battle. Russian soldiers managed to stop fraternizations at the launch of the great offensive of June 1917, but the echo of their repression acted as a detonator after its failure; renewed mutinies precipitated the collapse of the army despite the restraint and patriotic resurgence inspired by each enemy attack. During the negotiations at Brest-Litovsk, after October, the Russians wanted to fraternize with the enemy again – but the German high command's fear of revolutionary contagion effectively prevented it.

The combination of circumstances was different on the Western Front where there was no automatic link between fraternizations and the mutinies of April–May 1917. The latter, indeed, except in very few cases, had no revolutionary content. They were a cry of despair uttered against useless offensives by soldiers who could do no more, a formless outburst in favour of ending the fighting, even of peace. The earliest fraternizations, at Christmas 1914, could also be seen as such a formless outcry but they carried a different message. Essentially, they were a way to stop thinking about the war, to humanize it for these few moments when enemies met each other as brothers.

Although soldiers and officers thought, for a moment, that they could forget the war, the war itself had not forgotten them – and for that reason it punished them.

And as these particular fraternizations did not change the course of the war, many historians have, unwisely, ignored them. At best they have seen them as a sort of minor event, certainly a symptom of the mishaps of war, of its absurdities, but nothing more, and they have not thought them worth remembering.

The material in these pages will fill this gap.

# I

# The Christmas Truce 1914:
# The British Story

MALCOLM BROWN

Let's state the basic facts. At the first Christmas of a war that would last for over four years, and leave a long-lasting legacy of grief and dismay not only in Europe but across the world, German and British soldiers sang carols to each other, lit each other's cigarettes in the space between the trenches, exchanged souvenirs, took group photographs and even played football together. Some sort of friendly accommodation of the enemy, from cheerful waves and shouted greetings to full-scale fraternization, took place over two-thirds of the sector of the Western Front held by the British Expeditionary Force. Yet this amazingly 'Happy Christmas' took place following five months of fighting so bitter and brutal in nature, that not only had thousands of lives been lost but also the spirit of adventure and hope with which so many soldiers had gone to war had almost been destroyed. It should also be remembered that it happened against the background of a campaign of hatred and denunciation waged by the governments and the press, and endorsed by the peoples, of all the nations concerned.

The first British clash with the enemy was at Mons, in Belgium, on 23 August 1914. A second, fiercer action was fought on 26 August at Le Cateau. Thereafter, together with their French allies, the British were engaged in a prolonged withdrawal in the direction of Paris which would become notorious as the 'Retreat from Mons'. On 3 September a senior infantry officer, Major Herbert Trevor, wrote to his sister: 'War is a rotten game and none of us

13

would be sorry if it was over . . . where the fun comes I don't know.'
Similarly, although the early letters of artillery lieutenant Ralph
Blewitt to his future fiancée were full of an almost boyish antici-
pation, by 5 September – by which date the war was just one month
and one day old – he was writing to her: 'About this "Romance of
War" one hears such a lot about. Do you know anything about it?
Can't spot it here. However, I suppose it exists somewhere. . .'

The Retreat ended with the crucial battle that would become
famous in history as 'The Miracle on the Marne'. The British
played only a minor role in this great victory, of which the chief
architect was the French Commander-in-Chief, General Joffre,
who would become honoured worldwide for his achievement in
bringing the invading Germans to a halt and forcing them to go
back in the direction from which they had come. But they did not
go far. In the beautiful region of the Aisne valley the armies of the
Kaiser halted and turned to face their approaching foes. There
ensued a month-long, hard-fought battle which produced for both
sides a first taste of the kind of fighting that would soon become
the norm in Western Europe: siege warfare between opposing
forces living in trenches dug into the ground, only separated by
skeins of barbed wire and the dreaded danger-strip which would
shortly acquire the haunting name of No Man's Land.

That this really was a form of *siege* warfare was recognized by
a distinguished British officer who was there not to fight, but as
a correspondent on behalf of the British War Office to report on
the progress of the war. Colonel Ernest Swinton wrote his
dispatches for international circulation under the pseudonym of
'Eyewitness present with General Headquarters'. A soldier of long
experience, and well known as a writer and thinker on military
subjects, he soon saw the true character of the Aisne fighting,
pointing out that the Germans were using techniques which had
been specifically evolved for laying siege to the French capital. In
his report of 21 September he wrote: 'The present battle may well
last for some days more before a decision is reached, since, in
truth, it now approximates somewhat to siege warfare. The
Germans are making use of searchlights, and this fact, coupled
with their great strength in heavy artillery, leads to the supposition that they are employing material for the siege of Paris.'

Unable to use these devices as planned, as part of an urban assault, the Germans were now using them defensively in the field.

In October, however, the armies disengaged and there ensued a period of movement and counter-movement that would become known as the 'Race to the Sea'. The Germans tried to outflank the Allied forces, which immediately moved to counter them, so that the armies lurched northwards like grappling wrestlers until, almost within sight of the Channel coast, an even longer, bloodier battle was fought: the First Battle of Ypres. The result of this great effort by the French, the British and the Belgians was that the Germans gave up their attempt to force a victory in 1914. The consequence of that decision was entrenchment, with each side digging in where the fighting had stopped. Well before the year was over there were two parallel lines of trenches stretching between the North Sea coast to the Swiss border, from the Belgian seaside town of Nieuport to the French frontier town of Belfort. One English soldier and writer memorably called these trench lines 'a great livid wound that lay across Europe'. It was a wound which would bleed until 1918.

Yet it was in this new situation that the elements began to assemble which would bring about the remarkable phenomenon that would become known as the Christmas Truce.

## A Common Humanity

Romance might have been a casualty of the grim fighting of the first campaigns, but when the fighting died down, the guns fired less frequently and the opposing forces climbed down into their newly dug trenches, it was not long before men on both sides sensed a new and different atmosphere. For one thing these were not the sophisticated trenches that would later become the norm; they were often little more than scratchings in the ground that were extremely vulnerable to the excesses of the weather. And in the first winter of the war the weather was appalling. Rain and snow, accompanied by bitter cold, made life in the line miserable for both sides. One British officer wrote to his family:

'I have come to the conclusion that this damned place is a sort of second Venice. When you find a piece of dry land you think there must be some mistake. I was up to my waist in water two or three days ago – I tried taking off my shoes and socks but struck a few empty meat tins and desisted.'

A senior non-commissioned officer of a proud Territorial battalion, Colour-Quartermaster-Sergeant Robert Scott Macfie of the Liverpool Scottish, sent home the following description:

'I wish we could be photographed coming back from the trenches. I fancy we must resemble Siberian exiles rather than soldiers. We wear anything we like. We are not the least like a regiment in England, spotlessly clean, all dressed precisely alike, and every man erect, and every button in its place. We have woollen headgear, comforters that wave in the wind, gloves of various colours. We carry buckets and enamelled cups and mugs are tied to our belts with string. We do not walk erect or step out with a soldier-like stride. We slouch along, we hang our heads, march at irregular intervals in twos, threes and fours, and often a man falls gradually back, unable to keep up. Many are lame, and we would make a terribly depressing picture. Fortunately we move at night and nobody sees us.'

In such circumstances it is almost natural that enemies cease to be enemies; rather they become fellow human beings soaked by the same rain, frozen by the same frost, whitened by the same snow. Figures to be sympathized with, but also, being soldiers, to be laughed at and made fun of. Looking across at the German trenches, one young Territorial soldier summed up the attitude of many at that time:

'We hated their guts when they killed any of our friends. But otherwise we joked about them and I think they joked about us. And we thought: poor beggars; they're in the same muck as we are.'

A German officer, Rudolph Binding, recorded a practical consequence of this sympathy in his diary when in early December he noted: 'Friend and foe alike go to fetch straw from the same hayrick to protect them from the cold and rain – and never a shot is fired.' When soldiers begin to see those whom they are under orders to outwit and kill not as meaningless dots in the distance, as 'targets' for destruction, but as fellow men so close that they can hear each other talk, shout, sing, laugh, curse or scream with pain, a strange compulsion can begin to take over; they become companions in adversity, allies fighting the same grim conditions, and therefore, at a basic human level, almost friends.

## An Ancient Tradition

One of the most important British commanders at this time was Lieutenant General Sir Horace Smith-Dorrien. He was in charge of one of the two Corps which had made up the British Expeditionary Force from the beginning of hostilities. In charge of the other was Sir Douglas Haig, while the overall commander was Field Marshal Sir John French. (By this time two more corps had arrived, plus the Indian Corps, which had come straight from India, but these three were the dominant personalities at this stage of the campaign.) Smith-Dorrien had fought in the Zulu Wars in the late 1870s as well as in the South African War at the turn of the century. He had been in charge of the training of soldiers at Aldershot, the so-called 'home' of the British Army in the south of England, in the years before the war. He knew and understood the British soldier, his strengths and his gallantry, and also his weaknesses. He also had a deep knowledge of military history. He knew that one of the great temptations of the 'Tommy' if circumstances permitted was to relax his guard in relation to the enemy and to forget the purpose of the war which he was fighting. On 2 December Smith-Dorrien wrote in his diary:

'Weird stories come in from the trenches about fraternizing with the Germans. They shout to each other and offer to exchange certain articles and give certain information. In one place, by arrangement, a bottle was put out between the trenches and then they held a competition as to which could break it first. There is a danger of opposing troops becoming too friendly, but it is only too likely to happen and it happened in the Peninsula. I therefore intend to issue instructions to my Corps not to fraternize in any way with the enemy for fear one day they may be lulled into such a state of confidence as to be caught off their guard and rushed.'

In mentioning the 'Peninsula' the general was referring to what the British call the Penisular War, the long campaign in Spain between the army of the Duke of Wellington and Franco-Spanish forces during the reign of the Emperor Napoleon. There were stories from that war of French and British soldiers drawing water from the same wells, washing their muskets in the same stream, even sitting around the same campfire enjoying a game of cards. A famous British diarist of the nineteenth century, the Revd Francis Kilvert, described conversations with an old soldier named Morgan, who recalled occasions in that war when French and British sentries laid down their arms, met between their opposing lines and drank together. There were similar stories from the Crimean War, the American Civil War, the Boer War in South Africa, the Russo-Japanese War, even the Siege of Paris, where it is said the Prussians once invited the French to join them in a share-out of bottles of wine. Would this happen again, this ancient camaraderie of soldiers at war, especially at a time when the fighting had largely subsided and even the lowliest of soldiers recognized that there would not be any serious campaigning until the following spring? After all, if there was to be a natural break before the next season, why not give up trying to kill each other and have a good time? Let the war look after itself. There was no doubt the fighting would begin again, and in earnest, but for the moment why not, in the time-honoured phrase, 'live and let live'?

Smith-Dorrien was certainly right about the setting up of targets between the lines. Bisley has long been famous as the place in England where national shooting competitions are held. The *Illustrated London News* (the British equivalent of *L'Illustration*) commissioned one of its artists to make a drawing of an event which it described as 'An Anglo-German "Bisley" at the Front: a Friendly Match between the Rival Trenches'. The drawing showed, according to its caption, 'a German setting up a tin on a branch in the snow for our men to try their skill as snipers during a lull in the battle.' Ironically, the drawing appeared in the edition of the magazine published on 26 December. One can imagine the readers of this high-quality magazine being a little surprised at the bizarre antics of their representatives in the field.

One factor which helped this mood of inter-trench comradeship to grow was the presence in the German lines of many reservists who had worked in Britain until recalled to their divisions at the onset of hostilities. Most of them spoke excellent English and they were keen to maintain and show off their expertise. Many had worked as waiters in hotels and restaurants, so much so, that it was said that if a Tommy shouted: 'Waiter!' a mass of Germans would instinctively stand up in the German trenches and answer: 'Yes, sir'. Doubtless, it was thought that if they could, they would walk across with a tray and an aperitif.

Germans who had worked in Britain were eager to tell their enemies of their British connections. Captain Stockwell, a company commander in the 2nd Royal Welch Fusiliers, who were in the line near Houplines on the Franco-Belgian border, where the Saxon regiment opposite had a brewery almost in its front line, later noted in his diary: 'One Saxon, who spoke excellent English, used to climb up in some eyrie in the brewery and spend his time asking "How London was getting on?", "How was Gertie Miller and the Gaiety?", and so on. Lots of our men had blind shots at him in the dark, at which he laughed. One night I came out and called, "Who the hell are you?" At once came back the answer, "Ah, the officer – I expect I know you – I used to be head waiter at the Great Central Hotel."' A Scottish soldier, a Trooper of a Cavalry regiment, the Scots Greys, reported the following cheerful exchange between the lines: 'One day two of the Germans in the trench near ours asked if any of us came from Edinburgh and I shouted back that I did. They asked me if I knew a certain hairdresser's shop in Princes Street. They had worked there, they said. I replied that I had worked practically next door and had often been in the shop.'

Another Scottish unit, the 6th Gordon Highlanders, got into the habit of joining in singing bouts with the enemy. This was faithfully recorded in the battalion's official history: 'During the winter of 1914–15 it was not unusual for little groups of men to gather in the front trench, and there hold impromptu concerts, singing patriotic and sentimental songs. The Germans did much the same, and on calm evenings the songs from one line floated to the trenches on the other side, and were there received with applause and sometimes calls for an encore.' Certain episodes of this kind became so well known that when a young lieutenant of the 1st Hampshires, Michael Holroyd, arrived at the front just before Christmas, he was soon told of one particularly memorable example which he hastened to pass on to his parents (disguising the name of the battalion concerned by giving it an invented name; there was no Wessex Regiment in the British Army): 'There is a beautiful story of – the Wessex, say – who had a fine singer among them, whom both sides delighted to honour: so the Germans just shouted "Half time, Wessex", when desiring music, and everyone stopped firing. The songster climbed on to the parapet of the trench, and both sides joined in the chorus. If a senior officer of either side appeared, a signal was given and all hands lay doggo: then a fierce fusillade took place doing any amount of damage to the air twenty feet over the enemy's heads, and the senior officer went back delighted with his men's energy and zeal, not to say courage, in face of heavy fire. Then the concert recommenced.'

The Germans were familiar with British tunes, and were proud to show off their knowledge. On 8 December a young Tommy of the Royal Warwickshire Regiment, Private Tapp, wrote the following in his diary: 'Well the trenches have their bright side, for instance the Germans in their trenches have just sung our national anthem and then shouted "hurrah" and then several boos so then we give them a song and a cheer, sometimes one of our fellows shouts "waiter", "sausage", then sends five rounds rapid over.' The word 'sausage' was meant to be particularly demeaning, since the Germans were thought to be addicted to an especially spicy version of the sausage that was far more extreme in its taste than the English variety, and therefore believed to be particularly obnoxious. Indeed, it was not unknown for the Germans to be called by the Tommies 'sausage-eating swine'. In this case they were clearly not at all upset or fazed by the insults from the British lines. Private Tapp continued: 'The Germans seem to know who we are for they shout "Good old Warwicks" and our officer always tells us to give them a song back.' He added, prophetically: 'I think we shall we pals by Christmas.'

## A Pious Hope

As it happened, on the day before Private Tapp had written of his expectation of a friendly Christmas, the newly elected Pope, Benedict XV, publicly expressed his hope that 'in the name of the Divinity' the belligerent powers would 'cease the clang of arms while Christendom celebrates the Feast of the World's Redemption'. On the Western Front Private Tapp's expectation of camaraderie between the two sides would be realized far more fully than he could ever have thought possible. By contrast, the plea of the supreme pontiff was to fall very largely on deaf ears.

There were all sorts of difficulties in relation to this apparently reasonable and laudable proposition. The fact that for the Orthodox Churches Christmas fell on 7 January, not 25 December, added a serious complication to the possibility of any ceasefire on the Eastern Front. In the Middle and Far East the concept of a peaceful Christmas had no meaning at all in the case of Islamic Turkey (now engaged on the German side) or Japan (now fighting with the Allies). The German government did in fact accept the Pope's proposal, but only on the understanding that the other powers involved would make a similar commitment. For the western Allies this acceptance had little meaning. It was, after all, the Germans who had started hostilities and who were entrenched on other nations' territory and holding in thrall other nations' people. To cease fighting even by one day would prolong the ordeal of French and Belgian citizens under occupation, whom it was the bounden duty of the Allied forces to release as soon as possible. Writing on 13 December, one senior British staff officer, Douglas, Lord Loch, expressed himself almost in disbelief in a letter to his wife:

'What truth is there in the Pope proposing an armistice for Christmas? If true and accepted I don't think hostilities will be resumed – I don't think it ought to be accepted – We are out here for war and this cannot be mixed up with "Peace on Earth . . . good will towards men". War is a brutal and loathsome business and the soonest way to end it is to make war with guns whole heart and soul regardless of cost and regardless of all the amenities of peacetime.'

By coincidence the Pope acknowledged the failure of what he called 'our Christmas initiative' on the very date that Lord Loch wrote his letter, 13 December, admitting that it had 'not been crowned with success'.

Yet there were other elements in the wind: folk memories of ancient truces and understandings between enemies associated with Christmas seasons of long ago.

Shakespeare had famously fixed the claim for the special nature of Christmas in the first scene in his *Tragedy of Hamlet, Prince of Denmark*, in the speech of Marcellus on the battlements of Elsinore:

> *Some say that ever 'gainst that season comes*
> *Wherein our Saviour's birth is celebrated*
> *The bird of dawning singeth all night long:*
> *And then, they say, no spirit dare stir abroad,*
> *The nights are wholesome, then no planets strike,*
> *No fairy takes nor witch hath power to harm,*
> *So hallowed and so gracious is the time.*

Such was the potency of the Christmas myth, with its implicit assumption that this was not a season for wickedness and wars, that it is scarcely surprising that one or two voices raised the possibility that 'for Christmastide there will probably be something like "a truce of God" on the Western Front – if not by mutual agreement, at least by common consent'. This was the assumption of a writer in the already mentioned *Illustrated London News*, while one of Britain's leading provincial newspapers, the *Manchester Guardian*, commented on Christmas Eve:

'It will be strange indeed if one of those truces arranged tacitly by the men and winked at by the commanders does not occur tonight in order that, if possible, the Germans may find something to take the place of Christmas trees and the English something to take the place of holly in the trenches.'

In fact, there was no shortage of Christmas trees at the front that season, and if holly was possibly in short supply there was plenty of mistletoe to hand, traditionally used as a charm to win kisses from desirable ladies – indeed, published photographs of soldiers carrying mistletoe would cause some jealousy among sweethearts and wives at home, fearing that French and Belgian *mesdemoiselles* might be granting the favours which in normal circumstances they would have granted themselves. As for Christmas trees, the German authorities made it a special policy to send them to every unit in the German armed forces, even to U-boats. Additionally, the woodlands behind the lines, at this stage not turned into the ghost woods of later years, virtual moonscapes thinly populated by matchstick trees, could supply suitable branches if actual Christmas trees were lacking.

## Forces' Comforts

As if this were not enough to stir feelings of Christmas cheer, both Germany and Britain deliberately sent presents *en masse* to all their fighting men, so that they should enjoy the best possible Christmas in the circumstances. As the festive season approached countless British newspapers and magazines carried advertisements reminding their readers of the predicament of their men at the front and of their duty to give them a happy Christmas. The date of 12 December was announced as being the deadline for parcels; in the six days before that date 250,000 parcels were despatched from Britain to France and Belgium, while in the following week there were 200,000 more. Additionally two and a half million letters were sent to the fighting men in this period, while a steady stream of letters was also being sent to prisoners of war, at an estimated rate of 2,500 per day.

There were similar initiatives on the German side, supported by a countrywide campaign to send '*Liebesgaben*' – love gifts – to their champions in the field. Even the royal families on both sides participated. There were cigars from the Kaiser, while as well as a Christmas card from King George and Queen Mary all British servicemen received a special present from their daughter Princess Mary: a handsome tin box with tobacco and cigarettes, plus a pipe, or acid drops for the non-smokers. Since it was clearly the national will of both powers that their men should enjoy themselves, it is scarcely surprising that not a few men at the front on both sides would take this invitation further than was intended and settle for a Christmas of peace and goodwill rather than one of violence and animosity.

And then there was the strange case of the change in the weather. After weeks of cloud and rain, suddenly on Christmas Eve there was a hard sharp frost, the clouds dispersed and the sun shone out of a brilliant blue sky. This was 'Christmas card weather', as one ex-Tommy later described it: weather for celebrating in, for enjoying; weather that reminded people of home, and Christmases in time of peace – not weather for the rigours and hazards of war. In a matter of hours the whole aspect of the area of the trenches changed. The onset of the frost froze the mud, laced the jagged edges of ruined buildings and the barbed wire with rime, and turned the bare-branched trees into things of beauty. It had one other most welcome effect. It reduced the impact of the dismal cocktail of smells – from inadequate latrines, chloride of lime, and worst of all from the corpses of dead soldiers (following recent flurries of fighting) lying out between the lines – which by now had become the accepted, if hated, concomitant of trench life. Colour-Quartermaster-Sergeant Macfie of the Liverpool Scottish, whose unit was not in the trenches but billeted in the barns and workshops of a straggling village behind the lines, would be able to write home on Christmas Day: 'It was rather pleasant when I opened the big barn door this morning to see a typical Christmas scene – clear sharp air, and a white hoar-frost dazzling everywhere.'

Whether assisted by the frost or by the nature of the season, or by both, in many parts of the front Christmas Eve brought a sudden change of mood. Captain H G Hyslop, recently promoted to be commanding officer of the 2nd Argyll and Sutherland Highlanders, entrenched next in the line to the 2nd Royal Welch Fusiliers, recorded two contrasting events when writing in his diary under the date 24 December:

'I spent the day at Headquarters and walked over to Le Bizet with *padre* Stewart. There were a good number of our aeroplanes up, we saw seven at one time, and the Germans were shelling some of them hard. When we were returning through Houplines, the Germans put a shell or two over, and you never heard such a row as began from the civilians in the street. It was very crowded with women and children and every mother began screeching for her children to come in, and the children all screeched back, it was pandemonium let loose. This part of the town has had a bad time, so at the first sound of a shell I fancy all the inhabitants rush for the cellars.'

Then, suddenly, the whole mood changed: 'In the evening being Christmas Eve the Germans had a sing-song in their trenches, they even seemed to have a band of sorts somewhere near. One man had a fine tenor voice, and as our men could hear quite well they applauded the song, and he gave an encore.'

Meanwhile the Welshmen in the trenches next to the Argylls had had their own sing-song. Inspired by the occasion some of their number had painted the words 'Merry Christmas' on a large piece of canvas, added a doubtless unflattering drawing showing the German Emperor, Kaiser Wilhelm, and had hoisted it up in full view of the German lines. The gesture seems to have been accepted, for there was no attempt to shoot it down.

An artillery officer noted: 'About six o'clock things went positively dead; there was not a sound. Even our pet sniper went off duty.' There was an already well known phenomenon at that time known as 'the goodnight kiss'; the routine last attempt at dusk by a German sniper to achieve a killing before darkness set in. Significantly, that evening there was no 'goodnight kiss'. Such inter-trench greetings as there were would be of an altogether different variety.

Curiously, it seems that it was not until late in the day on 24 December that it occurred to the British high command that the Germans might use the festive season to mount a surprise offensive, charging the British trenches while their occupants were off their guard and hoping for a time of seasonal peace and goodwill. British Headquarters were at St Omer, some way distant from the firing lines. A signal was issued to be passed to all units with this message: 'It is thought possible that the enemy may be contemplating an attack during Christmas or New Year. Special vigilance will be maintained during this period'.

It was not until well after dark that this message was forwarded to the battalions in the front line. By this time in numerous sectors of the British front the Christmas Truce had already begun.

## Event or Non-event?

One of the standard myths about the Christmas Truce is that it was an event not acknowledged by the British authorities. It should not have happened, and therefore it did not happen. Surely this was an illegitimate gesture of which there would be no mention in the formal official records?

On the contrary, from the moment it began it found its way into official military documents. British units were under instruction to keep day-by-day 'a War Diary or Intelligence Summary', with the added instruction to 'erase the heading not required'. The following extract is from the War Diary of the 1st Battalion of the Royal Irish Rifles, dated '24.12.14 (Xmas Eve)', the words 'Intelligence Summary' having being crossed out in accordance with official orders: 'Nothing of importance happened until 8 p.m. when heralded by various jovialities from their trenches the Germans placed lamps on their parapets and commenced singing. Various remarks such as "If you English come out and talk to us – we won't fire", etc., etc., were shouted. On which our men came out and both British and Germans met halfway between their respective trenches and conversed. A good many Germans spoke English well. They were well clothed and clean shaved; good physique, rather inclining to extremes of age.'

The entry continued: 'The following reports, by OC 1/RIR [Officer Commanding 1st Royal Irish Rifles] on this curious situation – a "soldiers' truce" – were sent:

"8.30 p.m.: Germans have illuminated their trenches, are singing songs and are wishing us a Happy Xmas. Compliments are being exchanged but am nevertheless taking all military precautions."'

Perhaps the most important phrase in this report is the term 'a "soldiers' truce"'. It is evident that that ancient concept was still part of the culture of soldiers in war, and that the newspapers which had suggested that some such accommodation might occur at the Christmas season were correct in their assumptions.

The 2nd Scots Guards was another battalion which faithfully recorded what took place in its sector:

'On the night of Christmas Eve, the German trenches opposite those occupied by the battalion at Fromelles were lit up with lanterns and there were sounds of singing.

We got into conversation with the Germans who were anxious to arrange an Armistice during Christmas. A scout named F Murker went out and met a German Patrol and was given a glass of whiskey and some cigars, and a message was sent back saying that if we didn't fire at them, they would not fire at us. There was no firing during the night.'

This was only the prelude. The 2nd Scots Guards' War Diary would have much more to say about the events of the following day.

## As Told by the Tommies

Perhaps the richest source of evidence about the Christmas Truce is to be found in the mass of letters sent home by soldiers who had observed it or taken part in it. One soldier who was swift to record his impressions was Rifleman Oswald Tilley of a Territorial unit known as the London Rifle Brigade. It was in the line near Ploegsteert, just north of the Franco-Belgian border, though the Tommies, typically, made no attempt to use the Flemish pronunciation, calling it 'Plugstreet'; in fact they were in trenches on the edge of what they called 'Plusgstreet Wood', to the east of the town,

known locally, after a tiny village nearby, as Bois du Gheer. Tilley
wrote to his 'Dear father and mother' on 27 December, telling them
of the battalion's remarkable recent experiences:

> 'We have just returned from four days in the trenches – these
> have turned out to be the most extraordinary days we have spent
> out here – if not in my life. During Christmas Eve night the
> Germans started singing and showing lights and illuminated
> crosses in connection with their religious observances. Their
> singing was very good and sounded very weird.'

Tilley would also have much more to say about the following
day.

Even closer to the actual event was a senior officer in the same
battalion, Major Arthur Bates, who wrote to his sister on
Christmas Eve itself:

> 'Dearest Dorothy,
> Just a line from the trenches on Xmas Eve – a topping night
> with not much firing going on and both sides singing. It will be
> interesting to see what happens tomorrow. My orders to the
> Company is not to start firing unless the Germans do. Best love
> from your loving brother. Arthur.'

One of the best accounts of 'both side singing' at 'Plugstreet' that
evening is to be found in the reminiscences of another soldier of the
battalion, somewhat older than most of his colleagues, and, as will
be seen later (page 43), with a useful capacity to speak German,
Rifleman Graham Williams. Nightfall on Christmas Eve found him
in the front line but with his thoughts far away, back home with
his family in England:

> 'I was standing on the fire step, gazing towards the German lines
> and thinking what a very different sort of Christmas Eve this was
> from any I had experienced in the past. In the ordinary way of
> things, my father would be making Rum Punch from an old family
> recipe, which had been written out by his grandfather, and was
> kept, of all places, in the Family Bible! Earlier, after the evening

meal, we would have decorated the living rooms and hall with the traditional greenery, and would now be looking forward to wishing one another a "Happy Christmas", and toasting the occasion in the result of my father's labours. Instead of this, here was I, standing in a water-logged trench, in a muddy Flemish field, and staring out over the flat, empty and desolate countryside, with no signs of life. There had been no shooting by either side since the sniper's shot that morning, which had killed a popular young soldier in our company named Bassingham. But this was not at all unusual.

Then suddenly lights began to appear along the German parapet, which were evidently makeshift Christmas trees, adorned with lighted candles, which burnt steadily in the still, frosty air! Other sentries had, of course, seen the same thing, and quickly awoke those on duty, asleep in the shelters, to "come and see this thing, which had come to pass". Then our opponents began to sing *"Stille Nacht, Heilige Nacht"*. This was actually the first time I heard this carol, which was not then so popular in this country as it has since become. They finished their carol and we thought that we ought to retaliate in some way, so we sang "The First Nowell", and when we finished that they all began clapping; and then they struck up another favourite of theirs, *"O Tannenbaum"*. And so it went on. First the Germans would sing one of their carols and then we would sing one of ours, until when we started up "O Come All Ye Faithful" the Germans immediately joined in singing the same hymn to the Latin words *"Adeste Fideles"*. And I thought, well, this was really a most extraordinary thing – two nations both singing the same carol in the middle of a war.'

As it happened, Williams' battalion, the London Rifle Brigade, was next in line to the 1st Hampshires, the battalion of the newly arrived Lieutenant Michael Holroyd, who had been much taken with the story of the impromptu concerts of the so-called 'Wessex' Regiment. Almost certainly he must have heard something of the singing described by Williams, because that evening he wrote in a letter home: 'It is now Christmas Eve, and I've just been out with the doctor for an after-dinner stroll towards the enemy. The moon looks down upon a slightly misty, pale blue landscape, and bending my ear to the ground I can hear a faint whisper of German song wafted on the breeze from their trenches half a mile away. I shall be greatly surprised if they or we fire a shot tomorrow.'

A letter by a soldier of another battalion, Rifleman Ernest Morley of the Queen's Westminster Rifles, which was in the line some way to the south of Plugstreet, on the edge of Armentières, gives a similar high profile to musical exchanges between the lines. His account of what he elsewhere in his letter described as 'a perfect scream' begins with an attempt by the British, not, as was usually the case, by the Germans, to initiate Christmas celebrations, if not entirely in accordance with the spirit of Christian peace and goodwill:

> 'We had decided to give the Germans a Christmas present of three carols and three rifle rounds rapid. Accordingly as soon as night fell we started and the strains of "While Shepherds Watched" (beautifully rendered by the choir) arose upon the air. We finished that and paused preparatory to giving the second item on the programme. But lo! We heard answering strains from their lines. Also they started shouting across to us. Therefore we stopped any hostile operations and commenced to shout back. One of them shouted "A Merry Christmas, English. We're not shooting tonight." We yelled back a similar message and from that time until we were relieved on Boxing Day morning at 4 a.m. not a shot was fired. After this shouting had gone on for some time they stuck up a light. Not to be outdone, so did we. Then up went another. So we shoved up another. Soon the two lines looked like an illuminated fête. Opposite me they had one lamp and nine candles in a row. And we had all the candles and lights we could muster stuck on our swords [i.e. bayonets] above the parapet. At midnight we sang "God Save the King" and with the exception of the sentries turned in.'

Of the many letters surviving from that time, perhaps the most memorable was by Captain R J Armes, of the 1st Staffordshire Regiment, written on Christmas Eve itself; it is now certainly the most famous, in that it has appeared in a best-selling Christmas anthology and has been read at numerous Christmas services in recent years, even on one occasion being read in St Paul's Cathedral, London:

'I have just been through one of the most extraordinary scenes imaginable. Tonight is Xmas Eve and I came up into the trenches this evening for my tour of duty in them. Firing was going on all the time and the enemy's machine guns were at it hard, firing at us. Then about seven the firing stopped.

I was in my dugout reading a paper and the mail was being dished out. It was reported that the Germans had lighted their trenches up all along the front. We had been calling to one another for some time Xmas wishes and other things. I went out and they shouted "no shooting" and then somehow the scene became a peaceful one. All our men got out of the trenches and sat on the parapet, the Germans did the same, and they talked to one another in English and broken English. I got on the top of the trench and talked German and asked them to sing a German *Volkslied* [folk song], which they did, then our men sang quite well and each side clapped and cheered the other.

I asked a German who sang a solo to sing one of Schumann's songs, so he sang "The Two Grenadiers" splendidly. Our men were a good audience and really enjoyed his singing.

Then Pope and I walked across and held a conversation with the German officer in command. One of his men introduced us properly, he asked my name and then presented me to his officer. I gave the latter permission to bury some German dead who were lying in between us, and we agreed to have no shooting until midnight tomorrow. We talked together, ten or more Germans gathered round. I was almost in their lines within a yard or so. We saluted each other, he thanked me for permission to bury his dead, and we fixed up how many men were to do it, and that otherwise both sides must remain in their trenches.

Then we wished one another good night and a good night's rest, and a Happy Xmas and parted with a salute. I got back to the trench. The Germans sang "*Die Wacht am Rhein*", it sounded well. Then our men sang quite well "Christians

Awake", it sounded so well, and with a good night we all got back into our trenches. It was a curious scene, a lovely moonlight night, the German trenches with small lights on them. And the men on both sides gathered in groups on the parapets.

At times we heard the guns in the distance and an occasional rifle shot. I can hear them now, but about us is absolute quiet. I allowed one or two men to go out and meet a German or two halfway. They exchanged cigars, a smoke and talked. The officer I spoke to hopes we shall do the same on New Year's Day. I said, "Yes, if I am here". I felt I must sit down and write the story of this Xmas Eve before I went to lie down. Of course no precautions are relaxed, but I think they mean to play the game. All the same, I think I shall be awake all night so as to be on the safe side. It is weird to think that tomorrow night we shall be at it hard again. If one gets through this show it will be a Xmas time to live in one's memory. The German who sang had a really fine voice.

Am just off for a walk round the trenches to see all is well. Good night.'


## A Mass Fraternization

And then it was Christmas Day.

Rifleman Tilley's letter to his parents written on 27 December, already quoted for its brief description of Christmas Eve, had much more to say about what happened some hours later:

'On Christmas morning as we had practically ceased to fire at them, one of them started beckoning to us so one of our Tommies went out in front of our trenches and met him halfway amidst cheering. After a bit a few of our chaps went out to meet theirs until literally hundreds of each side were out in No Man's Land shaking hands and exchanging cigarettes, chocolate and tobacco etc.'

He then put into words a sentiment felt by countless men on both sides on that frosty winter morning:

'Just you think that while you were eating your turkey etc. I was out talking and shaking hands with the very men I had been trying to kill a few hours before. It was astonishing!'

Rifleman Morley, already quoted, had exactly the same thought when, like Tilley, he and his colleagues responded to the Germans' invitation to join them between the trenches: 'We went out and met them and had the curious pleasure of chatting with the men who had been doing their best to kill us, and we them.'

Tilley also mentioned that other key impulse behind the urge to hold a ceasefire at Christmas 1914, as already referred to in the letter by Captain Armes. For many the most important reason of all was the desire to give decent burial to their fallen comrades. The initiative, as reported by Tilley, came from the Germans:

'They arranged for one of our officers to meet one of theirs and they arranged a temporary armistice so that each side could bury the dead which lay between the trenches. Our fellows brought in five dead Germans to them and we had a joint burial service between the trenches. The German officer thanked "you English friends" for bringing them across.'

The War Diary of the 2nd Scots Guards suggested a similar mix of motives behind the ceasefire on its part of the front; friendliness on account of the season, plus a desire to give honour to the men who had died.

'Early on Xmas morning a party of Germans of 158 Regiment came over to our wire fence, and a party from our trenches went out to meet them. They appeared to be most amicable, and exchanged souvenirs, caps, stars, badges, etc. Our men gave them plum pudding which they much appreciated.

   Further down the line we were able to make arrangements to bury the dead who had been killed on December 18–19 and were still lying between the trenches. The Germans brought the bodies to a halfway line and we buried them.

   Detachments of British and Germans formed in line and a German and English Chaplain read some prayers alternately. The whole of this was done in great solemnity and reverence.'

Usually War Diaries dealt with military matters only, facts, significant details, careful assessments, but the writer of this diary, almost certainly the battalion adjutant, had no compunction on this occasion in breaking the normal rules, under the impact of the loss of some of his close comrades in a failed attack on the German lines made only a week earlier:

'It was heart-rending to see some of the chaps we knew so well, and who had started out in such good spirits on 18 December lying there dead, some with terrible wounds due to the explosive action of the high velocity bullets at short range.

Captain Taylor's body was found among them. His body was carried to the Rue Petillon where we buried him in our little cemetery. I talked to several officers and men. One officer, a middle-aged man, tall, well set-up and good looking, told me that Lieutenant Hon F Hanbury Tracey had been taken into their trenches severely wounded. He died after two days in the local Hospital and was buried in the German Cemetery at Fromelles. He also said that another young officer had been buried. He thinks this would be Lieutenant R Nugent who was reported missing. Captain Paynter [the battalion commander] gave this officer a scarf and in exchange an orderly presented him with a pair of gloves, and wished to thank him for his kindness.

Another officer, who could not speak English or French appeared to want to express his feelings, pointed to the dead and reverently said "*Les Braves*".'

A young officer of the 6th Gordon Highlanders, Second Lieutenant Arthur Pelham-Burn, took part in the burial service as described in the Scots Guards' War Diary, and was himself to become a fatality of the fighting in March 1915. In a letter home describing the event he wrote: 'It was an extraordinary and most wonderful sight. The Germans formed up on one side, the English on the other, the officers standing in front, every head bared. I think it was a sight one will never see again.'

Another significant burial took place in the area where the 2nd Battalion of the Bedfordshire Regiment was in the line. Its War Diary's account of the sequence of events noted under the date 25

December was particularly long and detailed, while also making it clear that this was a sector where the ceasefire was for one purpose only, and that there was no intention, on either side, that it should develop into a general fraternization:

'Christmas Day. "The Truce".

The following is the substance of a report forwarded by the CO [the Commanding Officer] to Brigade Headquarters.

"On the evening of 24 December 1914 at about 8 p.m. the Germans were singing in the trenches. There were numerous lights on their parapet apparently on Christmas trees. A voice shouted from their trenches and could be distinctly heard "I want to arrange to bury the dead. Will someone come out and meet me". 2nd Lieutenant de Buriatti went out with three men and met five Germans the leader of whom spoke excellent English but was not an officer. He said he had lived in Brighton and Canada. This German said they wished to bury about 24 of their dead but would not do so at night as they were afraid their artillery might open fire and they could not stop them and this would not be fair to us. No arrangement was made at the time.

This morning, the 25th, an officer and two men unarmed came out with a white flag and were met by Captain H C Jackson and asked to be permitted to bury their dead so we said we would not fire till 11.30 a.m. to give them time and this was done. My men had already buried some on night of 24/25.

It was noticed that the German trenches were strongly held, there being a large number of men sitting on the parapet during the time the bodies were buried. The men were a young lot from 19–25 years, well turned out and clean. I had given strict orders that none of my men was to go towards the enemy's lines without definite orders and that no one except those on duty were to be looking over the parapet. No Germans were to be allowed to come near our trenches. The German wire was loosely inspected and is as previously reported".'

Christmas Day was to produce a spate of accounts by soldiers of a whole range of units, reporting astonishing events happening between the British and German lines.

One of the youngest to experience the truce and to write eloquently about it was Rifleman Leslie Walkinton, a member of the well-established London Territorial battalion known as the Queen's Westminster Rifles (the battalion of the already quoted Rifleman Morley). Not many among those who had volunteered in the first heady weeks of the war found their way to France in 1914. Most became members of so-called 'New Army' battalions which would undergo months of training before being declared ready for active service; indeed, the majority would not take part in serious fighting until the Somme campaign of 1916. Walkinton, however, had filled a vacancy in a battalion and was sent to France in November because of the massive casualty count suffered by the British in the early battles. Countless men had enrolled hoping to be at the front by Christmas. He was actually *there* and proud of the fact, at, as he put it, 'the advanced age of 17'. He did not put pen to paper on Christmas Day itself, but he did the next day, and at length, knowing his parents and sisters would be eager to know how he had spent the festive season:

'My dear Father, Mother and Girls
     Just a line to let you know that I have had quite a merry Xmas and a very novel one. I have received two parcels of food and letters galore from you just lately.
     I do hope you had a very merry Xmas, if not try again on New Year's Day and write and let me know that you had a jolly time. As for me, I had a very novel, interesting, exciting and withal jovial day. Would you believe it – by mutual consent our battalion and the Germans opposite had a little armistice. We did not fire a shot all day. We met one another and had a chat halfway between the two lines of trenches and exchanged buttons, cigars and cigarettes. It was really funny to see the "hated antagonists" standing in groups, laughing and talking and shaking hands. I have got a German button and two cigars and a cigarette. One or two of them actually came from London and said they hoped to return after the war. Of course we did not talk about who was going to win or anything touchy like that. They were Saxons and were decent chaps apparently. Several had got Iron Crosses. We asked one chap what he had

done to win it and he did not seem to know. They had just heard
that the Germans had taken Buckingham Palace! Their clothes
were not very good and they seemed a bit jealous of our goatskin
coats. They had got half-Wellington boots and grey uniforms
and wore little round hats without peaks. Of course none of us
carried rifles. It was a beautiful day, the ground was white with
frost. Some of them were trying to arrange a football match, but
it did not come off. Talk about peace and goodwill – I never saw
a friendlier sight. We tried to explain to each other that we bore
no malice. One of their officers took a photo of a group of intermingled troops. They were not nearly as strong looking as
English fellows and some were much smaller even than I. I feel
much more confident about a bayonet charge now, although I
believe they usually run away before our fellows get within fifty
yards.

We are having a short rest now and I had a haircut, shave and
wash at the local barber's this afternoon.

Tons of love.

Happy New Year's. [sic]

Leslie.'

This battalion produced a number of chroniclers of the Truce.
Morley's has already been quoted. The following description is
from a diary by a soldier of the battalion whose name is unfortunately not known:

'Friday 25 Xmas Day: Freezing and a bit misty. We started
walking about behind the trench and after a bit we got out the
front and then we saw Germans doing the same thing, we waved
and they did until at last we got so close that five of us went out
to meet five of them and started exchanging keepsakes, buttons
etc. Went back for dinner and had Maconochie [a tin of
vegetables and gravy used as a standard ration in the trenches]
and Xmas pudding and potted duck. After went for a walk along
to our left towards the Rifle Brigade and on to the Lille Road.
Here I found about 200 English drawn up across it and twenty
yards further down about 300 Germans looking at each other,
in the end they all mixed up and started exchanging fags and

buttons. I got some fags, a cap badge, a button and some cigars. It seemed the weirdest thing in the world that you should be talking to the men you were trying to shoot the day before and, to crown all, a German officer got a camera and took our photos in a group. All tonight there wasn't a shot fired.'

Another battalion which took part in sustained fraternizing was the 2nd Gordon Highlanders; in fact it was their Chaplain, Revd J Esslemont Adams – also chaplain of their sister battalion, the 6th – who took a leading part in the joint burial service described by the War Diary of the 2nd Scots Guards. One of this unit's most eloquent letter-writers was Second Lieutenant Dougan Chater. He began his account of the Truce on Christmas Day itself, writing as usual to his 'Dearest Mother':

'I am writing this in the trenches in my "dug-out" – with a wood fire going and plenty of straw it is rather cosy although it is freezing hard and real Christmas weather.

I think I have seen one of the most extraordinary sights today that anyone has ever seen. About 10 o'clock this morning I was peeping over the parapet when I saw a German, waving his arms, and presently two of them got out of their trenches and came towards ours – we were just going to fire on them when we saw they had no rifles. So one of our men went out to meet them and in about two minutes the ground between the two lines of trenches was swarming with men and officers of both sides, shaking hands and wishing each other a happy Christmas. This continued for about half an hour when most of the men were ordered back to the trenches. For the rest of the day nobody has fired a shot and the men have been wandering about at will on the top of the parapet and carrying straw and firewood about in the open. This extraordinary truce has been quite impromptu – there was no previous arrangement and of course it had been decided that there was not to be any cessation of hostilities.

I went out myself and shook hands with several of their officers and men – from what I gathered most of them would be as glad to get home again as we should. We have had our bagpipes playing all day and everyone has been wandering about in the open unmolested but not of course as far as the enemy lines. The truce will probably go on until someone is foolish enough to let off his rifle – we nearly messed it up this afternoon, by one of our fellows letting off his rifle skywards by mistake but they did not seem to notice it so it did not matter.

I have been taking advantage of the truce to improve my "dug-out" which I share with D McCain the Scotch rugby international, an excellent fellow – we put on a proper roof this morning and now we have got a tiled fireplace and brushwood and straw on the floor. We leave the trenches tomorrow and I shan't be sorry as it is much too cold to be pleasant at nights.'

'On that day everyone spontaneously left their trenches and had a meeting halfway between the trenches. Germans gave us cigars and we gave them chocolate and tobacco. They seemed very pleased to see us! Some had lived in England for years, and were very bucked at airing their English again.'

Thus the brief account of Christmas Day written on 29 December by Lieutenant J A Liddell, later to win the Victoria Cross for gallantry in the air, at this time serving as an infantry officer of the 2nd Argyll and Sutherland Highlanders. His commanding officer, Captain H G Hyslop, already quoted for his description of Christmas Eve, had much to record when he wrote up his diary on the following evening.

'In the afternoon a curious thing happened, for the sniping suddenly ceased, and first one, and then two or three of the Saxons opposite came out of their trenches, then our men began to do the same, till soon the whole trench was lined with men waving and shouting to one another, presently a bolder spirit went forward a little and very soon the Germans and our men met halfway between the trenches and chattered away to each other not understanding each other in the least. Some of the Germans, however, talked English very well, and one had lived for years in Glasgow and other places. Our men gave them tobacco and knitted caps, while in exchange they got their little round military caps and some excellent cigars.

Several officers came out too from the German lines. The regiments in front of us were the 134th and 133rd of the 19th Saxon Corps. They looked very cheery but were mostly quite young and had few officers. They were asked if they really hated the English as much as was made out, but they said it was quite untrue and they were not Prussians. They seemed to think that Russia was completely done in and would trouble them no more, and some papers they gave us were full of great victories against the Russians. They were very anxious to have a football match but this could not be arranged. Altogether the men were out of their trenches for nearly two hours, but we parted before dark and the last words of a German officer were: "Well, it will be war again tomorrow".'

One of the best chroniclers of the Truce was the Medical Officer of Hyslop's battalion, Lieutenant Frederick Chandler. His letter written in the early hours of 1 January confirms and amplifies his commanding officer's account.

'In the afternoon [of Christmas Day] the Germans and our men shouted to each other and arranged an unofficial armistice – they got out of the trenches and met halfway and hobnobbed with each other, exchanged souvenirs and had drinks: they rolled a couple of barrels of beer over to the Welsh lines: and in one part two German officers came out with an orderly carrying glasses and two large bottles of Lager beer: they met one of our officers, shook hands, drank together and then decided they would have to call their men in: another officer – Stewart, had a box of good cigars given him: about four o'clock whistles blew and the men were called in but in our own lines and with the Germans opposite not a shot was fired the whole evening – everything was perfectly still and it was a bright frosty night – you can't imagine how delicious was that stillness and calm: for two months I have not had a quiet half hour and, oh, one does get sick of the crack of rifles. In other parts of the line they have no peace. They were Saxons opposite us, and they are good sorts I believe, they have no desire to be fighting the English. It is the beastly Prussians who have done all the harm.'

This was his comparatively brief report at the time. A year later he published a much longer account of his experiences of Christmas Day 1914, in an article printed in the *London Hospital Gazette* for December 1915. His day had begun with his taking advantage of what he assumed might be a quiet season to go out and 'get some photographs', since at that time cameras were not absolutely forbidden as they were later. The day at this time being misty, he went up the road parallel to the fire trench walking in the open.

'Several bullets came unpleasantly close, and I began to regret not having braved the slush of the communication trench, but as our Commanding Officer used to say, expressing the views of the men on the matter: "If you go up the communication trench you are bound to get your feet wet, whereas the worst that can happen to you if you go along the top is to get shot." However, I waited a moment, and as no bullets came particularly near, I felt reassured that the mist did really hide me, so proceeded.'

About to return by the safer if muddier route, he made a discovery of a kind that would become increasingly familiar as the war went on.

'Before getting into the trench I came across a couple of German boots sticking out of the side of the road; attached to the boots were a couple of German legs. I called attention to the legs, and investigation showed the rest of the gentleman imperfectly covered with earth; so he was propped into a more comfortable grave – a proceeding which delights the heart of every true British soldier. Some buttons were removed to remember him by, and he was snugly covered with earth and patted down. "Rest in peace, poor Fritz", thought I. "It is not you or your like who have caused this; there is not a combatant soldier in any of the combatant armies who would not make peace tomorrow; you have died bravely; and instead of Christmas in the warmth of the home you love, with your lager beer, your pipe, and your buxom haus-frau, and perhaps your little children, you lie stiff and cold with your feet sticking out of the roadside – this wretched, bullet-swept, shell-scarred roadside." I had no feeling of hatred in my heart at this time; later I was to see the effects of German asphyxiating gas, and this changed everything; but even now I have a slightly tender corner in my heart for the Saxons, and these were Saxons opposite us now.'

This was for Chandler the first moving episode of the day, shared by him and one or two Tommies; the second was shared by the whole battalion, his account adding some more choice details to the diary entry of his commanding officer.

'Many shots were exchanged that morning, but as the afternoon approached a most amazing thing occurred. All firing ceased and shouts were exchanged. Then came a tentative scrambling of a few men over the parapet, and a few Germans over theirs; then a scramble of dozens, then of scores of men of both sides; all met in the middle and talked and stared and exchanged cap comforters for the grey German trench cap, and bully beef for cigars. A German officer came out with an orderly with beer and glasses, little S—, our baby subaltern, was presented with a box of cigars. Two barrels of beer were rolled over to the regiment on our left, all was good fellowship and a pathetic friendliness. As dusk came on, and it came early, the men had to be called in. Shrill whistle blasts were heard everywhere and the land of death between the trenches was again deserted, and save for the grim barbed wire entanglements nothing but hard frozen mud and ice. But the men had made a compact. Not a single shot was fired, and that evening was one of the most beautiful, clear, starry, frosty nights that ever I saw, and there reigned a delectable entrancing quiet, the first quiet I had heard for months. Musical instruments were played and songs and carols were sung on both sides and Christmas dinners eaten. Our dinner was a memorable one: soup, a haggis sent from home, whisky, some sort of old hen, white wine, a Christmas pudding full of surprises with rum sauce, a savoury of sardines, port, an excellent cigar, and café au rum. This was luxury; later we learned to do ourselves well always, but we were only learning war in those days.'

## The Christmas Spirit

If dealing decently with the dead was an important motive behind the truce the Christmas spirit provided another. 'It doesn't seem right to be killing each other at Xmas time,' Private Tapp noted in his diary. Officers as well as men succumbed to the festive mood. Captain George Paynter, CO of the 2nd Scots Guards, having attended the burial service of their dead comrades, decided to join the festivities. He strode out to join a mixed group of British and Germans and with the cry: 'Well, my lads, a Merry Christmas to you! This is damned comic, isn't it?' proceeded to hand round a bottle of best rum which, one participant recorded, was: 'polished off before you could say knife'. It is hardly surprising that one soldier writing home would write of the day that: 'It would have made a good chapter in Dickens's *Christmas Carol.*'

Details which seem almost ludicrous enrich the story. A British Tommy met his German barber from High Holborn, London, and had a haircut between the lines. A German who had raided an abandoned house strutted about wearing a blouse, skirt, and top hat and sporting an umbrella. A Tommy who had found an old bicycle with bent wheels cavorted cheerfully around among the shell holes. For Rifleman Graham Williams of the London Rifle Brigade, out between the lines making good use of his German as a much valued unofficial interpreter, the day brought a particularly memorable, if almost comic, encounter:

'I was walking along when a German came up to me, and he actually greeted me with the words: "Wotcher cock, how's London?" I said to him: "You speak like a Londoner." And he said: "Well, I am a Londoner." I said: "What on earth are you doing in the German Army?" "Well," he said, "I'm a German, I'm a German Londoner," and apparently he'd been born in Germany, and had immediately afterwards gone to England with his parents, and they had a small business in the East End somewhere, and he'd been brought up in England and gone to school in England.'

Wherever there was fraternization there was much cheerful badinage and laughter, but the most striking effect of the day, for many, was the overall silence. As one soldier, Sergeant Self of the West Yorkshires, put it: 'There were no planes overhead, no observation balloons, no bombs, no rifle fire, therefore no snipers, just an occasional lark overhead.'

The absence of the sounds of war could, however, seem strangely disconcerting. Private Tapp commented: 'I miss the sounds of the shots going over, it is like a clock that has stopped ticking.'

## Football With The Enemy

One activity which, where it took place, could be guaranteed to break the unfamiliar silence with shouts and cheers was the playing of football. 'Footer', as the British often called it, was hugely popular then as now, in Germany as much as in Britain. It was almost automatic that when soldiers had time to kill, rather than kill each other, someone would suggest they should have a game of football. Behind the lines matches were constantly taking place. There were even stories of games being played by soldiers on the Somme front with shells passing over their heads. One contemporary report referred to 'the footballs which so many privates carry tied to their knapsacks'. Nor was football only enjoyed by the ordinary Tommy. On 22 December Major John Charteris, intelligence officer to General Sir Douglas Haig, having nothing to do 'turned out to play football for the Staff against a team of Cavalry. The Prince of Wales was playing . . .'

It was therefore entirely natural that as the peaceful atmosphere spread on Christmas Day the idea of playing football should be raised; the suggestion has been referred to in two accounts already quoted. However, against the general assumption – if British people refer to the Christmas Truce at all, they tend to think of it as 'the football match' – there was not one big international 'England v Germany' fixture, an impromptu European Cup game with eleven players on each side, a referee, and goalposts or their equivalent somehow magicked out of the ground. Rather there were a number of random, swiftly arranged matches, sometimes with caps for goals and scores kept (*The Times* reported a game won by the Germans with a score of 3–2, though it did not name the units that took part), while elsewhere they were just general *mêlées* with anybody who wanted to join in having a kick at the ball. Here and there genuine leather balls were produced, though at least one game, which the British claim to have won, was played with a tin can. A report by a German lieutenant explains why such games were possible: he wrote: 'We marked the goals with our caps. Teams were quickly established for a match on the frozen mud, and the Fritzes beat the Tommies 3–2.' In short, it was the sudden Christmas frost, making ground which would otherwise have been too soft to play on reasonably firm and hard, that made it possible that the attempt could be made. On the whole, however, far more games were proposed than ever took place.

Not everybody approved. One officer, ordered to prepare a more usable pitch for a possible future game by filling in shell holes, angrily refused to comply. This must surely be a very early case of a failure to create a level playing field. The proposed fixture was never played. Quite apart from any other cause, the return of the usual drenching rain in the days after Christmas made any such match unthinkable.

## The Necessary Distance

In the majority of cases, great care was taken not to let the enemy approach too closely to the British trenches. There were instances of German officers being deliberately 'seen off' – instructed to depart – for showing signs of being over-inquisitive. In other cases a more relaxed view was taken. Among the fraternizing battalions were units of the Meerut Division of the Indian Army (the Indians were the first troops from the British Empire to see action on the Western Front). Captain P Mortimer, attached to the Division as a Requisitioning Officer, observed the proceedings and described them in a diary entry written on the following day.

'The enemy came out of their trenches yesterday (being Christmas Day) simultaneously with our fellows – who met the Germans on neutral ground between the two trenches and exchanged the compliments of the season, presents, smokes and drinks – some of our fellows going into the German lines and some of the Germans strolling into ours – the whole affair was particularly friendly and not a shot was fired in our Brigade throughout the day. The enemy apparently initiated the move by shouting across to our fellows and then popping their heads out of their trenches and finally getting out of them altogether.'

Yet approaching too close to enemy trenches could have unfortunate consequences. Private George Ashurst of the 2nd Lancashire Fusiliers described the case of a solitary German who came out with a white flag high above his head.

'Having come about halfway to our lines, he suddenly stopped and waited. Then one of our men was seen to go out and meet him to bring him in to our lines. Unfortunately he had not been blindfolded, and consequently he had to be made prisoner of war. He protested and was awfully upset about it, but he had seen the position behind our lines and that must be kept from the enemy at all costs.'

That there were such variations of practice and behaviour points to one of the most significant aspects of the truce. It was not organized, nor, as it might be assumed, contagious, with units catching the spark from their neighbours. Rather it was the spontaneous product of a series of local initiatives. Thus peaceable areas could be interlaced with 'business as usual' zones where hostilities continued. This could have tragic results. One sergeant of the Monmouthshires crossing No Man's Land to offer cigarettes to a friendly German regiment was shot by a sniper from a regiment not involved in a ceasefire. He was officially described as 'Killed in Action', his 'action' being the distinctly unmilitary one of attempting to carry Woodbines to the enemy. The Germans sent across an apology.

This raises an important question. How extensive was the Christmas Truce in the British sector (at that stage not much more than thirty kilometres)? It would seem that there were sporadic examples of understandings with the enemy – ranging from friendly greetings between the lines to out and out fraternization – along about two-thirds of the area occupied by the British. Elsewhere, and, as already indicated, at points within the trucing areas, hostilities continued as usual. Thus in contrast to the accounts of men who enjoyed their Christmas, it is important to look at the experience of a soldier who obviously did not. The following extracts are from the diary of Gunner B C  Myatt, of the Royal Field Artillery, who clearly had no idea that his fellow soldiers only a few kilometres away were celebrating with their enemies rather than fighting them.

'Dec 22nd
  Raining and sleet all night and all day and terrible cold. I feel proper fed up, bad with cold in the head. I pray for this to finish, bags of shrapnel over and around us today.

Dec 23rd
  Snowing all night, cold to the marrow, and a heavy bombardment going on all day. Hard at it, no advance on either side, only a heavy artillery duel in which we came off best. Towards evening it got heavy firing, the French are too mad. The flashes from their guns can be seen, they don't take enough cover and they draw the fire.

Dec 24th
  It is now Christmas Eve. Not a very happy one either, a hot bombardment all night. We were firing at intervals all night, very cold, a bit of a frost going to snow again, hope to goodness it soon finishes, proper fed up.

Christmas Day. Not much firing all night but an hour's bombardment this morning, for a salute I suppose. We had a heavy frost all night which made the ground hard and better to get about. It came over very misty so we played the French batteries at a game of football, and beat them easy. A friendly game. We got a Christmas card from the King and Queen, a good souvenir, and also got tobacco, cigarettes and plum puddings from the [news]paper funds, but we had biscuits and bully beef for dinner, could have done with some fresh meat, never mind, roll on. Let's hope the next one ain't out here. Am wondering what the dear ones are doing at home, we had a bit of a singsong in the evening. Nothing to drink.'

Christmas Day had provided a remarkable experience for those fortunate enough to be able to share in it. But this was the darkest season of the year with the shortest days and as the bright blue of the sky turned to grey and the shadows lengthened it was obvious that the curtain would soon come down on this unforgettable, all-too-brief drama. It was time to say farewell.

Rifleman Eade of the 3rd Rifle Brigade had enjoyed a conversation with a German who had lived in London and who spoke good English. As they parted the German said: 'Today we have peace. Tomorrow you fight for your country. I fight for mine. Good luck!'

Captain Armes, who had written his long letter the night before describing the onset of the truce, had spent much of the day out between the lines. He told his wife: 'I left our friends on Xmas Day in a quiet mood. I stood upon the parapet and had a final look round and not a shot was fired.'

A member of the Queen's Westminster Rifles, P H Jones, noted that evening in his diary: 'Altogether we had a great day with our enemies and parted with much handshaking and mutual goodwill.'

A junior infantry officer, Second Lieutenant A P Sinkinson, in a letter later published in a national newspaper, described how in the friendly atmosphere of Christmas Day he had remembered the words of the prime minister in a speech calling for the utmost effort to bring the Germans to a humiliating defeat: 'As I walked slowly back to the trenches I thought of Mr Asquith's sentence about not sheathing the sword until the enemy be finally crushed. It is all very well for Englishmen living at home to talk in flowing periods, but when you are out here you begin to realize that sustained hatred is impossible.'

Not surprisingly most fraternizers on both sides came from infantry units; entrenchment had made them near neighbours and when the Christmas spirit took over they were only yards away. It was easy to respond in such circumstances.

The 26th provided an opportunity for men from other branches of the army to join the celebrations.

Second Lieutenant John Wedderburn-Maxwell, a gunnery officer, had come up to the trenches from the artillery lines late on the 25th. There he had heard, to his astonishment, of what had been taking place just a mile or two away from where his battery was stationed. Writing to his father, he told him that the accounts of his fellow officers had left him 'terribly jealous of having missed such an experience', and determined to make up for it at the earliest opportunity. He achieved this on the following afternoon, armed with a tin of cigarettes and accompanied by a Corporal from his battery.

'I made my way through the barbed wire in front of the trenches and when about halfway across waved to some of the Germans to come over, upon which two came to meet us and four more rolled up later. One was a German American who could talk fair English. I gave them cigarettes and was given a box of tobacco which I will send home as a souvenir of what is probably the most extraordinary event of the whole war – a soldier's truce without any higher sanction by officers and generals, with firing going on to the right and rather further away to the left. We strolled up and down for about half an hour, shook hands, said good-bye, saluted and returned to our lines.'

Another artillery officer who heard of the truce and was determined to experience it himself was Lieutenant Cyril Drummond. He and his telephonist went down to the front on the morning of the 26th at a point just to the north of Plugstreet Wood. The scene confronting them was such that it reminded him of the kind of exhibition that might be staged at London's Earls Court.

'There were two sets of trenches only a few yards apart, and yet there were soldiers, both British and German, standing on top of them, digging or repairing the trench in some way, without ever shooting at each other. It was an extraordinary situation. And so my telephonist and I walked down the sunken road in full view of everybody in Germany, with no one taking notice of us.'

He got into conversation with some of the Germans: 'They were very nice fellows to look at, and one of them said: "We don't want to kill you and you don't want to kill us. So why shoot?" I lined them all up and took a photograph.' (See illustration 3.)

## The Truce by Hearsay

Wedderburn-Maxwell and Drummond were fortunate in being able to hear news of the truce so quickly and indulge their curiosity almost at once. Men of innumerable other units, particularly ones based at a distance, either never heard of the truce at all or only some time after, by hearsay. This was certainly the case in the battery to which Royal Field Artillery officer Lieutenant Ralph Blewitt, who had mourned the death of the 'Romance of War' back in September, was attached. His second-hand, but generous and thoughtful, account of the episode was written on New Year's Day 1915, in a letter to his future wife; it should be noted that in his letters he frequently referred to the Germans as 'Deutsch' or, even as 'Dutchmen'.

'There is a fellow in the Welch who was posted from another part of the line. They had a terrific jolly on Xmas Day with the Germans. At dawn all the Bosches were seen sitting on the parapet of their trenches yelling to us to come out, after a Deutsch officer had walked out and spoken to a British one all the men got up and walked half up to the German lines where there was great handshaking and merry Xmasing. The Dutchmen gave our folk cake and cigars, and they had a football match with a sack filled with straw. That night they all sang carols together and next day (Boxing Day) it was the same till some officer came and said they'd had enough now so both sides retired to their trenches and started off sniping with increased vigour. The fellow I met had made a great pal with a Private of theirs who had been at Oxford as an undergraduate and was a professor at Munich. They each sent New Year's cards to each other's wives and the Dutchman gave our fellow a box of cigars!! They were all fed up with the war and wanted to know when we were going to give in! He (the

Dutchman) had great tales of Russian and naval victories which I suppose they stuff them with. Our fellow told us he didn't disillusion him as he didn't like to hurt his feelings.

It is typical rather of the feelings of the fighters on both sides as opposed to "hatred" and muck one reads about in the papers. Of course one can imagine if it wasn't stopped jolly quick I suppose it would spread all down the line and the armies would cease to fight at all. Then perhaps the O. C. Brigade and the haters and so forth would come out and have a scrap. It's a funny show, this!'

## Reaction From Above

On the evening of 26 December General Sir Horace Smith-Dorrien went down to the trenches. He was not pleased by what he found. He immediately circulated a stern memorandum which stated that he was 'struck by the apathy of everything I saw', excepting only the field companies of the Royal Engineers 'for whom I have nothing but praise'. Fortunately, he did not come across any cases of actual fraternization while at the front. When he returned to his headquarters, however, he was given news that confirmed his worst fears. He wrote in some heat:

'I was shown a report from one section of how, on Christmas Day, a friendly gathering had taken place on the neutral ground between the trenches, recounting that many officers had taken part in it. This is only illustrative of the apathetic state we are gradually sinking into, apart also from illustrating that any orders I issue on the subject are useless, for I have issued the strictest orders that on no account is intercourse to be allowed between the opposing troops. To finish this war quickly, we must keep up the fighting spirit and do all we can to discourage friendly intercourse.

I am calling for particulars as to names of officers and units who took part in this Christmas gathering, with a view to disciplinary action.'

Yet, curious as it might seem, no one was court-martialled following the Christmas Truce. Smith-Dorrien boiled with righteous indignation, but not a few other senior officers took a more relaxed view. A 'rest from bullets', as one of their number put it, allowed the troops to work above ground while improving their often inadequate trenches. Both sides appreciated the opportunity. A senior divisional commander, Major General Thompson Capper, saw clearly that a time of relative calm would allow the soldiers on whom the war depended a breathing-space in which they could improve their inadequate trenches – a courtesy, it should be noted, which was allowed to both sides. In a carefully argued report on operations in his sector for the period 22–29 December, he wrote: 'Recently, I have purposely kept things rather quiet, as so much work has had to be done at close range from the enemy, that I could only carry it out by exercising a certain amount of forbearance.'

At one point some Tommies, admiring the better progress made by the enemy opposite, went over and asked if they could borrow some of their tools; the Germans agreed.

One of the curious facts about the truce often overlooked is that once it started and became established there seemed no immediate possibility of bringing it to an end. As commanders like Major General Capper realized, there was a military case for continuing the ceasefire; but it seems there was also a very strong social one. Relationships had been forged and they were not easy to interrupt or break. Sworn enemies had become, almost, trusted friends. Second Lieutenant Dougan Chater had written a long account to his mother of the events of Christmas Day. He did not post his letter, however, and wisely so, for two days later he was writing again, with some even more remarkable details to tell her on 27 December.

'I am writing this back in billets – the same business continued yesterday and we had another parley with the Germans in the middle. We exchanged cigarettes and autographs and some more people took photos. I don't know how long it will go on for – I believe it was supposed to stop yesterday, but we can hear no firing going on along the front today except a little distant shelling. We are, at any rate, having another truce on New Year's Day as the Germans want to see how the photos come out!'

The last days of the year produced a range of comments and stories suggesting quite clearly that there was no instant desire on either side to resume hostilities. The CO of a Guards battalion, Lieutenant Colonel L R Fisher-Rowe, wrote in his diary on 28 December: 'I don't think that they want to start more than we do as it only means a few of each side being hit and does not affect the end of the war.'

On 29 December Captain Maurice Mascall, an artillery officer and an amateur artist, came up to the trenches from his gunnery battery with a view to doing some drawings, confident that he would be able to do so in perfect safety. He was certainly correct in that assumption. As he told his family in a letter home:

'I was sketching in front of our line, when suddenly a German appeared at the window of a ruined house opposite me, waving a cigar box in his hand. He was followed by several others, and then several of our men left our trenches, and the two parties advanced and met halfway. There was great saluting and bowing, and then an interchange of cigarettes, and then they separated with every mark of admiration.

Isn't this an extraordinary state of affairs. They seem to get more friendly every day, and heaven knows how they will ever start fighting again.'

Second Lieutenant J D Wyatt had another astonishing episode to report on 30 December. 'At about lunchtime a message came down the line to say that the Germans had sent across to say that their General was coming along in the afternoon, so we had better keep down, as they might have to do a little shooting to make things look right!! And this is war!'

Many were only too glad to take advantage of this most unusual and unexpected interlude, as Second Lieutenant Chater stated in his letter of 27 December: 'Yesterday was lovely in the morning and I went for several quite long walks about the lines. It is difficult to realize what this means but of course in the ordinary way there is not a sign of life above ground and everyone who puts his head up gets shot at.'

What was especially remarkable was that this was happening in a conflict in which from the outset the governments and the press of the nations involved had been engaged in a sustained campaign of vilification and hatred, which had been strongly supported by the civilian populations on both sides. Chater continued: 'It is really very extraordinary that this sort of thing should happen in a war in which there is so much bitterness and ill feeling. The Germans in this sector are certainly sportsmen if they are nothing else.'

One story which took almost a year to emerge, suggesting that Chater's view of the Germans had substance, was an account which survives in a letter by an Australian lady living in Germany, Ethel Cooper. It was written to her sister following a conversation with a soldier of the XIX Saxon Corps, Vize-Feldwebel (Lance Corporal) Lange. While on leave in late 1915 Lange described what had happened on the day following an intensive fraternization with a British battalion which had begun on Christmas Eve. The order issued by their officers to resume firing at the men with whom over the past two days they had become instant close friends produced a virtual mutiny: 'The difficulty began on the 26th, when the order to fire was given, for the men *struck*. Herr Lange says that in the accumulated years he had never heard such language as the officers indulged in, while they stormed up and down, and got, as the only result, the answer: "We can't – they are good fellows, and we can't." Finally, the officers turned on the men, "Fire, or we do – and not at the enemy." Not a shot had come from the other side, but at last they fired, and an answering fire came back, but not a man fell. "We spent that day and the next day", said Herr Lange, "wasting ammunition in trying to shoot the stars down from the sky." '

## The Case Against

One important question to raise is: what was the view of the local populace when they heard of the truce between the British and the

Germans; when they came to realize that the allies there to help their country defeat the enemy had been sharing a '*Joyeux Noel*' with them? The answer is that they were very angry. A member of a Welsh battalion which had taken part in the truce, Frank Richards, described what happened when they left the line: 'When we were passing through Armentières, all the French women were standing in the doorways and shouting about us fraternizing with the Germans – they didn't half give it us.'

The Tommies, though they might have understood the reasons for this angry reaction, were not of a kind to take such a rebuke without a sturdy reply – in fact, being soldiers, they issued a very outspoken, i.e. foul-mouthed one. According to Richards, 'The old platoon didn't half reply too – using about six languages. If they could have understood, they would have rushed into their houses burying their heads in shame.'

Yet there were many British who took a hard-line view of the truce and its aftermath, to whom any friendly relationship with the enemy was anathema. Captain Tom Ingram, a Medical Officer in an infantry battalion, expressed his anger in a letter to his family written on 6 January.

> 'All this friendly peace business at Christmas is rotten; we aren't here to pal up to the enemy and sing carols with him. One regiment especially distinguished themselves by their friendliness to the enemy at Christmas, and their second in command went and sang in the German trenches. This particular regiment is in our brigade and has not been so distinguished when fighting has to be done; in fact quite the contrary. Our men are awfully sick with them over the whole thing, and last night there was a bit of a scrap in the town between some of ours and the carol singing lot. Two or three other regiments who were too pally at Christmas have also had to fight their friends since; good thing too.'

Equally vehement in his views was Captain Sir Morgan Crofton, of the 2nd Life Guards, Cavalry Division, who set down his objections in his diary on 4 January, after becoming aware that the episode had been picked up and was being 'run' by Fleet Street.

'The London papers have been full of accounts for the last week or so of regiments of German infantry fraternizing with our troops on Xmas Day. Apparently the Queen's Westminsters did, but from many quarters there are the same reports of German and English soldiers mixing, shaking hands, exchanging cigars and cigarettes, even taking photos of each other. This is all very well but *ce n'est pas la guerre*.

Boshy papers of the halfpenny type slobber over this rubbish, but everyone out here condemns it. This is WAR, bloody War, and not a mothers' meeting. I am glad to say that General French fired in a snorter which should put a complete stop to these unsoldierly antics.'

Crofton preserved the C-in-C's 'snorter' with his papers. Dated 1 January 1915, marked 'Confidential', and signed by Lieutenant General C F N Macready, Adjutant-General to the British Army in the Field, it read:

'The Commander-in-Chief views with grave displeasure the reports he has received on recent incidents of unauthorized inter-course with the enemy and directs that the officers concerned be so informed.

It appears that our troops, under an improper use of a flag of truce and, on occasions, without that formality, have entered into communication with the enemy; it is to be clearly under-stood that on no occasion will any officer or man take such action except under the conditions laid down for flags of truce in Section 120 Field Service Regulations, Part II.

Any officer who may on his own responsibility countenance the opening of communication with the enemy, either on his own initiative or on that of the enemy, will report that matter at once to higher authority and will be held personally responsible for his action.'

Yet in the case of both Sir John French and Sir Morgan Crofton, it seems that an immediate anger gave way to a more moderate view. In his book *1914*, published in 1919, French wrote of the truce:

'When this was reported to me I issued immediate orders to prevent any recurrence of such conduct, and called the local commanders to account, which resulted in a good deal of trouble.

I have since thought deeply over the principle involved in the manifestation of such sentiments between hostile armies in the field. I am not sure that, had the question of the agreement upon an armistice for the day been submitted to me, I should have dissented from it.

I have always attached the utmost importance to the maintenance of that chivalry in war which has almost invariably characterized every campaign of modern times in which this country has been engaged . . .

In the swift and kaleidoscopic changes which occur in world politics, the friend of today may be the enemy of tomorrow. Soldiers should have no politics, but should cultivate a free-masonry of their own and, emulating the knights of old, should honour a brave enemy only second to a comrade, and like them rejoice to split a friendly lance today and ride boot to boot in the charge tomorrow.'

Surely such a sentiment – from a general often denigrated for his inadequacy, but who clearly still believed, in 1919, in concepts such as gallantry and chivalry which the war just concluded had turned into virtual laughing-stocks – is worth being accorded an honourable mention.

It would seem too that Sir Morgan Crofton might also have taken a more charitable view of the truce, not five years later as in French's case, but one, even though he did not say so in so many words. In Christmas week 1915, he was on board the Union Castle liner RMS *Saxon*, en route for Kenya where he was to join the British East African Expeditionary Force in its long campaign against German East Africa, where he would serve for two years as Provost-Marshal to the eminent South African soldier and statesman, General Jan Christian Smuts. On 28 December he wrote:

'There is a man in the Rifle Brigade called Swan on board. He is I think going out on Special Service.

He told me a lot of interesting things about the Xmas Truce which occurred last year in the trenches.

In some places, especially in front of the Yorks and Lancs Regt., it lasted six weeks. It began by the Germans (Saxons) on Xmas Eve putting little Xmas trees with lighted trees [sic] along the parapet of their trenches, the whole place, he said, looked like a regatta. In some places these were fired at and knocked over, but more generally they were not. For his part, he said, as he remembered the German behaviour to some wounded men of his battalion after the Battle of the River Aisne, he wished to have nothing to do with them, but some senior officers who had lately come out from home seemed more amenable to the truce.

The Saxons took advantage of this and began to swarm out into the No Man's Land between the trenches.

Lower down the line some British officers went out, after calling out that they were going to do so. The German search-lights were turned on them, and they were ordered to halt, when they reached the German wire entanglement. Here however they were soon joined by some German officers and soon after the fraternization became general.

The following day (Xmas Day) both sides walked up and down in the space between the trenches. The German officers clicked their heels and saluted all ours.

A lot of dead Germans in front of our trenches who had fallen in recent attacks were removed and buried, and cigars etc. were exchanged. The Saxons all professed to be already tired of the war, I wonder what they are now.

This unauthorized truce was more or less kept up for some time, both sides becoming very friendly, and there were occasions when one side borrowed the other side's mallets and wire to improve some of their entanglements. Some of the German officers, Swan said, were awful-looking ruffians; one especially, a red-headed enormous brute, who was nicknamed "Ginger" by our men.

Both their officers and men seemed frightened of him, he had probably shot a lot of the latter from time to time.

Ginger was bagged by one of our snipers, soon after the cessation of the truce.

At last the German officers came to the conclusion that the truce should end, but they found that they could not get their men back into the trenches, so they came over and proposed to our infantry that they should fire on them and thus drive them in. Naturally this they refused to do, and altho' they fired volleys they were all in the air, and were greeted with loud cries of "Good shot" from the Bosche who continued to sit in rows on the parapet.

Failing to persuade our infantry to help them in this respect they applied to our artillery, who, not being so near were not on such friendly terms. Chortling at the idea of such an unusual target they agreed, and a shower of well-aimed shrapnel ended this extraordinary truce.

The authorities on both sides, especially ours, were very annoyed at this lapse, and several punishments were meted out to the senior officers in charge, the Brigadier being sent home.

The Saxons, said Swan, kept impressing on every one who would listen, how much they hated the Prussians.'

As stated, there is no explicit approval in Crofton's account, but there is no explicit condemnation either. Perhaps after seeing so much of the cruelty of war – he had taken part not only in the First Battle of Ypres but also the Second, which saw the introduction of what we might now wish to describe as one of the first ever 'weapons of mass destruction', poison gas – Crofton, like French, saw some virtue in moments of humanity and respect between enemies even in a situation of all-out war.

## A New Dispensation

Sir John French's 'snorter' was not the only message from on high demanding a cessation of friendly dealings with the enemy.

On Christmas Day the BEF reorganized itself with Haig and Smith-Dorrien, now both promoted to the rank of full general, becoming commanders of two Armies; the First Army under Haig, the Second under Smith-Dorrien. Haig's Army included I Corps, IV Corps and the Indian Corps; Smith-Dorrien's included II Corps, III Corps and a newly arrived division, the 27th. There had been very little fraternization in the area of the front under Haig, whereas there had been much of it in the area under Smith-Dorrien. So the following terse, unambiguous order, issued on 1 January 1915, clearly carried the imprint of the latter's point of view and of his obvious impatience: 'Commander 2nd Army directs that informal understandings with enemy are to cease. Officers and NCOs allowing them are to be brought before a Court Martial.'

Under Lieutenant General Sir William Pulteney, III Corps had witnessed a great deal of fraternization. On 2 January, as if echoing his new master's voice, Pulteney issued the following signal:

'Informal understandings with the enemy are strictly forbidden. Any officer or non-commissioned officer proved to be responsible for initiating such understandings or acquiescing in any such understanding proposed by the enemy will be tried by court martial. Commanding officers are held responsible that all officers and non-commissioned officers in their units are made acquainted with this order.'

Yet it should not be assumed that all the British Army's leading commander generals took so strict and outspoken a viewpoint. The GOC of IV Corps, Lieutenant General Sir Henry Rawlinson, writing in his personal diary on 27 December, commented on the truce without the anger shown by some of his fellow senior officers:

'There has been a certain friendliness between our men and the Germans in the trenches. Christmas Day was looked on mutually as a peace day and both sides went out freely in front of their trenches and buried the dead which were still lying out in the fire-swept zone – Germans looked very clean and smart – Put on their best clean clothes for the occasion I fancy – They conversed freely and exchanged cigarettes – I am rather suspicious of them – But many of them expressed themselves as heartily sick of the war and anxious to get home to their wives and families.'

Another general, of somewhat lower rank, Brigadier-General Frederic Heyworth, whose brigade included such units as the 2nd

Scots Guards and the 2nd and 6th Gordon Highlanders, took a similarly indulgent view at this time. On 29 December he wrote in his diary: 'The Germans were outside mending their parapets, so we did and there was no sniping.' On 30 December: 'No sniping again and Germans and our men out working the parapets, although there was quite heavy firing going on in front of the 8th Division on our right.' On 31 December, there were festivities on both sides. Heyworth wrote: 'Dined with the Gordon Highlanders and danced reels afterwards. The Germans fired at the incoming of the New Year, but up in the air, and we did the same.'

However, by 1 January it was clear Heyworth had had enough. He commented: 'Our artillery shelled the German trenches and did them a good deal of damage.' On 3 January he reported an increase of hostility from the other side: 'After lunch we went down to the trenches and nearly got it from five German shells which fell about ten yards from us. They were evidently shelling a working party which had just finished.' On 6 January: 'A lot of Germans showing and doing work on their parapet. I have ordered firing to start at 3 p.m. so that will stop all that.' On 7 January: 'We have started sniping again which makes the Germans keep under cover.'

Yet to return to 'business as usual' was not as easy as it might seem. One factor which delayed it in some areas was the dreadful state of the trenches, made even worse in the first days of the new year by persistent wet weather. Captain Tom Ingram, in his letter of 6 January – as we have seen, a bitter opponent of the truce – recorded conditions so extreme that fighting was quite out of the question; conditions all the more galling for him because of a few days' break from the front during which he had enjoyed, among other things, the use of a 'fine tiled bathroom with a fixed bath and a shower bath'. He noted angrily:

'We have three more days of this luxury and then go to some perfectly horrid trenches. I went to have a look at them today. They are part of the same we had when I first joined the regiment. Since we were there early in November, the winter rains have flooded them completely, and now they are only dikes full of mud and water up to one's armpits. The men have to go about on top on both sides, and a sort of mutual armistice has come about, a sort of "If you don't shoot at me I won't shoot at you" kind of arrangement; comforting but not war.'

In such circumstances the only option was to allow a certain amount of 'live and let live' to enable both the British and the Germans to make their living conditions more acceptable; if they could not dig down, they could, as it were, build up. Wrote Ingram:

'At present both sides are engaged in building breastworks – i.e. sort of earth walls behind their flooded trenches – they will have their lean-tos behind this breastwork, and fire over the top, or through loopholes in it. At present neither side is firing at all, and each is busily engaged in building their breastwork. Unfortunately the Germans have built three-quarters of theirs, our people have only finished about a quarter of the place where we shall have to take over. It's a funny sight to see working parties of both sides not 200 yards apart not taking any notice of each other. As soon as the Germans have finished I bet they start and give us blazes; especially as the Saxon Corps in front of us now are going to be relieved in a day or two by Prussians. I quite expect we will have a bad time when we go in.'

The Medical Officer of the 2nd Argyll and Sutherland Highlanders, Lieutenant Frederick Chandler, reported similar conditions in the new year's first weeks, when his battalion too was building breastworks:

'The ground was a sticky bog in places and a turbid lake in others. These breastworks could never have been made at all, except through a tacit agreement between our men and the Germans. No one fired a shot and work went hurriedly on night and day. Our men and the Germans freely exposed themselves; they worked between the lines, putting up barbed wire, deepening the borrow pit and strengthening the breastwork. In some places the work was done within twenty yards of each other, and in one part souvenirs were freely exchanged. We could walk right up to the German line and say "Good Morning" to the German officers sitting on their parapet.'

## The Media Response

While all this was happening, the truce was being celebrated in the most remarkable way by the newspapers back home.

Far from denouncing the event, the British press celebrated it with a spate of approving headlines, such as: 'EXTRAORDINARY UNOFFICIAL ARMISTICE'; 'REMARKABLE CHRISTMAS DAY INCIDENTS'; and 'BRITISH, INDIANS AND GERMANS SHAKE HANDS'. Even the *New York Times* had the story as early as New Year's Eve, carrying a headline that arguably owed a little to the imagination: 'FOES IN TRENCHES SWAP PIES FOR WINE'. Leader writers and columnists mused thoughtfully about the event. In London's *Daily Telegraph*, the correspondent E Ashmead Bartlett (later to become dear to French hearts for his praise of the French defence of Verdun in 1916) wrote fulsomely about the event in the edition published on New Year's Day:

'Probably no news since the war began has made a greater sensation, and certainly none has made better reading than the accounts which have come through from the trenches of the unofficial armistice established between certain sections of the German lines and our own on Christmas Eve and Christmas Day.

All this seems incredible in view of the ferocity of the combatants during months past and of the authenticated tales of German atrocities and trickery. It seems to prove the assertion that the German soldier is a good-hearted peace-loving individual once he is outside the influence of the Prussian military machine.'

The *Manchester Guardian* on 2 January allowed itself a similarly rapturous response to the story.

'From its occasion, of course, it can be claimed as a truce of God, but it was not a truce of God in the sense that it was authorized and enjoined by the Church. It was a thing more hopeful than even such a truce would have been. It was the simple and un-examined impulse of human souls, drawn together in the face of a common and desperate plight . . . Those of us who are left at home may well think of the Christmas truce with wonder and thankfulness. For the men who kept it proved . . . that the human soul stands out a quite simple thing and of infinite good will.'

*The Times* of London also gave the event its formal blessing, on 4 January, albeit with ill-concealed contempt for the government of the country which had caused the war in the first place and had persuaded its soldiers to believe in the justice of their cause:

'We cherish no anger against the masses of our enemies. We pity them for the ease with which they have suffered themselves to be blinded and misled; but, as the wonderful scenes in the trenches show, there is no malice on our side, and none in many of those who have been marshalled against us.'

Occasionally, stories were published giving details of notable Christmas incidents in other parts of the front. The January edition of that ever popular magazine *The Lady* carried the account submitted by a correspondent of a remarkable occurrence deep in the French sector, one of a number of events in which the singing of a powerful single voice was the central element.

'I heard that in the French trenches in the Argonne the cold was intense, and, while a spiritless fire was going on at intervals, a village church bell sounded the hour of midnight on Christmas Eve, whereupon a voice, clear and beautiful, was heard singing, *Minuit Chrétiens, c'est l'heure solonelle* (The carol "O Holy Night" in English). And who do you think the singer was? Granier, of the Paris Opera. The troops, French and German, forgot to fire whilst listening to that wonderful tenor voice above the snapping of the guns, and for a few moments all was peace.'

That there were similar episodes elsewhere would not always emerge until later. A witness of an event in the German lines was none other than the German Crown Prince Wilhelm, Commander of the German Fifth Army in the Argonne region, whose war memoirs appeared in English in 1922. On Christmas Eve, feeling 'particularly drawn to my field-grey boys', he decided to visit them in the front line, to find there was no let-up in the intensity of the firing.

'The shells howled their monotonous and hideous melody, and from time to time the sacred silence was rent by the burst of a machine gun's fire . . . Nevertheless the spirits of the men were everywhere very cheerful. Every dug-out had its Christmas tree and from all directions came the sound of rough men's voices singing our exquisite Christmas songs.

Kirchoff, our concert singer, who was attached to our Headquarters Staff for a while as orderly officer, sang his Christmas songs on that same sacred evening in the front-line trenches of the 130th Regiment. And on the following day he told me that some French soldiers who had climbed up their parapet, had continued to applaud, until at last he gave them an encore. Thus, amid the bitter realities of trench warfare, with all its squalor, a Christmas song had worked a miracle and thrown a bridge from man to man.'

Similarly a letter only recently discovered, written by a Captain Guy Goodliffe of the 1st Royal Fusiliers, shows that the fine singers in the British sector noted by Captains Hyslop and Armes were not the only ones to cheer the hearts of the Tommies. After being moved to a different part of the line in January 1915, Goodliffe wrote: 'I miss the singing we had in our other trenches. We used to sing and the Germans applaud. Then they had a turn and you could hear everybody clapping. They had one right good singer too – a great favourite with our men. He was known as "Opera".'

Such musical overtures between the lines were not always so well received. It was reported that, when to the north of Ypres, the German 205th Regiment went up to the front on Christmas Eve they at one point spontaneously broke into the singing of *Stille Nacht*. Their Christmas 'present' was to be a continual hail of French grenades.

For the most part, however, the surge of stories relating to the amazing truce were benign and approving, especially in Britain. Newspapers from all over the country carried letters from ordinary soldiers, telling of their extraordinary experiences. Magazines like the *Illustrated London News, The Graphic* and *The Sphere* teemed with photographs and specially commissioned drawings. Before long the truce was being given honourable mention in the popular works of instant history which sprang from the presses from the moment the war began. In a weighty work about the 1914 campaign by one G H Perris, the author claimed that 'The vision of these hours of reconciliation will last when many a day of dear-bought but necessary victory has sunk into oblivion.' Perhaps the best and most ringing endorsement of the truce was that published in 1915 in a an early volume of a series about the war written by none other than Sir Arthur Conan Doyle, the creator of the world-famous detective Sherlock Holmes. He called the truce 'an amazing spectacle', and saluted it as 'one human episode amid all the atrocities which have stained the memory of the war'. There could be no finer claim.

## Back to War

Before long, however, it became clear that the interlude was, or soon would be, over. No longer was the space between the lines populated by fraternizing troops in khaki and field grey. What Lieutenant-General Rawlinson called 'the fire-swept zone' was precisely that once more, and it was about this time that it took on the name which would define it ever after: No Man's Land, soon to be called *le nomansland* by the French and *der Niemansland* by the Germans. For the war had to go on. The *Manchester Guardian* spoke the necessary words in an article of 7 January:

> '"But they went back into their trenches", a perfectly enlightened and quite inhuman observer from another planet would perhaps say, "and are now hard at it again, slaying and being slain. Evidently their glimpses of the wiser and better way was interesting but of no very great practical importance." To which, of course, we might reply with great reason that there was very much to be done yet – that Belgium must be freed from the hideous yoke that has been thrust upon her, that Germany must be taught that culture cannot be carried by the sword.'

In other words, there was unfinished business to be done. One famous participant who responded to the mood of the occasion was the cartoonist Bruce Bairnsfather, creator of the archetypal British Tommy 'Ole Bill', who took part in the truce as a front-line subaltern in the Royal Warwickshire Regiment. He was out between the trenches fraternizing happily on Christmas Day. But he knew that any 'peace' with the enemy could only be temporary. He later wrote: 'There was not an atom of hatred on either side that day, and yet, on our side, not for a moment was the will to war and the will to beat them relaxed. It was just like the interval between the rounds of a friendly boxing match.'

Yet it has long been a dream that if it had been left to the men in the trenches the war would never have developed in the way it did. Musing in his autobiography many years later, the famous English writer Jerome K Jerome – author of, among many other books, the classic humorous novel *Three Men in a Boat*, and, during the war, an ambulance driver at Verdun – put the point with simple clarity. 'A pity the common soldiers could not have been left to make the peace. There might have been no need for the League of Nations. I remember one midday coming upon two soldiers, sitting on a log. One was a French *poilu* and the other his German prisoner. They were sharing the Frenchman's lunch. The conqueror's gun lay on the ground, between them.'

Jerome was arguing with hindsight. As early as January 1915, a British infantry officer, Captain J L Jack, whose own battalion had not taken part in, indeed had not been aware of, the fraternization that had taken place both to the left and the right of their position in the line, mused in his diary along not dissimilar lines: 'These incidents seem to suggest that, except in the temper of battle or of some great grievance, educated men have no desire to kill one another, and that, were it not for aggressive National Policies, or the fear of them by others, war between civilized peoples would seldom take place.'

When the Medical Officer, Lieutenant Frederick Chandler, helped rebury the dead German soldier he found on Christmas morning, his comment: 'Rest in peace, poor Fritz; it is not you or your like who have caused this; there is not a combatant soldier in any of the combatant armies who would not make peace tomorrow', was expressing a similar sentiment. So was the speech of a former officer of the Gordon Highlanders, Major Murdock Mackenzie Wood, when, as a Member of Parliament in 1930, he contributed to a debate on the subject of conscientious objectors which revolved around the matter of killing in war. He had taken part in the Christmas Truce and was proud of the fact:

> 'A great number of people think we did something that was degrading. The fact is we did it, and I then came to the conclusion that I have held very firmly ever since, that if we had been left to ourselves there would never have been another shot fired. We were on the most friendly terms, and it was only the fact that we were being controlled by others that made it necessary for us to start to shoot one another once again.'

Yet ending the war without resolving the injustices resulting from it was, quite simply, not a tenable option. For the British, as for the Germans, it might be possible in theory to agree a ceasefire along the trench lines of the Western Front, to lower their guns, empty their rifles and declare an armistice. But the French had lost ten of their ninety *départéments* and much of their heavy industry, plus one of their greatest cities, Lille. Beyond the German trench-lines were countless of their fellow countrymen living in humiliating conditions and desperately clamouring for release. Their cry could not be ignored. That this was evident to some at least of the British serving at the front is clear from an eloquent letter by a Cavalry officer, Captain E W S Balfour, Adjutant of the 5th Dragoon Guards, writing to his family in the first days of December 1914. He realized that the occupation of so much of their territory – and by an enemy which two generations earlier had seized Alsace and most of Lorraine in the wake of the Franco-Prussian war of 1870–71 – had left the French populace in a state of fury. They had not simply lost areas on a map; they had lost part of their *mère patrie*:

> 'To the French it is their own home and it makes them mad. We somehow fight on with no increased animosity. If we were ordered to retire again tomorrow, I don't believe we should lose morale. The French really are giving everything and it makes one

wonder if people in England realize what the advance of an invading army over a country means.'

The same was true of the Belgians, left with little more than a foothold in their homeland. Nothing would induce them or the French to call a halt to the fighting, until the German invaders had been sent back whence they had come. By committing her forces to join the French and Belgians in the field, the British automatically signed up to a contract to do all they could not just to help defeat the Germans in battle, but to assist in expelling them forcibly from territories not their own.

## Last Echoes

Yet the mood of friendship established at Christmas 1914 was slow to fade in some sectors, particularly those where Saxon troops were entrenched, the largely correct assumption being that some German regiments, particularly Prussian ones, were more bellicose than others. Indeed one famous story of the truce is that at one point certain Saxon soldiers held up a message inscribed: 'We are Saxons, you are Anglo-Saxons. Why should we fire upon each other?' Captain Guy Goodliffe of the 1st Royal Fusiliers (see page 65), was reporting curiously unmartial incidents into the last week of January. On the 25th he wrote:

'There is rather a good story going about some [British] General . . . The General was very tall and was walking through the trenches where the truce still reigns. He however did not trust the Saxons and kept his head well below the parapet – as he thought. Suddenly a Saxon was heard to yell out "Look out Tommy, your general is coming round!"'

On 27 January Goodliffe had another incident to relate, one which he felt should be treated by his family as strictly confidential:

'I am told when the truce is on the Saxons have put up the Kaiser's flag, also a red and white one, presumably the Saxon one. In front of this is a small white flag and, so they tell me, there is also a tiny Union Jack put up. For goodness sake don't allow any of this sort of thing to get into the papers. There is awful trouble already about such things having come to pass.'

It was not until 5 February that he found himself writing: 'The Germans saw fit to attack us yesterday.' Even then the warfare thus launched seemed desultory rather than intense, a subject more for interest than anger, although it was quite close to his unit's part of the line:

'It was just a marvellous sight', he wrote. 'It was by night and wonderful to see the flash of flame from the firing guns and far off the shells exploding – and there was the noise of battle too. The "wump" of the high explosive shells and the "cheering" of the shrapnel as it hummed through the air. All the sky was lit up by the flashes. Then too there was the rattle of the rifles and the purr of the machine guns. Altogether it was a wonderful thing to see and listen to.'

In some areas the truce atmosphere persisted even longer. Ploegsteert, almost on the Franco-Belgian border, was one such sector. As late as 19 March Captain F E Packe, 1st Battalion Welch Regiment, back at the front in that sector after recovering from being wounded in the previous November, could write to his parents that this was:

'an absurdly quiet spot, it was one of those places where they fraternized with Germans at Xmas and a certain amount of the truce has gone on apparently, anyhow there was very little firing by day and never really heavy by night and I only had one man hit in two nights – not badly and he was the only casualty in the regiment! We never had a single shell the whole time I was there.'

What is significant about the date on which Packe wrote this, 19 March, is that not far to the south, at Neuve Chapelle, nine days earlier, on 10 March, the British had launched the first of a number of determined but unsuccessful attacks on the German lines to be made in 1915, each one of which would produce heavy losses. This was fighting of an altogether more savage nature than that observed back in January by Captain Goodliffe. Neuve Chapelle meant that the war was on, in full measure, and deadly serious. There would be few joyous interludes in the months and years to come.

Despite this the Germans made several more attempts to maintain the friendly relations that had been established since Christmas – at Easter. Captain Packe wrote in a letter of 8 April: 'On Easter Day [6 April] the Germans tried to fraternize showing white flags, etc. – they threw potatoes into one trench – but orders were very strict on the subject so we ignored them.'

Another, even bolder attempt at fraternization at Easter 1915 was described in a later memoir by Captain, then Lieutenant, E E H Bate, of the territorial unit the 1/2nd Battalion London Regiment, which had arrived in France early in the new year. Long before Easter they had enjoyed much entertainment from the Saxons opposite, with impromptu concerts and shouted exchanges: 'One chap regularly used to call out somewhat like this: "Hullo Englishman. This is X from Kensington. How's Chelsea doing?"' Though the mood was predictably different when a Prussian regiment took over, with bombs replacing badinage, at Easter the Saxons were back:

'On the Sunday they started climbing out of their trenches and kicking a football about with invitations to us to join them. Some of our chaps did go out and Marians [the Company Commander] sent word to Battalion HQ asking for instructions. The order came back: "Shoot every German seen", but we felt we could hardly do that; so having collected our chaps we lined the parapet and fired three rounds into the air, after which they retired to cover gradually.'

The 4th Battalion of the Middlesex Regiment had been in France since the Battle of Mons in August 1914, so that when the Germans opposite their section of the line at Easter began to show signs of attempting to initiate a break from the fighting, they were sternly rebuffed. Lieutenant T S Wollocombe wrote in his diary on Easter Day:

'At about 2 p.m. I got a message from the CO on the phone. He had sent it round to all companies. It came from the Brigade and ran thus:- "14th Brigade reports enemy using white flag in front of them. I instruct all trenches that no intercourse is to be permitted." I think the Germans wanted to celebrate Easter as they had done Christmas. They put the flag up in front of us at about 5 p.m., when we were standing to arms in the evening. We weren't having any nonsense and we watched for a bit, but the flag-bearers didn't appear so I told the men to shoot at it at 350 yards which I knew to be the correct range. They did so, and it disappeared, only to appear again after a minute. We fired again and it again disappeared for a second or two. They then tried to be funny and again brought it up to signal a miss by waving it above the head as we do for a miss on the range. Nothing more happened.'

It might be reasonably safe to conjecture that these desultory episodes finally brought down the curtain on the Christmas Truce of 1914.

### A Myth Refuted

Before concluding this account of the war's remarkable first Christmas, it is perhaps worth discussing one persistent myth, that units involved in the fraternization were punished by being withdrawn from the line or moved elsewhere to more dangerous theatres. It was not, for example, the case that German regiments participating were dispatched to the Eastern front, or that French formations were sent to Verdun, which, if anything, was almost a backwater at this stage, its terrible date with destiny in February 1916 being well over a year away. In particular, the German units involved, in accordance with standard German practice, continued to occupy the same sectors in Belgium and France; they would still be there at the following Christmas and beyond. One or two British battalions assumed they had been pulled out from the trenches for supposed misbehaviour, but they were soon back to 'business as usual' in the same front line. In fact, it is difficult to name anyone who suffered directly from taking part in the Christmas Truce, though two officers of an Indian Army battalion newly arrived from the sub-continent, Captains Kenny and Welchman, who had drawn the ire of an anti-trucing major for their convivial zeal on Christmas Day, had their long-awaited home leaves cancelled, and, before the ban on their visiting the UK was lifted, were killed in action at Neuve Chapelle.

The fact that the various units involved escaped censure, however, did not mean that they would be spared the punishing ordeals to come. On the contrary. Indeed, with the benefit of hindsight, it might be argued that perhaps the most moving comment about this strange first winter, with its interlude of uneasy peace that finally ended as the war got back into its stride, had been made weeks before by a thoughtful and articulate member of the Indian Army, Captain J W Barnett, Regimental Medical Officer of the 34th Sikh Pioneers. As far back as 21 December, four days before Christmas, he had written in his diary: 'I think we will win through, but our casualties will be appalling.'

What he could not have known was that he would be right on both counts, but that the winning through would take almost four years.

## A Significant Event

How important was the Christmas Truce of 1914?

In the matter of the basic task of the armies fighting in France and Belgium, it meant little. It was a brief holiday, a pause before the necessary burdens of the war were once again resumed. For, as has already been argued, the war had to be won. Peoples and territories held in thrall had to be liberated. There was no possibility that the governments and the populations of the belligerent countries would accept that there should be a general ceasefire and that their men should shoulder their arms and go home.

Yet it left a powerful legacy.

At Christmas 1915 there were the strict orders on both sides not to engage in any fraternization. This suited the attitude of many, such as, for example, Lieutenant Dennis Neilson-Terry of the 7th

Battalion the Queen's Royal West Surrey Regiment, who wrote in a letter to his mother:

'We had a very quiet Xmas in the trenches, no truce of any kind and we gave them a little artillery strafe in the evening which I don't approve of at Xmas time but still that can't be helped, can it, and then the next day we gave them merry hell with our "heavies" and everything we could send over, we were relieving that day and got pretty heavily shelled by the Huns [when] coming out into the open but luckily not a casualty in our Company.'

A briefer reference in the diary of an artillery officer with the Guards Division, Lieutenant E H Giffard, describes two abortive attempts to take advantage of the Christmas season:

'25/12/15. Christmas Day. Went down to [the front] and found our men and Germans fraternizing a little, but German shells on Rue Tilleloy put an end to it. Germans also asked for Armistice to carry away wounded from previous night's strafe: not granted.'

However, despite the less than festive mood suggested by the above reports, in one sector members of two battalions, the 1st Scots Guards and the 15th Royal Welch Fusiliers, did take part in a brief celebration. On Christmas Eve, as had been the case a year earlier, there were sounds of merrymaking and singing in the German trenches, with shouts of: 'Merry Christmas, Tommy', which were answered from the British lines by shouts of: 'Merry Christmas, Fritz.' The Germans clearly knew that there was a Welsh battalion present, because they serenaded them with the famous Welsh folk-song 'All Through the Night', to which the Welshmen replied by singing a favourite British Christmas carol, 'Good King Wenceslas' and various other carols. A young officer of the Welsh battalion, Wyn Griffith, later to become a distinguished writer, described what happened next:

'As soon as it became light, we saw hands and bottles being waved at us, with encouraging shouts that we could neither understand nor misunderstand. A drunken German stumbled over his parapet and advanced through the barbed wire, followed by several others, and in a few moments there was a rush of men from both sides, carrying tins of meat, biscuits, and other odd commodities for barter. This was the first time I had seen No Man's Land, and it was now Every-Man's Land, or nearly so. Some of our men would not go, and they gave terse and bitter reasons for their refusal. The officers called our men back to the line, and in a few minutes No Man's Land was once more empty and desolate. There had been a feverish exchange of "souvenirs", a suggestion for peace all day and a football match in the afternoon, and a promise of no rifle fire at night. All this came to naught. An irate Brigadier came splut-tering up to the line, thundering hard, throwing a "court martial" into every other sentence, and breathing fury everywhere. We had evidently jeopardized the safety of the Allied cause. I suspect that across No Man's Land a similar scene was being played, for later in the day the guns became active. The artillery was stimulating the infantry to resume the war. Despite the fulminations of the Generals, the infantry was in no mood for offensive measures, and it was obvious that, on both sides, rifles and machine guns were aimed high.'

In fact two officers *were* court-martialled in relation to this brief truce; members not of the Welsh battalion, but of the 1st Scots Guards. One was cleared, while the other, Captain Sir Iain Colquhoun, was considered to be so good an officer and so well connected – he had the advantage of being related by marriage to the British Prime Minister, Herbert Asquith – that his sentence, which was the mild one of being 'reprimanded', was instantly quashed by the BEF's Commander-in-Chief.

Nothing equivalent happened at Christmas 1916. Nevertheless as the guns kept on firing without the slightest concession to the season of peace and goodwill, a young artillery officer, Second Lieutenant Edward Beddington-Behrens, found himself thinking nostalgically of what had happened two years earlier and almost daring to hope that it might happen again. On 26 December he wrote to his family:

'Everything was done to prevent fraternizing between the two sides as the Boche would use the opportunity by getting useful information. Besides, things have gone past the stage when one can fraternize with the enemy, there is too much hatred flying about, it would also induce bad discipline in our troops. However I must say going to talk to the Boche in No Man's Land like we did at the first Christmas rather appeals to one's sporting instincts, don't you think so? Instead however, the artillery had a Christmas strafe at all hours of the day and night.'

But this young officer was almost certainly an exception. Long before this third wartime Christmas, under the impact of the arrival of poison gas as a weapon of war, and, even more significant, the ever mounting casualty lists caused by such long-drawn-out attritional encounters as the Battle of the Somme and the Passchendaele campaign, had almost wiped the story from the collective memory. To all intents and purposes, it was forgotten. After the war minds were concentrated on the remembering of the dead, on the building of hundreds of war cemeteries, and the commemoration of the missing. The most important cult of the post-war years was that of the Unknown Warrior, the 'Soldat Inconnu', a cult so strong that it continues to this day, adding new countries to the list of those who honour their national sacrifice in this way. There was no place in the popular mind for those distant figures shaking hands and lighting each other's cigarettes, or singing Christmas carols to each other when the war was only a few months old, unaware of the colossal sacrifice and the suffering to come. Thus looking back on that remarkable first Christmas from the standpoint of the late 1920s, a former infantryman who had shared the camaraderie between the lines could write:

'Men who joined us later were inclined to disbelieve us when we spoke of the incident, and no wonder, for as the months rolled by, we who were actually there could hardly realize that it had happened, except for the fact that every little detail stood out well in our memory.'

Here, as contributor I must inject a personal word. When I first researched this story some twenty-five years ago even veterans of the war assured me that the Christmas Truce did not take place. One former cavalryman told me to my face that the whole idea was 'eyewash', while a former infantryman wrote to me stating that the story was simply 'a latrine rumour': the kind of outrageous yarn that men often exchanged at their obligatory morning sessions in the latrine sap, such as: 'Have you heard our division is about to be posted to Samoa?' or: 'Do you know that next week we are to be sent to sweep the leaves from the lawns at general headquarters?'

Yet the Christmas Truce did happen, and increasingly evidence is being found confirming that this was no fairy tale, no fiction, but a genuine historical event, of much longer duration and involving far more men than was hitherto thought to be the case. As we advance into the twenty-first century we can look back at it with a gaze unclouded by the horrors of that sad, ancient war. We now have an awareness that since that time too many other wars have been fought and are being fought; too many people have died and are dying, and a gesture of protest and an assertion of common humanity, however ineffective they might have seemed at the time, are things not to be forgotten but to be celebrated and treasured. For the great fraternization of 1914 halted, if briefly, the juggernaut of war in its tracks, and gave some men at least an insight into the complex realities of conflict that they were never to forget, making them think again about the nationally inspired animosities to which they were expected to subscribe.

Indeed, nearly a hundred years later, the episode is arousing more interest than ever, tempting one to believe that perhaps in the fullness of time the Christmas Truce will seem as important in its way as the great battles that preceded and followed it. It never could have stopped the war. But if nothing else it asserted the often ignored truth that in the end mankind's survival depends not on conflict but on reconciliation, that we must somehow contrive either to live together on this planet or lose it. In a time of deep darkness it lit a candle of hope.

# 2

# Good Neighbours

## RÉMY CAZALS

The extreme violence of the Great War is well known. The variety of the massive means of destruction has long been examined and considered by historians – the desperate duration and intensity of the fighting, the dehumanization, and the traumas. Combatants on both sides of the front line have described the helpless waiting under bombardment, the impotent uncertainty of where each incoming shell might land, and the dismembered bodies. Their accounts also show the anguish before attacks, of waiting for the order to leave the safety of the trench, to join the waves of men being mown down by machine gun fire. The dreadful wounds and the rotting bodies in No Man's Land or hanging on the barbed wire are not forgotten. The death of comrades, families' deep distress, the long list of the dead on war memorials and the wild hope at finding a beloved name reported 'missing'; the distance, the despair, the exasperation, the hatred, the terror – every form of fear.

Tragic and unbearable images surge through the hundreds of published combatant narratives. French anthologies, assembled by Jean Norton Cru and André Ducasse around 1930 offer a glimpse of this material.[1] In his *Notebooks* a barrel-maker, Corporal Louis Barthas, described the horror of a war that was 'our century's shame, the withering of the civilsation that was our pride.'[2] His chapter titles used extremely explicit words: killing, massacre, charnel-house, hecatomb, bloody offensive, hell, blood-stained mud, abattoir, martyrdom, nightmare. Barthas, who was at the front from November 1914 to March 1918, experienced the violence directly, but the cooper from Peyriac-Minervois also offers a remarkably comprehensive overview of cases of comradeship between enemies, tacit or recognized understandings, mutual tolerance and fraternization.

Born in 1879, Louis Barthas was 35 in 1914 and a member of the Territorial forces. Mobilized immediately on 4 August, he remained at the depot in Narbonne, in south-west France; his age preserved him from the battles in Lorraine, the Marne and 'the Race to the Sea', the murderous opening months of the war as the armies covered great distances in advance or withdrawal and suffered terrible losses. On 2 October he was part of a detachment conducting enemy prisoners to Fort Mont-Louis in the Pyrenees, setting off so early in the morning that it was still dark. The Germans in their freight wagon were quiet and well-behaved, but tension between them and their French guards continued until the sun rose over the Mediterranean: 'A magical sight, a galaxy of colours, sun-rays, reflections, bursting through the grey tones of dawn.' The prisoners were full of admiration; the guards were proud because it was their sea and their sunlight. Later, the track ran beside terrain that was:

> 'so full of game that companies of partridge, squads of rabbits, columns of guinea-fowl and pheasants and quantities of other creatures, could be seen fleeing the noise of the train. Marvelling, French and Germans crowded to the wide open door of the wagon while we all pointed at the mass of wildlife vanishing into the undergrowth or the tree-tops.'

Soon the escort was sharing its food and wine with the prisoners. This 'friendly gesture', as Barthas calls it, was returned by the Germans when, on 30 October, the group of French soldiers was despatched from Mont-Louis to reinforce decimated ranks after their severe sufferings in the early months of fighting. Gravely, the prisoners saluted 'the victims who were going to suffer and to die'.

## The Christmas Truce

Barthas made no further reference to such overt comradeship between soldiers.[3] It remains relevant here as part of his narrative, however, for it recalled his first contact with the Germans before he joined the 280th Infantry Regiment early in November 1914 near Vermelles, in the Pas-de-Calais. Late December brought the extraordinary and well-documented episode of the Christmas truces between British and German troops. Barthas could only give an indirect description:

> 'The next night was the holy night of Christmas. As soon as night fell we settled well down in our holes, expecting a good night's sleep until dawn, but around 9 p.m. in the evening a rough voice ordered us to get up and pick up our kit as quickly as possible. In fact something entirely out of the ordinary was going on in the front line, we could hear singing and shouting and flares being set off at random, but no firing.'

Having seen nothing more for himself, Barthas handed the narrative over to his captain, Léon Hudelle, who in civilian life was editor-in-chief of the southern French daily paper *Le Midi socialiste*. Barthas kept a copy of Hudelle's account and included it in his fourth notebook, but unfortunately the cutting was lost and its exact origins are not known.

The unpublished correspondence between a private soldier in the 296th Infantry Regiment in the same sector, François Guilhem, and his wife, however, includes a letter dated 25 December:

> 'I will never forget this Christmas night: under moonlight as bright as day, and with the frost hard enough to split the stones, we were going up around 10 p.m. in the evening to carry timber into the trenches. You can imagine how astonished we were to hear the Boches singing hymns in their trenches and the French in theirs; then the Boches sang their national anthem and cheered. the French responded with the *"Chant du départ"*. All this singing from thousands of men right out in the countryside was truly magical.'

**Flooding and Fraternization**

In December 1915, Corporal Barthas was still at the front. A year had passed, including the attacks in Artois and Champagne, the notorious '*grignotage*' – 'nibbling away' – and increasingly intense shell bombardments. Barthas had not yet had his first chance to go home on leave to his wife and their two children. In the Neuville-St. Vaast sector, it was raining. It rained so much and so hard that the trenches and communication trenches were vanishing into the water. Dug-outs collapsed; nothing could contain the flood. On 10 December he observed:

> 'In many places in the front line, the troops had to leave the trenches to avoid being drowned; the Germans were forced to do the same, so that there was the remarkable sight of two armed enemies facing each other without a shot being fired.'

According to the corporal, no one fired. Men looked at each other; all were conscious of their shared sufferings. Then came smiles, exchanges of tobacco, wine or coffee, and words too, as far as was possible. There were handshakes. To fraternize was in itself an implicit condemnation of the war. Later, matters became even clearer when, after an announcement that only his compatriots could understand, one German broke his rifle in a gesture of rage. At this point, wrote Barthas, 'Applause broke out on all sides and the "*Internationale*" rang out.'

The 'big chiefs' soon intervened, however to 'put an end to any familiarity with the Germans', but the interdict was evaded at small outposts in front of the lines. One soldier, Gontran, continued to visit a German trench where the captain, 'a good family man', gave him a few cigarettes. One day Gontran was surprised by a French officer who threatened him: 'I've caught you at it, you will be shot tomorrow.' Terrified, the soldier leaped over the parapet and ran over to take shelter with the enemy.

This incident is confirmed in the original notebooks of another infantryman in the 280th RI, Léopold Noé:

> '21 and 22 [December 1915] Rain and rest. It wasn't a moment too soon to leave this Neuville-St. Vaast stretch. The Germans

and us, last week, came out of the trench every morning to warm up a bit when the sun came out; on both sides the artillery was under orders not to fire on the trenches. The men began to fraternize, from both sides; five men from our division went over to visit the enemy, and they came across to us or exchanged various items; but they weren't well fed like us; one of our unit went over, and when he came back the captain called him in to know what he had said to them and what they had said to him; then he told him he would put him in front of a court martial; the chap was scared stiff and went off again in the evening, he went over to the enemy and didn't come back again.'

## Outpost Number 10 in Champagne

In August 1916, Barthas had survived a week in the hell of Hill 304 at Verdun and was now in Champagne with the 296th Infantry Regiment:

'Our 6th squad went to occupy Outpost No. 10, which was nothing more than a barrage in an old tunnel trench . . . Six metres from our barrage, the Germans had set up their barrage. It was just a few strands of barbed wire between us, you could step across it in two or three strides, it was all that separated two nations, two races which were wiping each other out. There was even a covered sap which ended a metre from the German sandbags, if you'd stretched out your arms you could have shaken their hands.

Learning that he was condemned to spend twenty-four hours in such an outpost, a shirker or a good home-front citizen, no matter how patriotic, would have felt his hair stand on end and would certainly have written his last will and testament before heading up to such a deadly spot. How amazed he would have been, how stunned indeed, to see how calm and tranquil it all was in this little corner. One man smoking, another reading, someone writing, one or two bickering without bothering to lower their voices. And if these patriots, these shirkers, had listened a bit they could have heard the Germans coughing, spitting, talking, singing, etc. with the same lack of concern.

Their amazement would have turned to horror if they could have seen the French and German sentries sitting peacefully on the parapet, smoking their pipes and occasionally exchanging bits of conversation, like good neighbours taking the air on their front doorsteps.

Each relief passed on the local habits and customs of these little posts, and the Germans did the same – even if the whole of Champagne went up in flames, not a single grenade would land on this privileged corner.'

Such practices were common elsewhere, as shown by Captain Rimbault of the 5th Infantry Divison, from Rouen:

'Certain small posts were eight metres from the enemy posts. The men who occupied them, on both sides, did not want to hear anything that would lead to throwing grenades at each other. A tacit truce existed between the two sides, the Boche sitting on the parapet and smoking his pipe, and the Frenchman sitting opposite writing his letters. When one of the officers came round, the German would signal to his enemy and both men went back into their hole. Sometimes, when the enemy artillery started firing, the Boche, recognizing that there would be reprisals, shouted to the French:

"It's our artillery – murderers!"

At night, in front of the posts, barbed wire was set up out in agreement between the two adversaries, sometimes with one handing over missing items to the other. When a minor assault was being planned, the men warned each other and, showing their own grenades, made signs to make it clear that they did not expect to indulge in bloody excess.'

This complicity between men occupying the most advanced posts on each side, the hostility towards their own artillery, the advance warnings given to the enemy, can be found in many other accounts.

Louis Barthas describes the arrival of a sergeant from the neighbouring company who wanted to throw a grenade at the German sentry but was stopped by the the men. When an officer arrived to find out what was happening, he spoke calmly: 'So you're larking about with the Boche, is that right? Better be careful.' That night, Corporal Barthas asked his men not to answer the German calls.

At the same time, he posted a sentry to 'watch behind to see if we were being observed ourselves'. Another officer did indeed come storming up. He was taken for a German and, because he did not answer their challenge, a soldier threw a grenade at him, which bounced on his back without exploding. The enraged officer jumped into the trench: 'Who threw that grenade in my face?' Barthas replied that the sentry had done his duty, proof that they kept guard properly at the little outpost. Then the officer wanted to fire at the Germans to kill one of them. They pointed him in the wrong direction, he saw nothing, and departed muttering incoherently, which Barthas attributed to bad temper and a considerable dose of *gnole* (cheap brandy).

Nonetheless, the officers maintained their surveillance and one corporal was later caught and reduced to the ranks. On another occasion a lieutenant, cordially disliked by his men, brought down an over-confident German in cold blood, which drew direct reprisal fire.

> 'We began to cough heavily, to talk very loud, to joke and snigger to get the German sentries to show themselves. In fact, one of them was sufficiently intrigued to show his head, and then the French officer took aim slowly, carefully and shamefully and shot him through the head with a guard's rifle. Result: the Germans began firing, at any moment, all day long, with splintering rifle fire that tore through the sandbags, making guard duty impossible, and it was only by great good luck that none of our sentries was shot through the head.'

Barthas emphasised the opposition between 'the careless or perverse attitude' of the officers and the humanity among the soldiers. Of those who had not known life in the trenches, many could never under understand this tacit understanding, this brotherhood between enemies who were supposed to be watching each other all the time with their fingers on the trigger. But they should stop and think seriously about the fate of men who through the powerful and irresistible instincts of human nature were brought together in shared sufferings and dangers.

## Tacit Agreements

In the spring of 1915 near the front lines in Artois, the French soldiers of Barthas' regiment, the 280th RI, had occupied 'La Cuvette' (the basin), a shallow depression which provided shelter from rifle and machine-gun fire but not from shelling. On numerous occasions Barthas recorded how the Germans did not fire during peaceful activities such as labour, meals or sport.

During games of rugby – a sport of the greatest significance for men from the Languedoc – when the ball bounced into the front line wire the Germans refrained from firing on the bold player who emerged to recover it. Photographs taken on site and captioned by Captain Hudelle show a match in the Cuvette 'immediately behind the front line trench, 120 metres from the enemy'.[4]

After hours on guard or on fatigues the returning men needed a fire, which would have identified potential targets:

> 'Sparks, flames and smoke emerged day and night from hundreds of little fires, within sight of the Germans who tolerated them calmly because they were doing the same on their side.'

Elsewhere, fatigue parties worked at night on the barbed wire entanglements:

> '. . . in a little ravine with Germans on the other side who could certainly hear them working: yet not a rifle shot was fired: but this was reciprocal, there was virtually no firing on labouring parties from either side. How many thousands more victims would there not have been without this unspoken agreement dictated not by our leaders but by reason and common sense!'

And elsewhere again:

> 'the Germans having also installed their kitchens near the trenches, it was a matter of reciprocal tolerance and shared

interest that the unwarlike cooks on both sides were left in peace with their cooking pots.'

Louis Barthas also encountered the unspoken rules of 'good neighbours' in the mining war; men working night and day at the bottom of the mines ran a terrible risk of these small mines exploding, but a tacit agreement between the French engineers and the German engineers meant that there were very few victims. Over a long period, mines and small *camouflets* only ever exploded between two and six o'clock in the morning. This meant that the outposts and front lines were evacuated shortly before two o'clock every morning and, according to a widespread arrangement, calmly re-occupied four hours later.

Such examples from Louis Barthas should not imply that he recalled only peaceful episodes of the war. He also revealed some of its most violent moments which should have prevented any unspoken agreement or fraternization. The enemy nations were separated by an impassable new frontier, consisting of the lines of trenches on either side of No Man's Land, reinforced by barbed wire entanglements and artillery barrages. This frontier was under watch day and night, metre by metre, by hundreds of heavily armed men under orders to inflict the greatest possible harm on those opposite, in accordance with the rules of war, conditioned by a discourse that overflowed with hatred.

Such hatred probably faded among the fighting men themselves after the first months, as shown by many French, British and German combatants, but individual feelings of fear reinforced the general directive of 'Kill or be killed', and the enemy were sometimes perceived as devious and capable of treachery. An example can be seen in a letter of 28 April 1917 written by a man in the 80th RI:

'I have just been to see posts in advance of the front line, where the Germans are only twenty metres away, [from where] they even talk to us. They show themselves from the waist up. They have a nerve, there's one who greeted me and threw me a packet of cigarettes. But I didn't go out and pick it up because they are so deceitful, he could have shot me with his rifle. All the same, if

you don't bother them, they don't shoot us because they are as
fed up as we are. There was one who spoke very good French.'

It was the existence of so many obstacles to the 'establishment of
good neighbourly relations' that make many forms of such
relationships worthy of note.

## Official Sources and Trench Newspapers

There is a wealth of first-hand accounts as well as soldiers' notebooks and letters; and somewhere between the two come the
soldiers' own trench newspapers. The official framework of military life included the postal system and its surveillance, but extracts
from letters held in its archives represent the voices of the
combatant soldiers themselves. Consideration of official sources
must also take account of the leaden words of official language.[5]
In December 1914, stretcher-bearer Léopold Retaillau of the 77th
RI from Cholet began to copy into his own notebook the 'main
feats of the war' as reported by official communiqués.

In December, to the east of Reims, for example, in the middle of
a series of successful territorial gains and destruction achieved by
the artillery, the communiqué revealed German activity:

'On Christmas Day, the Germans emerged from their trenches
shouting, "Two days' truce!" Their trick did not succeed, almost
all of them were brought down by immediate fire.'

We may remark the words 'trick' (on the part of the Germans) and
'immediate fire' (from the French, vigilant and hostile to any form
of truce, for war must be 'total'). We know that the Christmas
truces existed, accepted or sought by both camps but, even without
a truce at specific points along the front, it is hardly likely that the
Germans would naïvely climb out of their trenches and let themselves be shot down.

On Christmas Day 1914 Retailleau himself mentioned that
French and Germans talked to each other in the trenches near
Ypres, and apparently even shared wine. Perhaps the contrast

between the reality of actual experience and the dead language of official texts induced the stretcher-bearer to abandon his self-imposed copying duty; he stopped early in February 1915.

Other official sources mention treaties and fraternizations in order to counter and condemn them. Some authorities appear to have had difficulty in believing that these deviations were possible, or tried to minimize their importance. Some officers' Journals (JMO, *Journal de Marches et Opérations*), mention them only briefly. For example, in the 30th RI on 27 December 1914:

'Situation stationary. The Christmas truce continues and the whole front is entirely calm. Along the two opposing lines, men do not hesitate to come out of the trenches. The Germans come over to meet our men, they exchange newspapers, tobacco and cigarettes. No other activity all day long.'

The JMO of the 56th Brigade for the same date reported the same atmosphere and activity in identical phrases.[6] As to the Christmas truce, complementary reports insist that the initiative came from the Germans, that the truce made it possible to bury the dead and to consolidate the trenches, to get useful military information and to impress the war-weary enemy with the French soldiers' determination.[7] It would appear, in fact, that the soldiers on each side reflected similar circumstances and feelings.

Lying somewhere between official texts, JMOs and the true feelings of the fighting men, trench newspapers were closely supervised and designed to sustain the *poilus'* morale and respond to their anxieties. They also added the occasional comic element. One of the most interesting extracts comes from *Marmita*, issue No. 1, dated 16 January 1915.

One morning, in an attempt to achieve closer acquaintance, a little circular was thrown over into the German entrenchment. Its text read along the following lines:

'You who are weary of struggling for a cause that is already lost, who dream of returning to see your bars and your girls, come over to us! You will come to no harm and you will have nothing further to fear from our 75s or our bayonets. Everything has been set up by the French for the welfare of prisoners. Men who suffer from bronchial problems are sent to the Côte d'Azur. Nerve sufferers rest in the clear air of Biarritz and the Pyrenees. If you like travelling you can go on a little trip to Algeria or Morocco. All the establishments reserved for German prisoners have the latest modern facilities, central heating, electricity and complete hydrotherapy rooms. Cigars, cigarettes, confectionery and sweetmeats are available in the canteens at the most generous prices.'

The proclamation continued in the same tone for around a hundred lines. From that moment, apparently, the conversations stopped and the enemy trenches were immediately relieved by other troops.[8]

Clearly, by mid-January 1915 it had already become possible to record 'brief conversations' which had been going on between the enemies 'for some time'. Use of the word '*loustic*', or 'joker', appears to indicate that this was neither serious nor generalized, for the word was not current in the language of the private soldier. It also appears, however, in the record of Major Bernard de Ligonnès, edited by Yves Pourcher:

'One *loustic* went out last night, he crawled as far as the Boche trench and talked to a Boche, telling him to come over, that things were very good in France: "A litre of wine every day, my German friend! Do you want some?"– "*Ja!*" He gave him a drink from his flask, the Boche gave him cigarettes, and they parted. Each one returned to his place, picked up his rifle, and the war continued . . .'

Both accounts, the trench newspaper and the Major's narrative, sought to minimize the affair: this was not a genuine fraternization, which *Marmita* and the authorities wished to avoid, but men exchanging 'semi-serious reproaches'. The little invented incident ended in the spirit of derision. Such trench journal items about exchanges between the two sides were designed to treat the enemy as a joke.

Two further extracts from these papers deserve comment. One is a humorous drawing showing an uncomfortable French trench full of water.[9] But the *poilu* in it, with water up to his knees, is entirely happy; with his left hand he holds up a sheet of paper while with his right hand he gestures over the parapet towards the enemy. He is shouting out 'Hallo there! You Germans, there's another laugh here, the *Gazette* is out again!' The drawing gives the impression that to address the Germans, to speak to them or gesture to them, was an everyday matter for the *poilu*. The actual words are ambiguous and can mean 'We French, we are going to laugh at you, the Boches, thanks to this new paper', or perhaps 'We'll have a laugh together, French and Boches'.

The other document is an extract from the trench newspaper *La Saucisse*, named after the sausage-like shape of a trench mortar shell or a barrage balloon. In June 1916 it adopted a serious and unequivocal note:

> 'This happened in a quiet sector. A thick mist blurred everything that morning. It was impossible to see two paces in front of your face. We had set up an outpost in front of our lines. It was cold, and drizzling; suddenly, a Boche patrol appeared out of the mist ahead. They were walking quietly, hands in pockets, rifles slung on their shoulders and smoking cigarettes. Dumbstruck, our men hesitated for a moment. That was when the Boche NCO suggested in a mournful voice: "Sad war, gentlemen! Sad war!" Then they disappeared back into the mist.'[10]

The mood of this short trench newspaper passage is not far from that of the soldiers' own writings.

## The Soldier's Voice

All sources, such as the notebooks written by the infantry corporal Louis Barthas, demand caution and a critical approach. With no education beyond the primary certificate, his writing talent was entirely natural, without literary effects, nonetheless his 550-page book sustains its energy to the end. Passages recording friendly contacts with enemy troops have been confirmed by other documents. But we may question the opinions that he expresses on these occasions. Was it probable that, as early as the occasion in December 1915, a soldier would have written a condemnation of the war, of its leaders and extremist belligerence? 'Ah!', exclaims Barthas, 'why weren't you there, our demented rulers, blood-thirsty generals, war-mongering ministers, death-declaring journalists, cowardly patriots at home, to observe this sublime spectacle!'

There seems to be no reason to question the corporal's sentiments, unless he had decided in advance that all French soldiers were bound to show consent to the war. In the real world, men evade any precise classification. It was not because the Socialists rallied to the *Union sacrée* (sacred union) that Barthas, socialist and pacifist before 1914, was bound to deny his previous position. Nonetheless he remained faithful to the cause. When in the Chamber of Deputies on 24 June 1916 the Deputy for the Allier, Pierre Brizon, justified his refusal, and that of his comrades Blanc and Raffin-Dugens, to vote for the war, Corporal Barthas was among those who sent him a letter of congratulation and who were brave enough to sign their names. A first letter has probably been lost, but on 17 August he refers to a previous exchange:[11]

'Dear Citizen Brizon,
    Thank you for the two brochures that you sent me. They are being passed round, and their effect is tremendous. Sometimes at a trench crossing a comrade reads them while two sentries watch out for a "watchdog" from our leaders.
    How your lines go straight to the heart of these men, who after two years are finally hearing, for the first time, words of peace, of hope, of faith and of protest against the greatest crime of all time against humanity . . .
    Esteemed Citizen Brizon, together with all my comrades, I send our most cordial brotherly sympathy.
    Louis Barthas, Corporal, 296th RI, 15th Company.'

Barthas defended this stance even as early as 1914. He was not alone in expressing profound hostility to the war at a very early stage. Such feelings are widely confirmed in the letters or notebooks of soldiers killed during the war, who had no opportunity to edit their material to reflect a possible change of heart after 1918. In

April 1915, for example, Joseph Bousquet cursed the war; on 8 January of that year he had already written: 'Everyone is demanding peace, shouting it out, myself the first'.

Such remarks convince us that it is not enough to extract an account of fraternization from a notebook or a letter. We need to know more about the author who is also the witness. We must enquire whether or not the text was designed for publication, and if so whether it appeared during the war or soon after, or whether the manuscript was uncovered decades later.

In his immense work *Témoins* ('Witnesses'), Jean Norton Cru describes some 300 books published before 1929.[12] Some texts were published just after Norton Cru's substantial book in 1929 while others have come out in the late twentieth and early twenty-first centuries, confirming the forecast made by Norton Cru himself. It could be said that the post-1978 success of the publication of Louis Barthas' notebooks marked the beginning of a significant renewed interest in books of this type.[13]

Some are rediscovered texts by notable French intellectuals such as Jules Isaac, or by other less well known witnesses – Louis Birot, Etienne Tanty. Other sources include notebooks and letters from peasants, craftsmen or workmen, such as Jean Bec, Xavier Chaila, Henri Despeyrières, Fernand Tailhades and Léon Vuillermoz. Some had never been published before. The vast array of accounts of fraternization does not offer any simplistic answers. What could be more dissimilar, in fact, than the 'life at war' of Sergeant Bec, of the volunteer recruit Binet-Valmer, the chaplain Birot, Colonel Campagne, the Franche-Comté ordinary soldier Léon Vuillermoz, or the antimilitarist libertarian Léon Werth? How did such a wide range of men describe friendly relations with the enemy?

A Catholic farmer and fervent patriot, Jean Bec left Béziers in January 1915 with the intention of fulfilling his duty to the nation which needed so many men to defend her against the invader who was occupying part of her territory.

In August, he hoped that the spilled blood would regenerate the nation and wash away the errors of the anti-religious government. On 25 September it had been decided to 'give a good sharp effort to bring it to an end . . . to chase the enemy out of France.' But he suggested it must be recognized that 'the Boches defend themselves in a way which brings credit on them'.

The horrors of the carnage, the absurd decisions of the leaders, their silly jokes, and the brain-washing in newspapers then took him further. Critical comments crept into the daily notes and soon occupied increasing amounts of space. 'Everyone is fed up' he wrote on 14 December 1915, at the same time as Corporal Barthas was fraternizing near Neuville-Saint-Vaast. On 3 March 1916 he was enjoying a quiet time in the front line on the Aisne: 'It's completely tranquil, not a rifle shot to be heard.'

In September 1916 he confirmed the existence of tacit agreements in the mining war, and in March 1917 detailed the encounter between German and French timber-carrying fatigue parties between the lines. On 8 April 1917 he described a sort of Easter truce: 'You might think that an armistice had been agreed on both sides, to spend this great festival without firing a single rifle or gun.' In the meantime, despite remaining faithful to his religious convictions, the sergeant was aware of angry protests:

> 'Oh! What torture! When can we expect the end of these sufferings? Our diplomats, those who are determined on a war to the bitter end, must come and share this life of every kind of misery with us, what the real *poilu* in the trenches has been enduring for more than thirty months.'

Two days later he reports:

> 'There too, there must surely have been some of our comrades in misfortune who will have paid with their lives for the pleasure of some cabbage sitting twenty or thirty miles away at the rear with his telephone . . . That's how a few more of the working class are sent out to a massacre.'

An ear ailment led to his evacuation on 18 July 1917. He wrote, 'Farewell to the front, my dream is coming true. I will do as much and more not to go back there.'

Léon Vuillermoz, a very young farmer from the Haut-Jura, was similarly self-righteous on the eve of war and did not hesitate to take careful note of any transgression against patriotic unanimity. In September 1914 he recorded a suicide. 'A sudden rifle shot was heard; we learned that it was a fellow from the detachment of the 35th who had blown his brains out.' In November, shirkers, profiteers and baggage-masters raided their comrades' mail. In January 1915 he reports two cases of insanity (one of two men, thought to be attempting to desert, was brought down by his sergeant). The notebooks for July contain a rejection of an order, an absurd distribution of decorations.

Near Bar-le-Duc in February 1916, before the German attack on Verdun, Vuillermoz recorded this laconic piece of information:

'Because some fellows in the 1st company had sung the *"Internationale"*, the company was given three days' punishment of additional fatigues.'

Another transgression is recorded in the same brief style, a truce near Confrécourt on the Aisne in March 1915:

'Only patrols kept things going on each side, but by tacit agreement no one fired on them, which produced a completely calm sector.'

In August 1915 he was somewhat more loquacious in referring to a message from the Germans, describing the method used to gain his attention (a 'missile' containing the text), and the translation undertaken by a man in his section who spoke German. The captain responded with the despatch of genuine trench-mortar shots, and the Germans retaliated.

In mid-February 1916, to the right of the Fort de Vaux in the Verdun sector, his unit picked up first a single German deserter, and then four more: 'They assured us of a major attack from their troops; they said that they and several of their comrades had just surrendered in order to avoid it.'

On 26 February Léon Vuillermoz' company was surrounded in Hardaumont Wood, and captured:

'They [the Germans] held out their hands to help us out of the trenches, calling us comrade . . . They did not maltreat us at all, did not search us, some of them gave us tobacco and cigarettes, they treated us like comrades, they said that we were lucky and that the war was over for us.'[14]

Louis Birot, Vicar General for the Archbishop of Albi, was a 'republican priest' who went off to the war at the age of 51 as chaplain to the 31st Infantry Division.[15] On 26 August 1914 he met his first Germans, three wounded Bavarians: 'I shook them by the hand; they returned the gesture warmly. They are Protestants'. On 30 August he intervened in favour of a score of men with self-inflicted wounds, and persuaded the authorities not to have them shot. His awareness of the particular sufferings of the heavy infantry came quickly; on 13 December 1914 he observed in his notebook:

'But the poor infantry! These infantrymen from the south, hacked about, weary, dragging their heels; the poor dirty, muddy, befouled infantryman, bent under his pack, sheltering under his groundsheet, wet through, his feet painful and frozen, his shoulders sagging under the weight of his kit, his rifle rusty: the infantryman who lives in holes full of water, who eats in them, who sleeps in them, who is living like a hunted beast, the poor heavy infantryman without escape, without life, who pounds the roads without knowing where he is going, who gets himself killed without knowing why: what an incarnation of weariness and suffering!'

Without approving it, the chaplain noted the outcome of this situation:

'Entire companies have surrendered like this, without military reason, out of weariness, cowardice or being led astray. This is a more reliable way of escaping the danger, and simpler than a self-inflicted wound.'

The gradual establishment of a friendly relationship with the enemy is delicately observed:

'First comes mutual insult: *Dirty Boches*, etc; then there are jokes and good humour and little tricks: soon there are cigarettes and sweets being sent across; in the end they are talking: the Germans say *"Kamarades, Kamarades!"* The leaders decide on a change of sector; the reasons for our move are complex. I stated one of them out loud: 'these over-extended contacts are not good for our men. Hatred, hostility, it all disappears. The enemy becomes *the neighbour*, often *the tempter*.' (9 December 1914.')

But Birot too was capable of change:

'Not one of them [members of the government] has the courage to get to the bottom of things, to undertake or propose the sacrifices which would make peace possible. And men go on killing each other! (1 August).'[16]

Colonel Campagne published his personal account in 1930. He suffered no doubts during the war and his book depicts a determined officer, forging straight ahead with unassailable conviction. He was certain that profiteers of all kinds and demagogue parliamentarians together had sullied the war. His book showed no lack of warrior spirit. At the same time, on the ground, the frank speaking allowed Major, later Colonel, Campagne to draw attention to the suffering of the troops, even to disobey a foolish order when its execution would unavoidably have led to carnage.[17]

His narrative includes three interesting episodes. During the night of 26 September 1914, French stretcher-bearers were rescuing the wounded. They were still at work when day broke: 'The enemy sent over a shell as a warning shot to stop us, then decided to let us get on with it.' At Christmas, men of both armies were singing in the trenches; but the stout-hearted officer thought it necessary to specify that, on the French side, they were singing 'Midnight Christians' while, 'opposite, they were singing hymns to the old German god, the barbarian god made in the image of the Lord of the war, Wilhelm II'. In December 1915, apparently in a sector near the one described by Louis Barthas, the struggle against the mud interrupted the war:

'The state of the trenches was lamentable [using the same word as Barthas] and it was almost impossible to get away from it. Taking advantage of this forced moment of peace, the regiment was opening conversations with the men opposite. They chatted from one post to the other, and threw bread in exchange for tobacco.'

Informed of this, the energetic Campagne reacted promptly:

'Two enemy officers appeared above the trench, their uniform revealing that they were artillerymen. Acting loyally, I had a rifle shot ostentatiously in front of them, into the air. They understood, and disappeared. Next day, when the rain had stopped, I made everyone go down into the mire, and the enemy did the same. The conversations had not yet begun again when one morning, at a barricade, the Germans asked why our attitude had changed and whether there had been a relief. A grenade-thrower and his sergeant answered.'

Surprised by an officer, the two 'delinquents' were sent to the Divisional General, who had them court-martialled, together with their Company Commander, an 'excellent lieutenant'. Campagne pleaded for the latter and obtained his acquittal; he said nothing about the fate of the soldier and the sergeant.

'To keep us going, and to keep the enemy alert, along our army front we kept up a series of the small operations known as raids,' wrote Colonel Campagne.

Léon Werth also spoke of patrols sent out to the enemy trenches, 'resigned to losing a few men' with no purpose except to arouse animosity: 'A useless patrol . . . an instructional patrol . . . A patrol to create more corpses in hatred.' The colonel and the private soldier might have been describing identical circumstances, but their interpretation was very different.

It was with full approval that Werth mentioned the gestures of comradeship towards enemy wounded or prisoners, exchanges of tobacco between the 'labourers of the two lines [who] sometimes feel obscurely that they are part of the same mass of men':

'There was a sort of armistice to bring in wounded men from between the lines . . . French and Germans alike came out of the

trenches and shook hands. The officers then had shots fired into
the air . . . the men returned, but for several days there were no
rifle shots across the parapets. Two soldiers with the Colonial
troops say that they had the same agreement between the two
sets of trenches. Men walked in front of the parapet, and one
morning the Germans signalled to them not to show themselves
so much because of their observation posts on the hillside
above.'[18]

On the jacket of his book *Mémoire d'un engagé volontaire*, Gustave
Binet-Valmer added the description 'citizen of Geneva' beneath his
printed name, yet he was above all a Parisian man of letters. His
war career was strange; he volunteered at the age of 39 as 'equerry'
to General de Trentinian and became sub-lieutenant in a group of
machine-gunners but ended up in the tanks. His dedication to
'Maurice Barrès whose work has never disappointed the combatants' matches various formulaic phrases scattered through the
book. A professional writer, Binet-Valmer sustained his literary
flourishes, notably in an account of fraternization in the spring of
1916. Earlier he had soberly observed a tacit entente to avoid
shooting, and the singing at Christmas 1915. He also described one
of the frequent scenes of fraternization after a trench flooding:

'As soon as I came over the crest I saw a strange spectacle.
Through my field glasses I could make out French and German
soldiers who were being forced out of their holes full of mud,
walking about between the trenches, using buckets to deal with
the flooding. A sort of truce was imposed on us by nature. As
long as a staff-officer did not think of ordering anyone to fire!
. . . The ammunition supplies were drowned, rifles and machine-
guns were threatened by rust. Germans and Frenchmen forgot
their mutual hatred and, in the desolation, looked at each other
across a few hundred metres . . . I came up from the rear, from
the village, I was fresh and ready. My own instinct was to seize
a weapon and bring down these figures.

"Fritz is working like us", muttered the men.

"And they are sympathetic, they feel for us what they feel for
themselves."

Believe me, the ferocity of this war is maintained by men who are not suffering.'[19]

## The Postal Censor

On its publication in 1917, Julian Arène's book was censored for its account of the Christmas Truce of 1914. In Louis Hourticq's narrative, the passage evidently 'suppressed by the censor' matched the description of good relations in the advanced posts. Notebooks which were not published before the end of the war or, in some cases, not until modern times, naturally escaped censorship; but trench correspondence and newspapers 'in the eye of the storm' were subject to censorship.

There was evidently a concern to avoid anything irregular. On 7 March 1916 Jules Puech of the 258th RI wrote to his wife:

'As you know, we were given very strict instructions to avoid being indiscreet in our letters, and I find that very restrictive because I would like to tell you what we talk about and what we do, and so on.'

Jean Tirefort, of the 50th RI, wrote:

'You will easily understand that I could tell you much more, more interesting details, but the censor is very severe and I would be punished and you would not even know the details, but we will catch up properly when all this nonsense is over.'

There was a specific account of early fraternization (14 December 1914) that Gervais Morillon included in a letter to his parents, begging them not to talk about it:

'Things are happening in the war that you would not believe! . . . the day before yesterday – and this lasted for two days in the trenches that the 90th are occupying now – French and German soldiers shook each other's hands; unbelievable, I can tell you! Not me, I would have regretted it . . . They came out of their

trenches, without weapons, nothing at all, with an officer in the
lead; we did the same and it was a real visit from one trench to
the other, exchanging cigars and cigarettes, and a hundred metres
away other men were firing over our heads from both sides; I can
assure you, we may not be clean, but they were really dirty, they
were disgusting, and I think that they are fed up with it too. But
since then, it's all changed; there's no more communication; I am
telling you about this little incident, but don't say anything to
anyone, we mustn't even mention it to other soldiers.'

For an episode of mutual understanding or fraternization to raise
concern in the postal inspection system, it was not enough for it
merely to have occurred. Descriptions meriting censorship required
participants or witnesses to describe the event, at the risk of having
their letters intercepted or of shocking the recipient at home. It had
taken some time for the postal censorship system to become organized; its primary purpose was to prevent indiscreet remarks about
positions occupied by military units, with the secondary aim of
assessing military morale – a feature which became increasingly
important as the war continued. A regiment's correspondence was
inspected on one day each month, and not in its totality. The
historian Jean-Noël Jeanneny has established that 180,000 letters
were read each week out of the correspondence of the nine French
armies – a proportion varying between one in forty items and one
in eighty.[20]
The rigour of the work undertaken may also be questioned. The
analytical process established in December 1916 had no heading
for 'understandings, tacit agreements, fraternizations'. Should
these accounts be sought under the heading B-6 'War-like or anti-
militarist feelings, vengeance for the dead, hatred of Germans' or
under B-9, 'Subversive Opinions'? They were often slipped into
B-10, 'Various' . . . And if, as Jean-Noël Jeanneny has calculated,
each censor had to examine 280 letters each day on average, based
on eight hours of actual work, and without taking account of
possible weariness towards the end of the day, that left less than
two minutes to read a letter, while also taking notes. No doubt
plenty of letters 'of no interest' could be skimmed quickly. But it
needed time to decipher the phonetic writing of some corres-

pondents or, at the other end of the scale, to follow the thinking of a few intellectuals such as Jules Puech, who used sophisticated codes to send information to his wife.

In their summaries several senior censors emphasized the 'blank-ness' of the letters. The riflemen of the 17th RCP 'say very little in their letters' (9 September 1917). 'The correspondence [of infantrymen of the 367th RI] contains nothing of any significance' (17 September). On the previous 28 May 1917 a report of the situation in the VIIth Army noted that:

'A misunderstanding of the censorship led a trooper to believe that his letters were suppressed purely and simply when he turned his attention even very slightly away from the line, above all when he thought of expressing what he called "truths".'

Most soldiers, however, kept their comments for their leave: 'I am going to tell you about it in a few days' time', wrote one *poilu* of the 143rd RI on 3 May 1917. And another, in the 118th RI, on 5 January 1918: 'I was at an advanced post with the lieutenant this afternoon. I have seen the Germans, but I will tell you about it later.' The same concern also explains the precautions taken in some accounts in which it is made clear that the initiative came from the Germans; the direct participation of the writer of the letters is concealed behind vague phrasing, or even denied when his friends took part in the fraternization.

The censors' reports were accompanied by somewhat unsatis-factory statistics. Proportional figures are given for letters that were 'good', 'bad' or 'without interest', the latter generally representing 90 per cent of the total. Soldiers who were accounted 'good' could write without any fear. Those who had expressed a 'bad' spirit dared to brave the censor and take a risk. The problem is that among the 85, 90 or 95 per cent, how many did not dare to write what they were really thinking, or to describe what they had seen?

In the extracts from 'bad' letters reproduced, one expression often appears: 'Everyone is fed up . . . everyone thinks the same as me'. This passage from a letter from the secretary of the colonel of the 202nd RI, intercepted on 18 October 1916, is extremely inter-esting on this point:

'Our men are charged to go tonight to deliver a manifesto printed in German which invites men to surrender and be taken prisoner, assuring them that they will be well treated until the end of the war. They surrender quite easily, but it is a reciprocal arrangement. Everyone values his own skin and surrenders at the first opportunity. I have seen it. And you only have to hear the soldiers talking and see them at work to be convinced of it. Everyone wants peace and seeks it out loud, and I can't understand how the French soldier can carry on marching, as he does, despite his independent nature. But the commanding officers observe that men are beginning to be tired and so we see them behaving carefully. General Joffre would like each soldier to go on leave at least every four months. Warm clothing is distributed and the soldiers are led to believe that people are concerned for their well-being, that's just beating the drum. It's time for it to come to an end, for everyone is completely fed up with it.'

Another non-commissioned officer, in the 131st Territorial Regiment, wrote about the farm workers under his orders in March 1917:

'They are tired of the war. All the men in our trenches are farmers, so they tell me, and if our wives are productive managers the war will last longer. Don't grow anything and the war will have to end sooner. That's their theory, I've heard it said hundreds of times around me.'[21]

There is a certain amount of rhetorical exaggeration here, no doubt. But to say 'everyone' has had enough implies quite widely voiced opinions from those who dared not write 'interesting' letters. In a letter to his parents on 18 May 1915, Henri Despeyrières writes that 'Everyone is fed up with the war'; and he insists on the clinching detail that he was referring to 'all of us here, officers and men'. Men who both gave their name and remained anonymous in letters to the socialist Deputy Brizon often mentioned that they were writing to him on behalf of a group.[22] Comrades in Corporal Barthas' squad made sure that he forgot nothing when he wrote his notes: 'You are writing about the life we are leading, you must not hide anything, you must describe it all.'

These observations offer proof of the lack of precision in the censor's statistics and the under-estimation of the amount of protestations favouring any form of transgression. This is evident in the case of a soldier in the 25th RI, a farmer in the *département* of the Manche, who wrote home in August 1917:

'We can see the Boches working away on their side as well, and no one is firing . . . Believe me, I don't feel good these days, and we are all the same because we are completely fed up. . . It's getting sad just now all round because I can't see the harvest brought in if it goes on much longer, between ourselves we wish that nothing more would happen, because that's the only way we can see an end of it.'

The discussion was evidently general within the squad, the section and the company.

The copious postal censorship archives may not be capable of giving us a full understanding of how transgressions, understandings and fraternization featured in the experience of life at war, but each series of letters examined can be read as a single item. Together they build a record of a specific regiment at a specific moment, revealing details of situations and events and, sometimes, contradictions which can in themselves be enlightening.

## Censorship in 1917: 'We are real friends with the Boches'

Inspection of the mail of the 217th RI on 24 January 1917 identified fourteen extracts which were queried. All agree: they are cold, but the sector is calm. The longest extract comes from a letter written by a member of the 19th Company:

'Fortunately the Boches have left us alone, no surprise there, the poor men are like us, they have often told us, they are the sacrifice for the outlaws who command them. It's only the artillery who are making war now, and we and the Boches, all day long and all night we walk about on top of the trenches. If anyone wanted they could fire at point-blank range but we don't do it any more. The Boches make signs to us with their rifles that they don't want to shoot at us any more; if they were forced to it, they would fire in the air [they would raise the butt end in the air, a sign of mutiny, or they would fire upwards]. My dearest wife, you can see how tired we are of the war . . . All this tells me that we heavy infantrymen are being messed about a bit too much. We are tired of putting up with it. We have had enough. Let Briand's gang, the men who want war to the bitter end, let them come and do it, but as for us, after two and a half years now, we don't want any more of it.'

This letter gives no indication of distance from the enemy front line, while others are more specific; two soldiers say they are thirty metres from the Germans, while one speaks of ten metres. Everyone describes the French and Germans coming out of the trenches and walking around in the open air, with no one firing, and barrages of barbed wire being set up in full daylight, both nations working alongside each other. French bread was exchanged for German cigarettes or cigars. 'We are friends with the Germans, in the morning we shake hands,' wrote one. 'We are good friends with the Germans' wrote another. And a third: 'It's the same on both sides, people say good morning, we're all comrades.' A corporal told how a German came to surrender:

'My man set his bayonet at his chest. He took hold of it and turned it away as he jumped into the trench and touched the hand of my man, and said: "*Bonjour Français*".'

Two further statements from soldiers go beyond a simple description of good understanding. 'We are desperate for this war to end because everyone is fed up with it,' wrote one man in the 19th Company, while a machine-gunner observed:

'Here I am again on the steps of a dirty and detestable sap. I wonder what these bastards are trying to do with us. Why don't they want peace, these murderers? It's because they are busy filling their wallets, the swine, and it makes us impotent, like

slaves, like feudal serfs . . . I'm looking for peace at any price.
There's plenty to be fed up with. Everyone's demoralised here.'

And what about the officers of the 217th RI? None of their letters
attracted the censors' attention. One might suppose that men fraternized without their knowledge, but the movement described by
soldiers was too extensive for the officers to have remained in
ignorance. They chose not to speak of it in their own letters, but they
mentioned it to comrades in the neighbouring regiment, the 221st.
On the same date, 24 January, the postal censors read a letter from
a sub-lieutenant in the 221st and picked up the following extract:

> 'These gentlemen of the 217th RI are telling us very interesting
> things. They are in the front line, thirty metres from the Boches.
> They can see each other all day long, the Boche soldiers salute the
> French officers in impeccable style. And no one, on either side,
> fires his rifle. This is in the interests of the French, who are in a
> less favourable position. It happens that the Boches are desper-
> ately hungry and keep begging for bread whenever they can, our
> men give them the crusts that the rats won't bother with, and the
> ends of pots of jam, in exchange for big cigars. The Boche officers
> laugh, and call the French officers "comrade" as they salute them;
> the soldiers even make the sign of breaking their rifles.'

Clearly, the 217th officers, at least the junior officers, knew all
about the fraternizations. And in speaking to their neighbours in
the next regiment they tended to play up their own part and to
denigrate their enemies, who are begging for food. They hint that
French soldiers did not genuinely fraternize with their equals; they
supposedly cheated the starving men by giving 'crusts' in exchange
for 'big cigars'. Yet this flatly contradicts the tone of the soldiers'
letters when they mention they had exchanged bread; one of them
even mentions white bread.

Further, not a single letter from an officer of the 221st RI
mentions the following incident, reported by a private soldier in the
regiment:

> 'How miserable we are, living like pigs . . . Yesterday, some of
> the men called out: "Down with Briand", they were singing the

"*Internationale*", "The 17th", etc., it went on for an hour. The officers did not say a word. They are equally fed up.'[23]

The officers said nothing, they wrote nothing. And so the postal censor reported the situation in the 221st, having examined 533 letters of which twenty-one were 'good', only four 'bad' and 498 'of no interest': 'Morale good, although there are plenty of complaints of frozen feet and cold food.'

## 'It's Better Than the *Chemin des Dames*'

On 2 July 1917 the censor looked at letters written between 24–29 June by the 25th Battalion of the *Chasseurs à pied,* seen as élite infantry troops. This unit was based in a quiet sector in Alsace. 'This little stretch is entirely calm just now. The weather is superb, we are enjoying a veritable health cure,' wrote one man. Another wrote that, 'I am rewarding myself with a splendid holiday that I certainly could not have afforded in civilian life.' While a third soldier wrote:

> 'We are in a nursery sector, very peaceful, no shooting allowed. We have our meals on the parapet, and Fritz does the same. From here you can see fellows from the companies [who] spend their day talking with the Boches. It's certainly better than the *Chemin des Dames*.'

This soldier does not say who had forbidden them to shoot, but from other sources it seems that the decision was taken at their base, confirmed by a fourth extract:

> 'It is strange to see how well we get on with the Boches. Last night the Boches came over to lay barbed war a few metres from our sentries, we did the same, not a rifle shot between us. [Soldiers to] our right chose to fire on the Boches working party, it was shelled in return.'

Those who did not respect the truce were punished with reprisals.

## Boche *poilus* and French *poilus*

In September 1917 the Argonne sector was very quiet. 'It's not really what you would call war', wrote an Auvergnat, and a Parisian noted that 'the sector is peaceful, the Boches do not worry us'. The fraternization is classic: men see each other, they do not fire, they say 'Hallo', they talk together, they exchange things. And, clearly, everyone enjoys it. 'If I ended the war here, I'd be almost sure to go home in good health,' wrote a *poilu* from the Doubs. A corporal who witnessed this friendly scene did not hesitate to describe it in admiring terms:

'Yesterday we witnessed a pretty little session in the front line between German and French soldiers. It was all quiet around 6–6.30 a.m. At about 6.30 a.m. we suddenly heard someone shouting, a German voice, very German, saying, "*Kamarades Franzouses*", twice. A great devil of a Boche, very upright, imperturbable, showed all the upper part of his body out of his outpost. As was proper, and fully in line with his duty, the sentry took aim at him and was about to press the trigger when a 'friendly' soldier (from the Engineers) intervened and stopped our good defender in his destructive work, then this friendly type, imitating the Boche, stuck first his head out of the post, then the top of his body: "What's up, Comrade Boche?" he asked, and the Boche replied: "I'd like to hand over our *Gazette des Ardennes*, if you'd like it, do you want it?" On the affirmative, the Boche picked up a stone, wrapped it in the newspaper and then balanced it on the parapet . . . This chap, who was certainly no green youth, jumped on to the parapet and, standing upright, slowly, picked it up. While he was doing this, six other Boches had deliberately shown themselves while a score of our men had flooded into the outpost. . .

Then the Boche soldier turned to his friends and asked them something in German. He went from one to the other, then came back to his first position and shouted in very good French: "Do you want any more papers?" Then he threw over seven papers. Everyone disappeared, one after another, and we did the same. Yesterday, a German soldier started singing while I was on duty. We answered him with a shout of "Good pig".

The same thing happened every day. When we took over from the *poilus*, cigarettes were passed to and fro and men even had a drink together. I should say that the distance from this Boche outpost to the French is barely a dozen metres, they came out to share a drink there at the bottom of a mine crater.'

The postal censor for the 226th RI for 13 October 1917 discovered a fresh example of tacit agreement after a flooding. The extracts retained by the censor fell into two groups. Three examples clearly evoked an agreement not to fire, as seen in this letter to an address in the Deux-Sèvres:

'For some time now it has been raining all the time; at this moment we are up to our knees in water, we have to climb out on top of the trenches; it's lucky that this is a quiet sector, otherwise I don't know what we would do. It's the same for the Boches, if not worse, we can see them walking along the trench tops, we don't fire on them because they could do the same to us.'

Five extracts describe the flooding and its consequences, without referring to the Germans: 'It never stops raining; it's getting really awful'; 'If you could see me now, how I am writing to you, the water is up to my knees'; 'All the tunnel-trenches are falling in, the shelters along the lines are all flooded'; 'It's been raining for three days now without stopping . . . We are wet through to the marrow of our bones; we have to get the water out with our shovels . . . In our shelters, the water is nearly up to our bunks'; 'Between the Boche trenches and ours, there's a real lake.'

### 'All Good Neighbours'

The expressions 'neighbours' and 'good neighbours' appear frequently in the extracts to illustrate the range of situations. That it was possible to refer to the enemy as 'good neighbours' in the context of such a merciless war raises questions.

The two sets of infantry, both vulnerable, faced the same enemies in terms of weather conditions and their consequences. Indirectly, the enemy of the men in the trenches might be the artillery on both sides, and even 'them', the officers considered responsible for a violence that the base did not intend. These conditions could be sufficiently marked for the sociability established on one side of No Man's Land to be extended across both sides.

## Life in the French Trenches: Friendliness Versus Dehumanization

Away from towns, villages and houses, the soldiers lived in and under the ground, sometimes at the heart of woodland, or what remained of it after shelling. Too far from the kitchens and too near the latrines, along with lice, flies, rats and sometimes corpses. On 28 June 1915, when the historian Jules Isaac was a corporal with the 11th RIT in Champagne, he described the typical conditions:

'Three and a half hours marching, carrying full kit on one's back. The men are heavy, weary and suffering. A vague smell rises from the ground, which is full of bodies. Improvised cemeteries every-where, full of little wooden crosses . . . At first light, between 2 a.m. and 3 a.m. in the morning, we reached this new mole's burrow along winding tracks. I don't know how to describe this extraordinary place for you . . . at the bottom, a wretched little stream runs close by, naturally disturbed, polluted with the ordure of the thousands of men who have lived here and are still living here. All along the river, flies in their billions gorge them-selves on flesh . . . All the other side of the little hillock . . . is hollowed out, worked through, inhabited, honeycombed with holes and hide-outs of every shape and form. Planks, stones, sticks, corrugated iron, all cobbled together roughly.'

Then he adds that 'you can hear the blast of bombs and machine-guns all night long.' Isaac summed up the situation a few days later: 'It is the chaotic swarming of humanity returning to semi-savagery.'

As quickly as possible, using whatever came to hand, the ordinary soldier struggled to organize his life despite the complete lack of amenities. *Cagnas* and *gourbis* – dug-outs or bolt-holes – became improvised lodgings. But gradually they were consolidated and furnished with whatever could be pillaged from the shattered villages. Haversacks were not left lying about on the ground, they were hung on a bayonet stuck into the sides. Another bayonet stuck into the ground acted as a candle-holder. The light represented 'civilisation'. It was possible to build a fire. One lieutenant even decorated his shelter with a few roses, using an empty grenade as a vase. Empty 75 shell-cases could hold whole bunches.

Soldiers from a squad lived together in their dug-out. Early in the war, as a the result of the regiments' regional recruitment, these men knew each other well. Shortly after reaching the front line, Louis Barthas was

'. . . posted to the 21st Company, claimed by his captain Léon Hudelle from Peyriac . . . in the 13th squad, consisting entirely of men from Peyriac or the surrounding districts; this was the Minervois squad.'

They spoke Occitan together; they exchanged news from home, from their local area or village. Food parcels were divided and shared. Men from the Drôme, from Vézelay and many other localities did the same. They helped each other: taking a friend's place for sentry duty; finding a 'war godmother' for an orphan or for a soldier from the occupied territories of the North. A teacher wrote letters for an illiterate comrade. In the name of his friends, Corporal Barthas wrote to the Socialist minister Marcel Sembat, drawing his attention to the poor organization of the soldiers' bread distribution, and to congratulate Deputy Brizon on his brave stance.

Intellectuals such as Jules Isaac or Jules Puech discovered the friendships formed among men who had lived and endured for so long together. Naturally there were exceptions. Etienne Tanty, another intellectual, had the misfortune early in the war to find everyone unbearable in his squad of the 129th Regiment. Later, in the 24th, he was to find true comrades, 'in full mutual confidence'. Within a squad a confidence evolved in which news was exchanged, tall stories and continual humorous insults passed from young men to their seniors and from the older men to their juniors, as Jules Isaac observed on 24 December 1914:

'Luckily what saves us is the French temperament, equable, a liveliness of character which provides moral resources, finding something to laugh at whatever the circumstances, even tragic, an almost irresistible drollery; back there in the trenches, in the darkest and most awful nights, I have been reduced to uncontrollable laughter, weeping with laughter!'

The sharing of experience from the older men to the newcomers was important and introduced the younger soldiers to 'common practice' in relation to the 'neighbours' opposite. This determination to create a living place despite war and death is proof of an impressive capacity to adapt, yet this also softened the aggression towards the enemy and a modicum of dignity was rediscovered which strengthened morale.[24] The men who lived in these underground holes and mole-runs were 'rehumanized'. Were those men over there truly the animals described in propaganda? Verification was possible; they were there, close at hand.

### 'They Cough and We Cough'

This softening of the mutual spirit can be seen in letters retained by the postal censor; the trenches of the two camps were often close together, and the advanced posts very close. 'We are twenty metres away from the Boches, no more', wrote a soldier in the 52nd RIC in October 1917. A Parisian posted to the 143rd remarked in April 1917 that:

'I wish you could see where I am just now. It's a tunnel trench blocked by a barrage made of sand-bags, fifty centimetres thick and 1.20 metres high, and Fritz is a few metres away with his own barrage. They are Bavarians, good fellows, luckily, because otherwise it would be impossible to stay there. Don't fire, that's what they said, we won't fire either. I'm sure they don't have much to eat because they keep asking for bread. They give us cigarettes, and yesterday evening they sent me a card. I have kept it, I will show it to you when I'm on leave. It will remind me of them. We've been here for four days now, and never a rifle shot between us.'

Even unseen, the German presence opposite could not be ignored. They were audible: 'They cough and we cough.' (Pierre Champion); 'The Boches must have heard us laughing.' (Louis Mairet); 'At night, we can see them lighting their cigarettes and we can hear them chatting and singing' (Germain Cuzacq). A Parisian soldier posted to the 29th Battalion of Senegalese riflemen wrote that:

> 'There is one place where, when the black men make a noise, the Boches demand silence. We do the same thing, so it doesn't look much like war.'
> (30 June 1917.)

The soldier-hero of Pierre Chaine's book *Les Mémoires d'un Rat* watched a German. This tiny silhouette was a soldier like him who was carrying out the same work in a different uniform. Both ran the same dangers, suffered from the same bad weather, worked on the same fatigues. Even though these similar activities were devoted to opposing causes, in fact they created a communality of life and of concerns which was enough to create a point of contact that created a kind of obscure sympathy despite the surrounding hostility.

Pierre Paraf used the expression 'disconcerting sympathy': 'We were in agreement to accord the German soldiers a certain degree of esteem that was clearly a consequence of the shared experience of inexpressible sufferings.'

As Marcel Papillon remarked after the capture of a prisoner,

> ' "Poor buggers who are swimming in it like us and who must be sick of this wretched trade," said some soldiers, suddenly caught out by this disconcerting fellow-feeling. They are just like us, they must be absolutely worn out.'

This was written on 30 January 1915. On both sides, the infantry had not yet reached the end of their wretchedness; and neither had their enemies.


## Mutual Enemies

'Here we are living almost like good neighbours with the Boches,' wrote a soldier in the 59th Regiment in January 1917. 'It isn't Fritz who's the enemy, it is the winter.' Already in October 1914 Jules Isaac had referred to the mud as 'our worst enemy'. It became a regular feature in soldiers' letters. 'When we came down from the lines we were in a pitiful state, just ragged walking mud,' according to a soldier in the 120th RI in October 1917, who observed that their German enemies were in the same condition:

> 'Luckily the Boches are like us, otherwise we could not go on because we are forced to get up on the parapets, and the Boches do the same and we don't fire on them just as they don't fire on us.'

It was a matter of common sense for the infantry not to fire their rifles or throw grenades, but it also showed that they were not blinded by hatred. The artillery reacted differently; the gunners 'did their job'. 'The two sets of infantry remain quiet, but the artillery fire is still lively,' noted an artilleryman, Captain Pastre, in the spring of 1917 in Lorraine. Earlier he had recognized the different conditions:

> 'What a life of sacrifice it is for the fine fellows in the infantry! We certainly have our own tough times in the artillery, a session with a battery under bombardment undoubtedly lacks charm; all the same, there's no comparison between our miseries and what's happening to those fine fellows.'

'It's the poor footsloggers who are on the receiving end' observed Ladislas Granger, a sergeant in the 313rd. He wrote again in his notebooks that the French artillery:

'. . . were beginning to irritate us with their firing . . . that they sh** on the Boches without stopping, so they get angry and send over their heavy stuff.'

The same forthright language can be seen in the letters from Etienne Tanty to his parents:

'I still have nothing amusing to tell you. The artillery never stop sh****** on us, today and last night, no doubt for us to celebrate the 14 July [1915], and for the Boches in answer to their polite messages.

All day long the 75 has been sh****** on the Boches without let-up – and on us as well, apart from the fact that it is unbelievably wearisome to hear the shells fired, and whistling and exploding, splitting the air, and fire attracts fire and provokes enemy shots, the 75 salvoes are often badly aimed and end up landing in our own lines as much as in the Boche trench.'[25]

'It's only those wretched artillerymen who disturb us,' wrote a soldier in the 247th in October 1916 when a barrage interrupted an episode of fraternization. 'In this set-up, when the men hear the guns fire, it doesn't matter which side is firing, they shake their fists,' added Pierre Champion. Captain Rimbault reported Germans saying to the French: 'Our artillery . . . murderers.' 'The bombardment is starting up again; it's our lot who have started it, what bastards they are!' complained Léopold Noé. Whether the artillery was following the rules of war which required them to kill the enemy, or whether they had received specific orders, it made no difference to the infantry.

Many, along with the private soldier Despeyrières in the 14th RI, wrote or thought in June 1915 that:

'If our generals, if our staff officers joined us in an attack, if the general charged at the head of his army and the colonel at the head of his regiment, the war would soon be over and peace would be near; but those fellows don't understand.'

Léopold Noé's notebook records on 27 January 1917:

'There's a copse about 500 or 600 metres away, we went there to get wood but we ran into a bunch of sentries who took it from us and stopped us getting any more. It belongs to a big landowner round here, and our officers are billetted there, and we mustn't touch the wood, we who are putting our lives at risk for everything that there is in France. Our officers are well warmed and we don't have coal or wood to burn, it's appalling. If only an aircraft could come over and drop a nice little bomb, well aimed, on their château, that would make us proud!'

In July 1915 Etienne Tanty went further:

'If only they could spend just forty-eight hours in a trench, all those idiots who want to "hold on to the end"! A few 120 long guns, about 210 Boches, a team of gunners aiming their weapons on the Elysée, on the Wilhelmstrasse, on Parliaments, on the salons, the newspaper offices and that old toad of a Pope, it would be a game for the gunners and deliverance for us!'

And Lieutenant Desabliaux reported a dialogue in which a soldier in the 129th RI condemned the 'crew back at the rear who are swimming in the blood of the *poilus*.' According to the same soldier:

'All the soldiers are the same poor beggars, whether they are officially friends or enemies; they all carry the same vermin and the same misery. Well! I can bet one thing: put a hundred Boches on one side and a hundred French soldiers on the other, they would all say the same, *Vive la paix!* Let's have peace!'

In the course of a fraternization in December 1915 Corporal Alfred Joubaire commented that the Germans still loved their Kaiser. 'All the same, one of them said, "*Wilhelm, Poincaré, kaput!*"' 'Let them do the fighting, then, Poincaré and Wilhelm', exclaimed a soldier in Paul Cazin's hearing.

   The fierce disapproval of the men at the front extended to profiteers, men who enriched themselves, to gendarmes, to the 'officers who are too clean', whom the *poilu* Despeyrières no longer wished to salute.[26] René Naegelen summed up the thinking of the men in the trenches:

> 'Those Germans opposite are suffering the same fate. These men are too wretched to wish each other ill. In their shared misery they come closer to each other than to the men at the rear who flatter them, glorify them, encourage them – and get rich themselves. And if they could understand each other and speak to each other, they would shake each other by the hand.'

This concept had been shared in some quarters from the beginning, while for others the idea developed slowly; in some cases it was intermittent, but the length of each man's stay in the trenches was relevant.[27] Consent to the war was less profound and less generalized than has sometimes been asserted, but other forces were opposed to revolt.[28] Nonetheless, they could not prevent the men in the French trenches from extending their neighbourliness towards those opposite.

## Comfortable Relationships

In most cases, the first living Germans seen by French soldiers were prisoners. 'Their faces are much like our own,' wrote Pierre Champon, and, according to a friend of Paul Lintier, 'They don't have such ugly mugs as I would have expected.' Near Douaumont, in October 1915, Sergeant Granger watched a 'sad file of wounded men, so hard for the stretcher-bearers to carry through this quagmire . . . The volunteer German stretcher-bearers help our men, and they all shake hands afterwards.' In September 1917, also in front of Verdun with the 287th RI, Chaplain Lissorgues remarked that:

> 'I often observe with astonishment the almost familial relations between our soldiers and the prisoners. They try to understand and embark on limited bits of conversation.'

Conversation with the prisoners reveals the propaganda at work in both camps. Emile Devoize, from Romans, a soldier in the 252nd, wrote in his ten-centime notebook that:

> 'Yesterday we took a prisoner, a very pleasant man. He told us that we French torture our prisoners. What a distortion of the truth! It's the same as if we were to say that in general they, the Germans, kill our wounded men. A French corporal spent four days in the wood when he was wounded, he had nothing to complain about in the way of bad treatment; quite the contrary, they gave him water, and when they left him they shook his hand.'

No doubt to raise French morale by proving that their enemy was weakening, an officer included letters from German prisoners in a report. The result was not what he intended:

> 'They are the same as us. Wretched, despairing of peace, the monstrous stupidity of all these things, these wretches are just like us. The Boches! They are the same as us, and misery is the same for all of us.' (Etienne Tanty, 28 January 1915.)

These letters also helped to confirm the similarities between their circumstances.

For one of the men in Jolinon's squad, the man on the other side was 'the other poor bugger'. For others, they were 'poor buggers', 'poor fellows on the other side', 'brothers in misery'. Looking at their own image in the mirror, the men could be sorry for themselves.

Referring to someone else as 'that fool' when feeling a fool oneself was not insulting; nor was speaking of 'the Boches'. The German soldier was individualized with an informal name: 'Fritz is working like us', said a soldier to an officer, Binet-Valmer, who wanted to fire. 'I'm looking at Fritz, Otto and Wilhelm going quietly about their business,' wrote Jules Isaac. An unnamed sergeant in the 366th RI, whose letter was read by the censor on 17 March 1917, played on the familiar image created by the popular 'Alsace' novel of Erckmann-Chatrian:[29]

> 'The Boches are not harsh any more and they leave us in peace, no doubt they have to put up with a good deal too . . . We have

good relationships and we don't have anything to be afraid of, because there's a sort of understanding with friend Fritz, we see them coming out of their trenches about 200 or 300 metres away.'

As they watched the enemy, the French soldiers evidently began to recognize the enemy's human worth and courage. He was humanized. Truces would observe rest periods and mealtimes, his duties and leisure hours. On 23 April 1915 Roland Dorgelès wrote to his partner:

> 'Yesterday evening, or rather last night, the Prussians opposite us were relieved by the Saxons. They had hardly arrived before they began shouting: "*Kamarad* French, into your dug-outs!" They were telling us that we could sleep peacefully, that they were not planning to attack us; the Saxons and Bavarians are not quick to pick a fight.'

The minimal comfort that each side tried to introduce into the trenches was respected by the enemy, winning similar respect in return:

> 'The fire is kept going all day, and even most of the night. The Boches must be reasonable too, because we are in the front line, in fact they do the same.' (A soldier in the 297th, February 1917.)

Like Barthas, a man in the 132nd commented in October 1917 that:

> 'in some places we are four metres away from the Fritzes but they aren't unreasonable, and what's good is that our cooks can come to within fifty metres of us to get our meals ready, so we can always have it hot.'

Scarce water supplies were frequently used in turn by French and Germans soldiers, described for example in books by Jacques Meyer and Jean-Marie Carrié. Roger Dantoine's description can stand for all:

'At the centre is No Man's Land, with a stream running through it. The water is used by both sides. The place where the stream is easiest to reach has become a place for fraternization. Dusk falls, we go for water. Opposite, they are doing the same, in the same way. Each one waits till the first-comer has filled up, and then takes his place. Each one heads off in his own direction undisturbed.'

Other fatigues were undertaken without confrontation: 'The men go out at night to gather wood between the lines. Sometimes they meet Boches, who are doing the same for their units.' (Sergeant Bec, March 1917); 'Luckily the Germans don't fire and the working parties with food or trench supplies going up to the front line are not disturbed, despite the moonlight.' (Sergeant Brès, October 1914). This was evidently not always the case, if orders were strict.

Less frequent was the growing of food in No Man's Land. References to this practice were picked up by the postal censor for the 2nd BCP on 22 October 1917: 'We can see the Boches and they can see us, people walk around in the front line, and gardens are cultivated in front of the lines.' On 2 April 1916, Henri Charbonnier's unpublished notebook written in a Vosges sector only partially confirms this statement:

'The men are not very cautious either. They have been told that the Boches won't fire and off they go to pick salad leaves between the lines.'

Cases are recorded where the enemy was respected at his toilet or with his trousers down, taking a bath in a stream – provided it was a solitary observer and not a group of men. It was indeed a great blessing to be able to come out of the ground and walk around in the open.

There is frequent mention of truces to bring in wounded or bury the dead, with an implication of silent agreement from the officers. The brave Major Bréant, a career cavalry officer, refused a truce in November 1914 after a battle:

'We only had two men wounded. But the Germans lost men killed, and plenty of wounded. In the morning, two non-commissioned officers and a German soldier approached the trench. All three were wearing arm-bands and they waved a very large white flag with the Red Cross on it. They asked to take in their wounded. We took them prisoner. With such an enemy as this we cannot allow a truce or suspension in the fighting. No negotiations are possible . . . And the dead are there, unburied, fifty metres from the trenches, and the wounded are dying; sometimes we can hear them moaning.'

What would he have done if the French had suffered greater casualties than the Germans? Other officers did not take this attitude, as can be seen in examples too numerous to cite here.[30]

The ultimate consequence was that French and German troops not only respected their opponents' labours but helped each other. Galtier-Boissière evoked in general terms those tacit truces through which the adversaries could strengthen themselves in parallel, sometimes even obligingly lending each other their tools. Henry Nadel gives a more precise description:

'We redoubled our networks of *chevaux de frise* in full daylight. The Germans were working on theirs at the same time. One of their teams even gave a hand to ours, and lent them their wire-clippers.'

Even a captain, Paul Rimbault, was able to see that:

'. . . at night, in front of the posts, setting up the barbed wire was done in accord between the two enemies, one sometimes passing a missing item of equipment to the other.'

## Celebrations

In times of peace, festivals mark important cultural moments; in times of war, each side made efforts to celebrate such occasions within their own community. Some festivals were not suitable: the 14 July celebrations for the French, when the Germans would merely send up a heavier bombardment than usual; the Kaiser's birthday for the Germans or the celebration of a victory. In the

A classic image of the Christmas Truce: two Tommies of the London
Rifle Brigade (left and centre) posing with Saxons of the 104th and
106th Regiments. The photograph was taken by a fellow LRB man and
sent to London for publication. Courtesy of Imperial War Museum
Q70075.

Germans and British photographed *en masse* between the trenches,
Christmas Day 1914: an image which appeared in several British
newspapers in January 1915.

Boxing Day, 1914: a group of friendly enemies photographed by artillery subaltern Cyril Drummond. 'One German said "We don't want to kill you and you don't want to kill us. So why shoot?" . . . I lined them up and took a photograph.' Courtesy of Malcolm Drummond, Imperial War Museum HU35801.

'An Awkward Encounter': drawing published in *The Graphic*, 30 January 1915: a rare image of Franco-German fraternization at Christmas 1914. Spades and the presence of dead soldiers imply that this was a ceasefire strictly for burial purposes.

German soldiers singing carols in the trenches: a photograph taken on the Eastern Front but precisely reflecting what happened on the Western Front at Christmas 1914. Courtesy of Ullstein Bilderdienst.

Trench layout and conditions: soldiers of the 6th Queen's (Royal West Surrey) Regiment eating dinner in the trenches near Arras. Snow and the presence of steel helmets, not introduced until 1916, suggest the photograph was taken in the winter of 1916–17. Courtesy of Imperial War Museum Q4846.

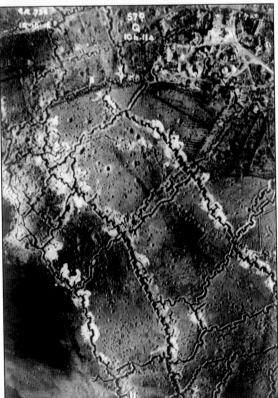

The danger zone known as No Man's Land: aerial view showing trench lines at Beaumont Hamel, Somme battlefield, 1916. British trenches, bottom left. Courtesy of Imperial War Museum Q61479.

Christmas Eve: 'Got 'im!': Christmas Day: 'Salaam Salaam'. Cartoon impression of the Christmas Truce by an Indian Army Officer, Captain E. R. P. Berryman, from a letter of 1 January 1915. Courtesy of Imperial War Museum Documents E.R. Berryman Collection, ref. 66/77/1-50.

'Talkers' (i.e. soldiers) and 'Fighters' (i.e. civilians). An American view of the Christmas Truce, *New York Evening Sun*, 22 January 1915.

The camaraderie of captors and prisoners: a British soldier offers a German prisoner a drink of water from his bottle as other German prisoners look on. Courtesy of popperfoto.com BOP30143099.

Battle of the Ancre, November 1916. A wounded German being helped by a British Tommy. Note the presence of the French camera crew, suggesting that this was effectively an early media event. Courtesy of Imperial War Museum Q4502.

Friendship when the firing stops: a Scots Guardsman giving a wounded German soldier a drink after an attack, August 1918. Courtesy of Imperial War Museum Q6983.

Eastern Front: the war between Germany and Russia. A German soldier comforts a wounded Russian, June 1915. This front was to collapse into chaos following the fall of the Tsar in 1917. Courtesy of Getty 3275606.

French trenches, even if the menu of the day was improved, the soldiers remained sceptical. 'I don't mention our national feast day, which will be celebrated only by the artillery,' wrote Pierre Champion. 'That's too formal; the true festival will be our deliverance, the end of our sufferings.'

On Wilhelm II's birthday, the Germans could be heard singing and, further to the rear in a French village occupied by the Germans, the church bells rang. In both camps, particularly in the early days, there were shouts of delight at the announcement of a successful offensive, the capture of thousands of prisoners, a new ally entering the war, in the hope that the good news would help to hasten the end of the war.

The main Christian feast days, on the other hand, concerned all combatants along the western front. In the sectors held by the British, the Christmas Truce of 1914 was an extraordinary occasion, completely contradicting the hatred which all kinds of propaganda were designed to develop, and the violence of fighting in the preceding days. The truce between French and Germans was on a smaller scale; it was still too early to fraternize with enemies who were occupying part of national territory and who had committed atrocities. Yet there were friendly conversations and exchanges even before December. And everyone saw Christmas as a sacred moment. Many no doubt agreed with Julien Arène: 'You cannot kill each other on Christmas night.'

The atmosphere of truce stretched along both sides of the front held by the British, all of it entirely spontaneous. In the north, near Ypres, stretcher-bearer Retaillau was only an indirect witness; he was told that French and Germans talked together, that three infantrymen had a drink with the enemy, that some enemy soldiers came over to the French trench to hand out cigars, that a major and a private soldier took the opportunity to be taken prisoner.

South of La Bassée, Gustave Berthier was personally involved in a fraternization which was instigated by the Germans:

'I was the one who went out to three or four metres from their trench, where three of them had come out, to talk to them. Both sides agreed not to fire their rifles, and there were some exchanges. A little further to the south, at Carency, French soldiers in the 26th RI were said to have sung German hymns with their enemies.'[31]

Various accounts describe truces in other sectors. In the Somme, a postman called Marius Nublat was not in the line but heard it said that:

'In certain trenches German and French soldiers smoked cigars together. The four Frenchmen who had been over to the Boches came back, but we kept the Boches. Eugène told me, in his letter, that they were singing on Christmas evening and that the Boches applauded them: "Bravo *Français!*"'

A Territorial soldier in the Aisne, Victorien Fournet, described a truce which seems to have lasted from 12 December to mid-January:

'And the Germans opposite us did not fire. They showed themselves and made signs to us not to fire and even better than that: yesterday lots of them came out on top of the trench. And it was the same from our side. They made signs to each other. Then the German proposed to come halfway across, he set out like us to shake hands. Then, first, off they went. They saluted each other, they talked together . . . And, in the afternoon, they played music; until the evening, they were dancing together, you could see them from the waist up in the trenches. I don't know now whether they wanted to play a trick on us or whether they were beginning to feel fed up. But, anyway, I can't be sure, I didn't watch them for long. But the artillery were not all that out of touch, shots came down from time to time.'

In Argonne, the singer Kirchoff gave a recital to the 130th Wurtemburg Regiment. Well wrapped up, the French soldiers in the opposite trench climbed out on the parapets and applauded so much and so well that Kirchoff repeated the song.[32] At Les Eparges, Eugène Lemercier heard another fine singer, an unnamed tenor:

'What an outstanding night! – a night beyond compare, where beauty triumphed, where despite its bloodstained failings humanity showed the reality of its conscience. I must tell you that along with the intermittent rounds of fire, there was singing all along the line, all the time! Opposite us, an impressive tenor announced the enemy's Christmas. Much further away, behind the ridges, where our lines began, the "*Marseillaise*" responded. The amazing night was full of stars and flying stars. Hymns, hymns everywhere. It was the everlasting search for humanity, the unquenchable springing of order in beauty and harmony.'

Elsewhere, according to Eugène Pic, the French took the initiative in the matter of song:

'At midnight, a few fine voices chanted the "*Minuit chrétiens*". They responded over there and a choir rang out in marvellous harmony with "*Stille Nacht! Heilige Nacht!*"'

Roland Dorgelès reported this episode involving the 74th RI in his letters, as did another soldier, Charles Toussaint, and the regiment's official daily record. Dorgelès recorded the events in different ways, according to the identity of his correspondents; and, curiously, he did not return to the incident in his novel on the period, *Les Croix de bois*.

The account from the soldier who was not a professional writer is more sober and more precise. It begins with the religious singing on both sides, during the night of 24–25 December. On Christmas Day a German envoy came to announce his comrades' decision not to fire and to request the same of the French, who readily agreed. Then something happened that resembled the best moments of the truce between German and British troops; hundreds of soldiers came out, from both camps, so that No Man's Land became the setting for a sort of village fête with gifts being exchanged, food, beer and wine.

The NCOs did nothing to interfere. It needed the regiment's commanding officer, Lieutenant-Colonel Brenot, to take the decision to end the truce by arranging for artillery fire, high enough not to wound his men or, of course, the Germans who were with them. The liaison officer Charles Toussaint was at the command post and heard the order being given by telephone. It may be noted that the official daily record for the 74th RI, which was laconic in its reference to the fraternization itself, toughened the official response:

'As soon the Colonel heard of these regrettable incidents, he gave the order to bring the men back and to open fire immediately on the Germans.'

Yet it seems that during the night of 25–26 December there was continued singing and visits between the camps. Toussaint reported that a Frenchman who had drunk too much was brought back to his trench by the Germans. During the day photographs were taken, as happens between friends and as happened with the British and Germans further north. The British press published some of these shots. General Mangin, in command of the 5th Infantry Division, ordered the confiscation of all such photographic records of the truce, and forbade the presence of cameras in the trenches.[33]

Although the French could not go quite as far as to say – like some of the English or Scottish troops – that the Germans were 'terrific chaps', it is probable that, wherever a truce occurred, the image of 'the enemy' softened to reveal men with human feelings, the same traditions and holy days, who knew how to rise above the limitations of warfare.

The Christmas truces in 1915, 1916 and 1917 are less well recorded than the events of 1914. What happened at the first wartime Christmas was a surprise for the leaders; afterwards they took matters in hand and gave strict orders, yet the spirit of *entente* between the infantrymen in the two camps was undiminished.

Then in 1915 there were fresh breaks in hostilities with French singing applauded by the Germans. Perhaps because he was not at the front in December 1914, Pierre Champion, a sub-lieutenant with the 288th RI, devoted a full and emotional page to Christmas Night 1915:

'Among other occasions, I remember 25 December 1915. I had spent the whole day in our tunnel trenches that were full of water.

The moon was visible through the shifting clouds; a great peace fell with the gentle milky light that surrounded us. What a silence! Nothing to be heard except the wind in the dry branches. Our men whistled, like bird-calls. The Germans, joining in the good mood, did the same. And our neighbours on the right, Territorials from the Auvergne, sang the chorus of "*Minuit chrétiens*" with great meaning and whistled the "*Marseillaise*".'

'Leaning on the fire-step, in our turn we sang the "*Noël*" by Adam, complemented with little harmonies from the flute played by our machine-gunner lieutenant . . . Were they thinking of their Charlotte, their Catherine, their Minna, their Louise, those men just a few metres away in front of us? It is heart-breaking to think of the dreams of so many poor men who were far away from the line in their thoughts that night. And I feel that I can see the tears in the eyes of some of my sentries, during that night-watch full of silence when not a single bell sounded over our countryside.'

Nothing fresh was recorded in 1916 or 1917. There was singing to be heard. Two soldiers from the 102nd RI went to celebrate with the Germans during Christmas night 1916, and did not return.[34] A soldier in the 2nd Engineers told his parents of a scene without surprises in 1917:

'On Christmas Night the Fritzes bellowed all night long, and it was the same with us. If anyone wanted to fire overhead from one side to the other, it would be a gesture without response. The heavy infantry on our side threw over bread, and they threw big packets of cigars and cigarettes. It was only the artillery which was firing.'

Without the specific date, this would have resembled any ordinary tacit truce. In fact, this occasion probably was just such a silent and mutually understood break in hostilities which had already lasted for a while and which Christmas rendered more colourful.

The other religious festivals had less emotional impact. Truces were observed at Easter and All Saints, but on a much smaller scale. As for the 'feast of deliverance' which was so long and fervently hoped for – 11 November 1918 – it was hardly a propitious moment for fraternization. It was a day of victors and vanquished. The French had received strict orders: 'Do not speak to them'; 'All friendly gestures are forbidden'.[35] Among the extracts from trench newspapers which escaped the spirit of propaganda and irony towards the enemy, the following may be cited:

> 'Military bands struck up suddenly, loud and strong and, from the German trench, like a jack-in-the-box, Germans sprang out, hands raised, they walked across towards us shouting: "*Kamarades*, the war is over!"
>
> They were singing, their faces were joyful. My goodness, they looked happier than we did, these losers. But I looked at their faces bending down towards us where, as on our faces, there was a passionate warmth of deliverance. After all, we all share the same thoughts today, we are the same, men who are finally released.'[36]

## Allied Talk

Some Germans and a few French soldiers could speak their enemy's language, quite apart from men from Alsace who were present in both armies,[37] and opening friendly relations between the two sides was sometimes hampered by language differences; as one *poilu* of the 201st RI exclaimed when his trench was only a few metres from the enemy, 'If only I could speak Boche!' But the barrier was not insurmountable. Various forms of communication were in use, successively or simultaneously, and might begin with apparently unfriendly exchanges.

## From Insult to Lightheartedness

When the enemy armies dug into the ground in the autumn of 1914 they had just gone through several weeks of desperate fighting. Their spirit was weary and shots continued to be exchanged from one front line to the other. The enemy was safe from rifle fire but was within range of the human voice; fusillades to stop him raising his head alternated with disparaging insults. Chaplain Birot observed: 'Mutual insults first . . . Then came humour, light-heartedness, playing tricks.' In the trenches to the right of those occupied by Jules Isaac in May 1915, men:

> 'exchanged insults and challenges with their Boche opposite numbers in the Homeric style which is always up to date. In the end the Boches brought out the *mot de Cambronne* ["merde", shit] in a terrible accent. General laughter.'

The classics formed a considerable part of the education of any writer who had qualified as a secondary-school teacher with an *agrégé* degree in history; he had lived with Achilles and Hector, the Achaeans and the Trojans. His contacts with men in the trenches taught him a great deal, not least the ability to find humour even in tragic circumstances. The stone-dresser from the Drôme, Louis Chirossel, with nothing more than his certificate of primary education, wrote of one of his friends who was also at the front:

> 'He is working a little to our left and so close to the Boches, that they do nothing but squabble with each other all night long, as well as with the Boches. Apparently it's quite funny.'

Louis Hourticq described a conversation punctuated with rifle shots and interrupted by shelling: 'After the bombardment, the verbal insults carried on, the supplies were inexhaustible.' The cook was as 'voluble as a machine-gun'. But another soldier had to admit:

> 'As he was tossing out insults with a heavy provincial accent, one of the Boches told him rudely in Paris street slang to go and learn proper French.'

Maurice Genevoix recorded another battle of insults that ran to German advantage, during which one of his comrades sought desperately for fresh ammunition: 'Who knows a Boche swear-word, real Boche, in Boche slang?' That brought laughter on both sides, even as the rifle shots continued in the full knowledge that they would not reach their target.

Rumour reported that Louis Hourticq's cook armed himself with a large kitchen knife before advancing on to the parapet to confront the enemy. In Verdun in 1915, Jules Puech witnessed a scene of bravado which he described to his wife:

'Yesterday evening, we were barely settled in and watching night fall, with lovely moonlight on the trees, when Sub-Lieutenant Parison came up to show the sergeant some levelling work to be done. Then he got up on the parapet in order to explain things more clearly – which was unwise, because it was not yet completely dark. Running like a rabbit he went to examine the *chevaux de frise*, which were exposed to potential enemy fire. We were so close to the lines that when he returned we could hear German voices. I couldn't make out what they were saying, but someone confirmed that one officer was speaking French.

'I don't know whether P. was stimulated by his little act of imprudence, or for some other reason, but he started to shout to the enemy in German, moving from one place to another, and then he fired off a dozen rifle shots. I could hear clearly, "*Deutsche Kamarade*" and . . . "*zurück*" ['back']. I could also hear someone responding in French, something like, "You are silly", which my comrades told me they heard too.'

The men in their trenches followed the spectacle of aerial combat high about the trenches, and applauded their own side's victories. On 5 November 1914, in the days before his enthusiasm had cooled, Henri Despeyrières wrote to his parents with an account and some interesting comments:

'I have just been very impressed. I have just seen one of our aircraft fall after being hit in full flight by a German shell. He was mortally struck . . . It's the first aircraft that I have seen brought down since the beginning of the campaign. By bad luck it was a French one . . . The pain at seeing one or two of ours fall also includes a sort of scorn. A shell that is fired on us often creates more than two victims. But the Germans do not know this; they do not see it. This morning they saw and we heard them, from our front line trenches, applauding wildly. Oh, if only we could bring down their machines!'

And two days later, he wrote:

'Yesterday evening we heard the news (to be confirmed?) of the Austro-German retreat. At the colonel's order we sang the "*Marseillaise*" and shouted *Vive la République* and cheered with enthusiasm in the front line trenches. The Germans responded in turn with a tremendous row. They shouted: "Down with France", in French, and quite a lot of other things, sometimes in French and sometimes in German, and each one accompanied by the music of . . . shots (sorry, the Germans were also playing the flute, as they do quite often).'

A theme emerges; each side proclaimed its victories to the enemy, and the addition of fresh allies on their side of the war. For any 'information' received, there would be an answer:

'We sent them a little note saying that the Russians had taken 200,000 prisoners, that must have pleased them. The next day they answered our comrades to say that they were not Austrians and that they were waiting for us.' (Postal censorship, 247th RI, 1916.)

Large notices carried the same themes: 'Come on over, we are waiting for you' (Pastre) or 'Warsaw taken' (Castex) . . . The French 'wrote this notice on a large board: "Death to the Boches". And the Boches fired on it . . .' (Dorgelès). Combat in the form of insults and boasting turned into a game. Rifles were to hand; they were part of the game. It was a matter of defacing an enemy notice, but also of showing skill in target shooting.[38] In the trench opposite Le Rutoir (in the Vermelles sector of northern France) on 23 November 1914, Valdo Barbey observed that the Germans were waving their shovels, with only the tips visible, 'to show us whether or not our firing was accurate'. In an anecdote from a soldier from Agen, the French awaited the withdrawal of human targets before firing:

'It has been snowing for two days, and it's not melting. The Boches set up snowmen in front of their trench, and that's enter-taining. We demolish them with rifle shots.'[39]

More generally, the proximity and the extended sociability provided opportunities for shared laughter, even – and perhaps particularly – over the most trivial incidents. One morning, at dawn, Lieutenant Marcel Etevé appreciated the talent of a 'Boche artist' who was giving an impressive imitation of a hen laying an egg. Captain Tuffrau observed a show that went on for 'more than a quarter of an hour' in the trenches not far away:

'The French sentry showed himself from the waist up, blew his whistle and the German appeared; both of them were laughing and making comic gestures, and then disappeared. Then it was the German's turn to begin.'

### Intermediaries and Fraternization

The exchange of insults and bragging was a conversation of sorts. On both sides, it could happen that men took up the game and laughed promptly and without showing themselves. In the case of the two sentries making others laugh with their grimaces, it is not known which one first dared to show himself or what signs helped to set up a climate of confidence. The situation described by Captain Tuffrau was, moreover, more complex. It was not merely an interval, a fragile peace treaty between two individuals: the inci-dent was part of an ensemble of practices that involved the participation of the whole section and even connivance at battalion level.

Jacques Roujon tells of one such brief but complex incident:

'An interval: the Germans imitate animal cries, roosters, dogs, calves, pigs. We ask for news of the Kaiser. They reply: "He's well thank you; see you soon in Paris." Then we retort with a single word. Opposite, they shout out again: "Happy Christmas. Send us some wine." And they sing the "*Marseillaise*".'

Music and singing were widely evident. Philippe Barrès records that by the Aisne in January 1917 the French troops heard a German playing the harmonica. They called out to him: 'Comrade, do you know 'Puppchen', do you know 'Lorelei'?' The musician apologized for his poor instrument. 'That doesn't matter!' shouted the French. Elsewhere it was a French soldier who sang and a German wrote home that it made him forget the war. In a similar anecdote Henri Despeyrières wrote that:

'. . . in our trenches, one of our soldiers was singing and when he had finished there was a distant sound of clapping came from the Prussian trenches opposite.'

In May 1916 the postal censorship picked out this extract from a letter written by a soldier in the 401st RI:

'We have a concert every evening; the Boches begin while we sing the "Marseillaise" or the "Brabançonne" [the Belgian national anthem] and all sorts of songs, they even play the accordion; each side applauds the other.'

It is not known whether the practice, which was noted on two nights, continued; it was clearly the intention to have a concert 'every evening'. Roger Boutefeu recorded the same circumstances.[40] Gabriel Thivolle-Cazat could hear the Germans opposite him singing the 'Internationale' in French.[41]

One very distinctive situation appears in the postal censor's records for the 2nd Regiment of African chasseurs for 15 March 1917. The summarising report stated:

'These cavalrymen hold the trenches on the extreme right of the front, right up against the Swiss frontier, as shown in a photograph that was taken and sent to the General Staff. This particular situation gave rise to a curious incident: a Swiss military band had come to the meeting point of the three frontiers. The Germans and French came out of their trenches to listen to the concert.'

Caution in the face of censorship kept the soldiers from describing too much in their letters – except for one man in the 3rd squad:[42]

> 'On Sunday morning a Swiss band came and gave a concert at the extreme edge of their territory, which lasted for three-quarters of an hour. Germans and French came out of their trenches to listen to the band and applaud the performers. It was strange.'

This incident is confirmed, indirectly, in a rather later letter (19 April 1917) from a corporal in the 6th African *chasseurs* occupying the neighbouring sector. The Swiss must have continued their recitals, since the two letters do not refer to the same 'concert':

> 'At a distance we heard the Swiss bugles. What a change so near us! Here, everything was quiet. At 8 o'clock everything was shut down while next door the neutrals were making plenty of noise, they had lights on and were far from unhappy, at least that's how they sounded.'

According to Maurice Gandolphe, the Bretons who formed a squad within his company decided one day to dance in the open, to accordion music from the German trenches. Henry Nadel describes a genuine fraternization, quite lengthy and complex in form, which arose from a Paris waltz whistled by a French sergeant and taken up by 'a whistler opposite'.

> ' "Thank you" said the Frenchman.
> "It's nothing, at your service," replied the German, a former Paris café waiter.
> Next day, a despatch of cigars was not enough to dispel all distrust: were they poisoned? Wouldn't the next gift be a grenade? Then came a piece of paper weighted with a stone: "Don't fire, we won't fire either – let's give it a try." A hand appeared above the enemy trench, then a head, two heads, five heads, groups of heads along about 500 metres of parapet. Then curiosity won the day. Our men showed themselves in turn, stood up to waist-height above the parapet, to watch this strange spec-

tacle of enemies smiling at us, making friendly signs . . . It was agreed that, at night, no one should be out in the open and there was the right to fire on any patrol. When an officer went by in the enemy trench, the soldiers disappeared, but not without warning us. We exchanged gifts. The Boches kept us supplied with tobacco, we sent them our surplus bread . . .

They also gave warning of the existence of a mine, but the French colonel appeared unexpectedly and he insisted that "the masquerade" must cease: "You will be so kind as to kill some of them immediately or I will put you up in front of a Court Martial. Wait! Go and tell your sergeant to order a round of fire, that will bring down more of them."

It took two minutes to set up the first salvo, which was followed by three more. Before firing, the sergeant signalled to the Germans to take cover, for it would have been "an abuse of trust" to kill them.'[43]

When a fraternization was about to begin, there might be an exchange of a message, whistling, or a shot in the air to attract attention. The censors for the 1st mixed Zouaves, infantry and 9th Zouaves on 6 February 1918 picked up one Zouave's letter:

'Their way of operating was as follows – fire in the air to see us standing upright and in range to say, "Friends let's begin to understand each other why are we going to kill each other, the war is over for us, it's up to those who started it to stop it. We can see each other, twenty metres away for the nearest, and we won't fire." We want peace, and the Boches want it.'

In some cases a white banner was waved, or the Red Cross flag. In the case of the latter – apart from the fact that it did not always work – the truce was limited to the evacuation of wounded men or burial of the dead.

Whoever initiated an approach took a considerable risk, as in the incident described by Louis Pergaud:

'We did not wish wounded men to die between the lines, as happened the first time. It was truly dreadful for us. Would they

fire on him, and on the stretcher-bearers? Too bad. He hoisted
the Red Cross flag and, armed with nothing more than his
doctor's armband, he stood up out of the trench. I held my
breath. This brave little doctor was such a kind and charming
comrade . . . The Germans behaved very correctly. They stood
up above the parapet, and we looked across at each other.
Mistarlet advanced, followed by his men, he got near the
wounded men, six metres from the Germans, to whom he gave
a military salute, in old-fashioned ceremonial style, then he dealt
with the wounded man and, while he was being carried away on
his stretcher, he saluted again, in the same way, the enemies
returned his salute. He came back into our lines; heads disappeared down behind the parapets, silence reigned again and not
a rifle shot was heard for the rest of the day.'

Both sides had been impressed, and the silence of the rifles
honoured the courage of the doctor and, at the same time, the attitude taken by each side.

Many texts use the word *culotté* for the man who took the first
risky step, meaning 'brave' or 'full of nerve'. This example from a
soldier in the 330th RI dates from March 1917:

'A *culotté* Fritz, having had his fill of wallowing in mud, called
us and very soon after we saw Fritzes and Frenchies standing out
on the plain armed only with picks and spades, I can tell you our
work went with a swing and it wasn't war any more, it was more
of a quick-fire burst judging by what got done.'

When a soldier was sufficiently courageous or foolhardy to
emerge and shake his enemy by the hand in the middle of No
Man's Land, after the repeated exchange of signals, his section
comrades watched him protectively: "No doubt more than one
finger was on the rifle trigger, ready to fire if either of the two
activists moved too suddenly." If, as in this case reported by
Antoine Redier, there was an intention to move on to genuine
exchanges, the signals operated in both directions and fraternization ensued.

Henri Robert described a similar scene on 2 April 1915:

'Finally, after making signs, two bolder men slipped under the wire defences and advanced warily towards each other. The Frenchman was a little seventeen-year-old, the baby of his troop, and the Boche a big plump fellow; we were afraid that this great warrior would drag our little man into his trench – we had our rifles ready. But they met and looked each other straight in the eye, then they exchanged their gifts, shook hands briefly, and fled back each to his own trench. It all happened very quickly: no officer was involved and luckily it all passed off without a hitch.'

Courage was also required to take water from the jealously coveted spring which lay between the two lines. As recorded by Jean-Marie Carré:

'One day a man in the 147th Regiment, desperate for water approached the spring at the risk of being shot. He had left his rifle in the trench and the Germans did not stop him coming . . . An hour later a Boche came out of his hole in his turn and advanced towards the spring, carrying his empty can. Our men debated: "Should we shoot him?" It's a fine opportunity! "No, that would not be right." Even in war, good manners prevailed.'

## Finding the Right Words

Once fraternization was engaged, it might not be possible to find the right words (Elie Vandrand, 9 May 1915): 'We chat together but we don't understand each other much, we often say Comrades, cigarettes, tobacco, cognac', or men would use the words learned at school, or a German who had worked in Paris would bring out his slang. In all cases, hand-shaking was a clear signal and the exchange of items, without money changing hands, could also be undertaken without much need to talk. Barter of French bread for German cigarettes and cigars was the most usual practice.

The Germans had little difficulty in making themselves understood – as a sergeant in the 88th RI wrote to Paris, probably to his wife, on 19 July 1917:

'As I wrote to you yesterday, I was on watch from 2 a.m. until 6 a.m. in the morning. At 3 a.m., around daybreak, the Germans greeted us at the forward posts and tried to talk to us. Oh, they aren't far away here, barely twenty-five metres. We manage to understand them, with gestures or a bit of chat. They were starving, we showed them bread, that's what they wanted.'

Some soldiers mentioned exchanging French pipe tobacco for cigarettes; it was more unusual for the Germans to offer food. Alfred Joubaire recorded on 15 December 1915: 'A Boche brought some rum over to the French trench. A Frenchman and a Bavarian linked arms and had themselves photographed.'

One man in the 29th BCP received some ham: 'We still talk with with them, we smoke Boche tobacco and they eat good bread with us. They give us ham and plenty of other things.'

The later event happened in October 1917 when food supplies were severely affected by the blockade. Later still, on 11 November 1918, a *poilu* in the 163rd RI recounted that he had received some German sausage. In order not to upset his contact opposite he also received German bread 'which we accept for appearances' sake, but not to eat because it's not good and it's all black'.

The most elaborate conversations touched on food, family, and peace-time life. The Germans were encouraged to surrender, and sometimes their deserting was discussed (Léon Werth):

'One night, a French-speaking German announced that he and four of his comrades were fed up with the war and wanted to surrender. The sergeant who was in command of the French advanced post showed him which trench he would be in next day. They agreed a time. But only three of them came over. They said that they had taken advantage of a sleepy sentry. They apologized for their two comrades, just as one apologizes for two friends who fail to honour an accepted invitation. At the last moment the two missing men had been ordered away on kitchen duty.'

The wild hopes that kept emerging in conversations in the French lines reappeared when German soldiers shared in the discussions: peace and the end of suffering. In January 1917, for example, the French soldiers in the 5th RI and the Germans were unable to reassure each other. In June, the Germans told the *poilus* of the 75th RI that the war would finish in August. 'The war may soon be over', wrote a soldier in the 132nd at the end of July 1917. 'It's a Boche rumour and I think it's true.' Abbé Lelièvre, a chaplain, described an exchange of messages in March 1915 in which each one defended the relevant country's positions. Addressing the French in such expressions as 'brave comrades' or 'worthy comrades', the Germans inveighed against the English and above all the 'Russian tsarism which is the enemy of all freedom and all human feeling'. And their final message ended with this appeal; 'In any case, work with all your strength, with us, to establish a lasting peace.' All were agreed on who was responsible: 'Yesterday evening I was talking with one man who spoke French. He told me: "French comrade, war capitalist".' 'It's always the little men who are in the trenches,' the soldiers in both camps agreed.

For everything to be clearly understood, gesture was added to words. In September 1917 the 350th arrived in the Vosges. The men in the departing regiment had 'sent a signal not to fire'. Indeed, at dawn the Germans signalled their intentions:

> 'We saw the Boches who shook their helmets and then showed themselves. We did the same, then they indicated that they would shake our hands. Then one man took his rifle and waved it in the air and finished by putting his rifle to his cheek but he turned round and aimed towards the rear. It was very clear, and we understood from this that it wasn't at us that they should be firing, but at those who were in command.'

When a threat hovered over good understanding – the arrival of an officer or an order to start firing again – it was still possible to make use of explicit signs to warn a German on his way across for a visit to turn back and return to his trench or to warn of a bombardment as happened in July 1917:

'They made signs to us that at 7 a.m. the artillery would open up on us, and they were right, it was pouring it down on us until 11 a.m.'

## Codes of Behaviour

The shift from the occasional contact to a practice of this length indicated the development of a recognizable set of 'rules' for acceptable behaviour. Actions such as firing rifles or detonating mines met the requirements imposed by higher command but, in reality, were part of an implicit code between enemies who had decided not to harm each other. Experienced combatants knew that weapons could be used either with or without the intention to kill, and the old hands explained this to the novices. Sometimes, when mines exploded and firearms were making a tremendous noise, what external observers saw as a lively confrontation was in fact no more than communication between enemies, telling each other that they had no genuine intention of fighting.[44]

Ordinary soldiers did not always take the trouble to describe such secret codes, but traces can be perceived in their writing, more frequently in the case of mine warfare. Under an energetic commanding officer, a man always alert to beat down the Boche, it was difficult to acknowledge the existence of such customs; they do not, for example, appear in Colonel Campagne's book.

Rifle or machine-gun fire could be intense, but regulated to pass well above enemy heads, according to Jean-Pierre Biscay in the French army. The German officer Ernst Jünger wrote that:

'Brief comments, not without a certain basic humour, fly between the lines – "Hey, Tommy, you still there? – Oh ay! – Well, get your head down, I'm going to fire".'[45]

A shot 'for form's sake' was recounted by Gaston Top, a doctor serving with the 27th artillery. In the words of Lieutenant Ségard of the same regiment, who was sent out on observation along the trench:

'I was crouching there beside my telephone with my binoculars set across the parapet, when all at once I heard a voice opposite shouting: "Hey, hey, comrades, French comrades! Can we come out?" At the same time a handkerchief was being waved frantically above the Boche trench! One of our men waved his in return, and straight away a large man stood up twenty metres away, then another, then a third, pipe in mouth and hands in pockets; our men did likewise . . . and they chatted together!

The Prussian who first called out, and who spoke with the purest Paris accent, a former café waiter in Paris, was keen to talk – "Well! So you slept well?" – "Yes, not badly!" – "We left you well alone, we only fired for form's sake!" – "Well, that's true!" – "Look at that old fellow over there, he's still half asleep!" An old sweat kept laughing – "You got children, old man?" – "Yes, three!" – "Ah, me too. Do you think that we will be finished with this stupid war by Christmas?" – "Don't know – It's pretty miserable, isn't it?" – "That's true!" – "Tell us then, you French, do you still have bread to give us?"

Well, they were just about ready to invite themselves to dinner, when suddenly a shell swept in from a French 75, which knocked out the armistice.'

This account becomes even more significant when the date is added – 15 November 1914 – and with the added detail that Doctor Top was so keen a patriot that for the publication of his book in 1917 he withheld from it 'matters which are not timely to describe' out of respect for the army. What he described came very early in the war and for these infantrymen it already seemed normal. The artillery, however, were taken aback and it was they who broke the truce.

In time, however, the artillery also took part in ritualized combat. On 1 May 1915 Doctor Top rode past a stretch of land entirely churned up by shells. 'Fortunately,' he wrote, 'it was not the moment; they bombard it from 3 p.m. to 4 p.m., and it was only half past two.'

Gabriel Chevallier described a quiet sector:

'Once a week, four German guns sent over some thirty shells in a scattering of fire. Once this distribution was over, we could be certain of being left in peace for a week. Our own firing was more imaginative. From our second lines, winding along the hillside, I could sometimes see our 75s firing freely, breaking down German banks or bursting in the open country. But there was little intensity on either side; the artillery set off simple demonstrations, because it was a custom of war to fire guns.'

He continued:

'In the infantry, they took care not to disturb such a peaceful sector, such pleasant countryside. We avoided provocation, unless orders came from the rear to act aggressively.'

In August 1916 Captain Jean de D, to the east of Pont-à-Mousson, describes 'a ridiculously quiet sector: two or three shells per day on our front lines, with our guns firing the same number back.' Lieutenant Binet-Valmer evokes another scene where 'men would prefer not to harm each other'. He adds,

'Don't imagine that we are fraternizing. That's not at all the way with the cavalry. But we let each other get on and forget the war, we polish up our weapons so that they shine and not for them to be ready, and the rifle shot which breaks the silence could equally come from a casual poacher. At particular moments, which are known in advance, our guns and theirs send a few shells over the staff headquarters, shells which do not reach these gentlemen but which we hear with a smile of complicity.'

Perhaps because the mining war was perceived as particularly unpleasant, the soldiers did not hesitate to subvert it, and to conceal this subterfuge. Examples can be found in the *Notebooks* of Corporal Barthas. Other notebooks, which have remained unpublished, contain further evidence such as this incident narrated by Henri Charbonnier on 30 November 1916:

'The enemy warned us that they were going to explode a mine . . . A certain degree of connivance exists between German and French soldiers so that they warn each other when something is going to happen. They have absolutely no interest in getting hit for the pleasure of a Mr Big tucked up nice and warm ten kilometres in the rear, who suddenly decides he wants to see a show of destructive fire.'

The same complicity emerged in oral accounts recorded by Jules Maurin and Claude Marquié,[46] and the postal censors intercepted many other examples. In February 1917, for example, three soldiers in the 85th RI 'noted conversations and exchanges taking place in the trenches with Germans'. The summary chose not to touch on the other point but some soldiers showed no such hesitation: 'They passed on excellent cigars to us and, what's better, they warned us every time a mine was going to be exploded.' Another man, in the 85th RI, added that, 'The Boches are becoming as disgusted as we are.'

When three other regiments were subject to postal surveillance at about the same time, (the 95th, 107th and 114th), the same feelings emerged in the form of passing on the words of a song; later it was to become known as the 'Chanson de Craonne', echoing the bloody setback to the offensive of 16 April 1917 on the Chemin des Dames.[47] Historians who were familiar with La Guerre des soldats (The Soldiers' War) by Raymond Lefebvre and Paul Vaillant-Couturier, published in 1919, knew that this song was already in existence in 1915 under the title of 'Chanson de Lorette', from the equally bloody fighting that year to the north of Arras.

The censorship for February–March 1917 registered three versions, in which the refrain evoked other hot sectors. The modified line was 'It was at Lorette/in Champagne/at Les Eparges/at Craonne, on the plateau . . .' For Verdun, another version appeared: 'It was at Verdun at the Fort de Vaux'. What was important was that the line-ending must rhyme with the final line: 'Qu'on doit laisser sa peau' – 'That's where we leave our skins'.

In mining warfare, the handling of explosives was a delicate matter – and the management of a tacit truce was equally delicate. Sprains or 'accidents' might occur, sanctioned by reprisals, unless 'excuses' were offered and accepted. A case of the former comes in Pierre Chaine's book:

'The winter of 1916–1917 passed for us without any incident except for periodic reliefs. Mines and *camouflets* were fired off efficiently every morning, but the tradition gradually became established that they would only be fired between 6 a.m. and 7 a.m. in the morning, the critical moment when everyone left the shelters. There was only one misunderstanding, and we expressed our discontent in such a way that the Boches did not do that again.'

A veteran of the 96th RI told Jules Maurin of an even more striking situation which he experienced in December 1916:

'At Vauquois, in general, the mines were set off in the morning while the forward observation posts were evacuated, before being reoccupied after the explosion. One day, however, a mine blew up at midday. A moment later, a banner emerged from the German trench with the single word: "Accident". The French wrote a responding poster: "Yes, many dead". And the Germans answered: "Here too".'

Apologies were also exchanged between British and German troops, as would occur between good neighbours over an involuntary breach of the unspoken etiquette of social life. As for reprisals, they were the price of transgression. But were not understandings and fraternizations themselves deviations in relation to the war-time norms, fixed and reiterated time after time by the authorities?

## Breaking the Rules

Under the particular norms of war, forcing the enemy to admit defeat required the application of the greatest possible degree of damage. This might be through propaganda, blockade, shelling cities, or other means. At the front, however, it was a matter of killing, wounding or capturing soldiers. The strongly hierarchical structure of the army made matters even clearer; commanding officers punished the deviation represented by friendly contact with the enemy and sought to prevent any such activity. This was their role and their capacity to exercise their authority was at stake. For this reason, one way of ensuring that deviation did not exist was to deny it, to affect ignorance or to minimize its extent.

From another point of view, soldiers who struck up tacit or declared agreements with the enemy faced several problems. First was the potential personal risk of punishment by their senior officers. Second, infantry soldiers needed the potential complicity of junior officers, the artillery and relieving troops.

War meant no understanding with the enemy, no fraternization and the rule was constantly repeated. Even as early as 5 December 1914, Etienne Tanty wrote of a reported note condemning familiarities: 'The General reminded us that the only relationship permissible [with the enemy] was via a bayonet . . .'[48] Surprised by the scale of the truces at Christmas 1914, the leaders of all armies gave strict orders to prevent any repetition. But such interdicts needed to be reiterated. The penultimate paragraph of General de Villaret's order of 8 January 1916, in command of the VIIth Army, is particularly interesting:

'Subject: Relations with the enemy.

The attention of all Corps and Divisions of the Army has already been drawn to the serious failings represented by the relations occasionally established at certain points along the front between French and German soldiers. These relations are inadmissible with an enemy whose crimes have soiled and ruined a large area of the national territory.

Repeated reports have established that such practices, once very rare, are beginning to occur more frequently. This is how understandings are sometimes established between the stretcher-bearers of the two armies bringing in their dead and wounded. Elsewhere, certain men have warned enemy operatives of the opening of fire by our 75 gun to enable them to take shelter in advance, and have obtained in exchange warnings of firing opening from the German *Minenwerfer*.

Such facts are evidence of a weakness or a criminal connivance on the part of the officers who have tolerated them. They must cease forthwith and completely. Generals in command of army

Corps or Divisions and officers of all ranks must therefore call the attention of all men to the extremely serious nature of such practices which relate to the Code of Military Justice (articles 205 and 206).

In their instructions to their men they do not, of course, need to go into any detail of the various forms which violation of military duty may take; such a course could give too clear an idea of what should not be done to men who had not yet thought of it . . . Further, they will make all necessary dispositions to ensure that a rigorous system of surveillance is established in the front line; they will give an account of these dispositions.'

General Pétain gave similar orders, specifying on 12 September 1916 that the crime of 'intelligence with the enemy' entailed the death penalty.[49] After his promotion to General in Chief of the French Army, he returned to the question again, notably in his notes of December 1917, at the end of a year that had been particularly rich in fraternizations.[50]

Nonetheless, in practice the sanctions were not severe. Corporals and sergeants were reduced to the ranks; ordinary soldiers were punished with imprisonment. In October 1917 a soldier in the 132nd RI was involved in another kind of punishment:

'I think I'll soon be able to go on leave and I'm very happy because I have just been punished: ten days more to do and the company commander is currently under arrest. I can't explain all this to you in this letter.'

But he added, writing across the lines: 'For doubting whether we fraternized with the Boches. We are barely four metres apart in some places.' Elsewhere, as punishment for two *chasseurs* of the 29th BCP who were caught exchanging bread for cigars in November 1917, their lieutenant proposed only a week in prison. It is true that the penalty was raised to twenty-five days by the colonel and to sixty days by the general, but it seems that there was a general desire to limit the significance of the affair.

## The Temptations of Understatement

As already indicated, the postal censor's summaries confirmed this tendency. In 1916, such summaries often used the conditional ('the supposed inter-trench relationships, between our soldiers and the Germans.')[51] In the end the actual episodes were recognized.

At the front there were tacit agreements 'which the officers wished to ignore', 'stories of French soldiers talking with the Boches' which, preferably, should be 'buried'. Officers rejected any accusation of fraternization in their units. Stilted official language was fully engaged: '. . . in the 288th RI, there was fraternization with the Boches with rifle shots.' In order to prevent evidence of the Christmas Truce in 1914 from being recognized, General Mangin enforced the seizure of photographs.

An officer who could not deny his men's transgressions would defend himself either by condemning a state of affairs which existed before his arrival, or by emphasizing his own duplicity: he took advantage of it to improve their positions; he had obtained information on the enemy; he had added to the enemy's demoralization.

Some cases reveal details of the arguments for the defence. In his report on one of his soldiers, an officer of the 344th RI insisted on all the extenuating circumstances: it was a foggy day, 26 January 1918, the soldier was trying to get warm by stamping his feet; he had set his rifle on the parapet; suddenly shapes in the fog had thrown something at him; he did not have time to pick up his weapon; the packet contained cigarettes. He had given some to his comrades. In his own defence the officer added that: 'it was only an isolated case' and that the soldier was a 'poor fellow'. Result: sixty days in prison.

According to his captain, another soldier, Victor B, of the 121st RI, had done nothing wrong beyond being addressed by a German who asked him for chocolate. Of course, the Frenchman had not replied. The officer related the incident in a flood of warlike words:

'The formal order to fire on any German who might show himself had been given. This order was carried out and, for the sake of example, the officer on watch at advance post no. 6 on the 17th in the morning [November 1917] himself successfully shot a

German non-commissioned officer who showed himself very deliberately on the enemy trench. A German soldier was brought down in the same way a few moments later. From then on the struggle was continuous, with grenades and rifle fire. The Boches responded vigorously with ribbed grenades which killed and wounded our men. The battalion leader can confirm that no conversation took place and will never take place with those opposite as long as the the regiment is in occupation of this sector. Our men have too much hatred for the Germans not to respond with rifle shots or grenades to any gesture of friendship from those people.'

The affair of A, of the 65th RI, developed out of the postal censorship. This soldier had written to his parents in December 1917:

> 'We are still very quiet, you'd think we weren't even at war, here the French and Germans talk together just like in peace time. The Boches give cigars and cigarettes to men in the front line, and on our side we give them bread and wine, so that everything goes wonderfully well.'

The letter was seized. In the ensuing enquiry A defended himself saying that, as his parents had five sons under arms and were very worried, he had wanted to reassure them that he was not in any danger. He had invented this story from what he had heard from other soldiers, who were not identified. Among his comrades, some had neither seen nor heard anything; others mentioned vague German proposals that were not accepted, copies of the Germans' French-language magazine *La Gazette des Ardennes* being thrown into their trench; a sergeant said that he had heard, in front of a sector next to his own, an enemy sentry shouting after a shower of fire: 'Comrades *Franzôses* pigs, much firing' (this sentry had immediately suffered several grenades).

The conclusion of the lieutenant-colonel commanding the 65th RI was clear:

> 'No exchange took place. Further, the many star shells sent up that night by the enemy, the heavy shooting and machine-gun fire

by both sides at the slightest noise, do not indicate any act of fraternization.'

A more serious case was that of Sergeant J of the 18th BCP, whose letter of 7 November 1917 to his parents in the Doubs contained the following passage:

'It rains every day, which is not at all pleasant, particularly in our sector. But the Boches are like us. Men walk about in the open, just as if there wasn't a war going on. But I don't think that it can last long, there are grumbles already. The men must fire, whatever happens, and they don't want to. It's the officers who are forced to take the rifles. But they are like the men, they have to appear above the parapet and I think they are going to be picked out by the Boches. It appears that the men in the front line have passed the word to the Boches, so that every time an officer is going to show himself, on either side, they will do their best to bring him down. But I'm afraid that they are mistaken.'

The sergeant was reduced to the ranks. His defence at the enquiry appeared unconvincing: supposedly, he had seen nothing himself but had interrupted a conversation at night between men on fatigues whom he did not recognize. His captain however had fully grasped the more dangerous implications: that soldiers could hate their officers, or what they represented, a great deal. He treated the words of J as a 'tissue of lies' and insisted that:

'On the subject of understanding between elements of opposing front lines to fire only on officers, this seems practically impossible. It is extremely difficult for a sentry without field-glasses to recognize an officer, whose trench uniform differs little from that of the men in the ranks.'

The commanding officer approved. J's letter was without foundation and should not be taken seriously. Nonetheless he was to be condemned for his behaviour:

'He did not behave in a way which is suitable for a French soldier, and even less for a non-commissioned officer.'

At senior levels, the affair was minimized:

'It is undeniable that at the beginning of November, when continual rain had transformed tunnel-trenches and communication trenches into rivers of liquid mud, impossible to use, men had to move around across the fields, on both the French and the German sides; the latter held back for some time from firing, hoping for reciprocal behaviour for what they had done automatically; but this state of affairs did not last; Major V, in command of the 18th BCP, gave the order to fire on any German who showed himself; he was obeyed, I was able to confirm this personally on several occasions.'

The conclusion was that: 'the only response to the German who wants to talk is a rifle shot full in the chest'.

What a wonderful thing is official language! But how could the officers prevent understandings and episodic fraternization? Various methods existed, the most certain being to create situations so aggressive that they entailed reprisals, which in turn provoked a revival of violence.

## Agreements and Sanctions

The tendency to deny, ignore or minimize situations of camaraderie with the enemy delayed official awareness. Nonetheless, as soon as the facts were confirmed, the reaction was to move the guilty unit. 'As soon as it was known, we were sent to a different sector,' said a veteran of the 142nd RI questioned by Jules Maurin.[52] On the other hand, Henri Désagneaux evoked the arrival of his unit in a sector that was too quiet, under 'orders to put an end to this state of affairs' because:

'they were going so far as to fraternize with the Boches, cigarettes were being passed from one trench to the other, men were making music together.'

High command sought to pin guilt on the ordinary soldiers by asserting that fraternization was sought by the Germans in order

to weaken France. In 1917, after the Russian Revolution and disso-
lution of the Russian army, official texts used the fear of similar
insurrections to obtain the same result in the French army.
Certainly, in the fourth winter of the war, Germans threw appeals
from Lenin and Trotsky into the French trenches, written and
printed in French.

This practice was both like and unlike previous exchanges of
newspapers with the enemy. It was no longer a question of boasting
superiority, but of appeals for peace. On the other hand, the intention to weaken enemy morale was unchanged, despite the
long-standing practice of conversations between French and
Germans concerning the war as a capitalist plot and the universally
longed-for peace.

The reaction of one particular *poilu* is very interesting. It was
discovered through the postal censorship, which intercepted a letter
written in pencil on the back of a sheet printed with the Russian
government's proposal for an armistice and immediate peace,
dated 28 November 1917. The unnamed soldier's letter is dated 5
December:

> 'You can't imagine how anyone could keep going with this
> cold, day and night outside, nothing hot to eat, with one's feet
> dead with cold . . . We are sacrificed, exiled from the whole
> world . . . We will be relieved when we have suffered 60 per
> cent losses. I am writing this in a shell-hole and tonight, believe
> me, it's none too warm, with the frost. Luckily my leave is
> getting nearer, because this time I won't come back here. Well,
> I must go now, and dance about a bit to warm myself up. You
> can get this read out to all those people who keep shouting "On
> to the end" and tell them to come here for a bit to do like me,
> leave behind their fat and maybe their skins . . . Here is a leaflet
> that the Boches sent us yesterday, I don't know but I think they
> are right.'[53]

The most effective way to break a truce was to take the initiative
with hostilities. 'Hatred must not be allowed to weaken,' wrote
Gabriel Chevallier. To this end, orders were given to fire on the
enemy working-parties (and to receive the same in return).

Lectured from those much more highly placed, a junior officer would come to the advance post and coolly kill a German whose confidence had been won in the atmosphere of *entente*. There would then be reprisal victims: 'That earned us a shower of ribbed bombs creating deaths and woundings.' (Jean Safon.)

The philosopher Alain, who served with the artillery during the war, noted that:

> 'Sometimes through the artillery field glasses we could see the infantry sentries sitting down on the parapets and starting up a conversation from one trench to another. The order was to start shelling immediately. This firing was against the peace, much more than against the enemy.'

The practice of raids or single incidents was also intended to break the peace and destroy confidence. The French Colonel Campagne was no dupe when he remarked that this form of war was promoted 'to keep us and the enemy up to the mark'. He criticized the actual organization of the system; the men charged to undertake the raid left the site once the raid was over, to enjoy various advantages (rest, leave, decorations); the ordinary soldiers, 'reduced to the role of trench-guards and labourers', suffered the reprisals.

The threat of reprisals was in fact significant in bringing understandings to an end. Each camp knew what the other could do in the way of destruction. As Paul Vaillant-Couturier observed, 'If we bother Fritz, Fritz is going to give us a bruising because he has what he needs to do it' and, in the words of Max Buteau:

> 'The Boches are out in front, a hundred metres away. If you don't say anything to them, they will leave you in peace.'

An unnamed soldier in the 172nd RI wrote that: 'In order to have peace ourselves, we leave them in peace.'

Any interruption of the peace by one of the adversaries was met with an immediate riposte – unless there was an explanation of any misunderstanding, as happened in August 1917 in the sector held by the 26th BCP in Alsace. A calm sector; but then, suddenly, the truce seemed to be broken:

'Until now the sector was quiet; we chatted with the Boche, we laid our barbed wire entanglements together, we shook hands, everything was fine. But yesterday, we still don't know why, we were greeted with a hail of missiles 1.60 metres long; then the 75s joined in, the 88s responded, then it was the 120 long guns, in the end for more than an hour we were under intense shelling. We thought it was an attack and we held ourselves ready, but nothing happened and it all went quiet again. What was worst for us, it was our own 75 gun which was firing right on to us. By lucky chance, we only had one man wounded, and not badly.'

The author of this letter, which was intercepted by the postal censor, wrote first of his surprise, then he remarked on the matter of reciprocity in shelling and, on top of that, the mistake of the 75s. Another soldier gave the explanation in a letter to his family in Nantes: 'They pulled something off on us the other day because they thought that we were going to attack, they told us about it next day.' It was a mistake, and good relations were able to re-surface. Next day, French and Germans were talking together again.

Other soldiers' letters from the same battalion, written on the following days, confirmed the restoration of good neighbourly relations: 'We are working on the parapet and chatting with the Fritzes'; 'The *Fridolins* are pretty good to us; we get cigars and cigarettes from them nearly every day; they come over and find us, almost in our trenches.' One of the extracts describes an unusual exchange:

'Yesterday I did an exchange with a Boche; I gave him three little bars of soap, and he immediately gave me a porcelain pipe with some cigars. It's extraordinary, the trade we carry on between the two sides.'

In his neutrally worded account, Lieutenant Morin described a truce in which a German would throw a few grenades, which did no great damage. But, one day, one of his corporals was killed by a rifle shot. 'It must be from an officer' was the reaction of his soldiers. Morin organized reprisals. They were bloody. Then good neighbourly custom was restored and the French officer wondered whether the men might perhaps have explained to the Germans the reasons for the aggressive phase. Whatever the circumstances:

> 'This re-establishment of good relations was confirmed in fresh exchanges: objects began to fly across the canal again, silhouettes appeared once more in the dawn light, but the weapons were silent.'

Morin, still a sergeant in the spring of 1915, mentioned *crapouillots* (trench mortars), unpopular with the infantry who swore at them ferociously and objected to their fire because they invariably and almost instantly attracted reprisal shots from *minenwerfers* or even the artillery – for negotation went on within each camp as to levels of aggression or silence in response to enemy fire. The infantry was particularly vulnerable in this respect, while junior officers were torn between two loyalties, the world of the senior command and that of the fighting men.[54]

## Establishing Rule-breaking in Camp

A stretcher-bearer, Ormières, described the effect of the trench mortars:

> 'In this sector we have the *crapouillots* which are part of the concert and don't leave us alone. One day I was in the line at the aid post as usual, when we were visited by three *crapouillot* men. The major wasn't there, and as I was in shirt-sleeves the men mistook me for him. I didn't enlighten them, and gave them each four days excused from duty. When the major returned he laughed and we had four quiet days: the Germans were not at the receiving end of our shells and so they did not fire on us.'

The infantry suffered from its vulnerability, for it could not compete on terms of equal fire-power with the full force of the enemy. As a result, it was the infantry which was most open to

understandings with the other infantry. A sergeant in the 366th RI
wrote about this in March 1917:

> 'The Boches are not always unreasonable and they leave us pretty
> well alone, no doubt they have had enough of it already and if
> there was only the infantry I think that friendly agreement would
> soon be reached.'

Yet the truces were fragile: 'It was sometimes enough to have a
change of troops on relief, a different officer, for the real war to
break out again,' wrote Jean-Pierre Biscay. During a substantial
truce the trench occupied by Lieutenant Morin's section was on the
receiving end of a few grenades that were 'no doubt thrown by a
junior officer on a round, who found this camaraderie altogether
excessive'. In order to escape the explosion the soldiers jumped on
to the parapet 'without even coming under rifle fire'.

Officers who broke truces were sometimes held back by other
officers or became objects of disapproval. It might happen that a
lieutenant showed himself to be more reasonable than a corporal
who wanted artillery fire to disperse German troops at work in
the open area: 'Let the Boches alone. We need peace too when we
are working on the barbed wire.' Alternatively, a captain might
show himself as more 'pacific' than a young and headstrong
lieutenant.

No single pattern of behaviour can be attributed to the officers.
Some deliberately interrupted understandings, others slept in their
dug-out and did not want to know what was happening at the
forward posts, many stood back and allowed events to carry on.
For Captain Rimbault the 'game' should not last too long, but it
could exist. A captain in the 88th RI in July 1917, according to a
soldier's letter, did not want his men to get out of the trench for
exchanges but 'all the same he did not stop them, for a conversation'. Lieutenant Calvet wrote that he could not 'tolerate these
talks' but the interdict was only applicable if he was present, and
his description proves that he heard a good deal (May 1916):

> 'Thus it was that, yesterday, they told us of the success of the
> Austrian offensive against the Italians. When one of our men was

coughing, they sympathized: "Ill, *Kamarad*?" But I cannot tolerate these chats. So when I am around, my men keep quiet; and the Boches are surprised.'

In October 1916 a soldier of the 23rd RI reported an unlucky incident affecting a German:

> 'There is one who came over to bring us the Berlin newspapers every morning. One fine day he bumped straight into an officer, so we were forced to take him prisoner. That morning we didn't pay for the papers. Since then they haven't brought us anything. Perhaps they will return later.'

It is of course possible that this unfortunate surprise encounter may have saved the soldier's life.

Captain Tuffrau recorded a very illuminating incident near Orvilliers, in July 1917. Having heard rumours of fraternizations, two officers went to observe and saw soldiers come out into the open and throw something towards the enemy trench. A German 'came out calmly to look for it'. In turn, the Germans threw a message which was read by the French. Then men signalled, from both sides. One of the watching officers then fired on the Germans:

> 'At the shot, Boches and French disappeared. After a moment the two Frenchmen stood up and, turning their backs directly on the enemy from whom they feared nothing, they tried to see. De Gislain fired in their direction, but above their heads. They disappeared.'

Lieutenant T, in charge of the guilty section, admitted:

> 'Oh, I must tell you, there's an arrangement. When they come out to lay their wire, we go out quietly to lay our own. No one fires. It's tremendous. And then we get information . . .'

There was bitterness among the colonel's staff 'about this business' which brought one officer in front of a court martial and poisoned relationships within the regiment between accusers and accused.

Better if the matter could be dropped – but a conflicting tradition insisted on the importance of self-justification. It was all the more significant that the regiment that relieved the 246th had itself denounced the practices that it encountered:

> 'The Boches began by welcoming the 317th, then declared that they hoped the 317th would leave them in peace as the 246th had done . . .'

Charged with intelligence with the enemy, T defended himself, saying that his section had done no more than send the Germans newspapers showing a Russian victory, as it had done earlier by order, at the time of Romania's entry into the war . . . At the court martial the defence lawyer 'made everyone weep, including the jury', and T was acquitted.

In this case, connivance extended to the whole section under T's command, and even to the 4th battalion of the 246th Regiment. It did not however reach the regiment as a whole, nor the relieving unit. It was here too that traditions were passed on from veterans to beginners. The customs of a sector could be passed on to the relief. Captain Dubarle, of the 68th Battalion of *chasseurs alpins*, stated in the Vosges in December 1914 that:

> 'A hundred and fifty metres away, the German trench: to the left, a wood; to the right, Cernay plain which is still occupied by the Germans. There were a few Boches around; but a convention had developed, it appears, between our predecessors and the enemy. There is no firing unless one is attacked. If it is only a matter of bringing in supplies, undertaking trench maintenance, no rifle shots. And in fact the day passes quietly.'

Soldiers in the ranks wrote: 'An agreement, an understanding reigns between the French and German forward posts. The necessary word is passed to the reliefs not to fire' (postal censor, 350th RI, September 1917). On their side, the Germans behaved in the same way. In his book *Trench Warfare 1914–1918*, Tony Ashworth notes the details given by a French officer to his British colleague who was coming in to take over his sector, in order 'to let sleeping dogs lie.'[55]

The system did not work perfectly. There were hitches, immediately punished by reprisals. There were moments of defiance: 'We don't know what kind of Boche we have facing us, so we are on our guard' (28 July 1917). Sometimes the Germans themselves informed the French of the state of morale in another unit: 'They often tell us: "the Company beside you, not comrades . . . bad Company".'

The artillery was entirely different, however, and initially it refused to believe in the fraternizations. On 8 October 1914, Ivan Cassagnau wrote:

> 'We are hearing a strange bit of news that we cannot believe. On the Xth corps front, apparently on several occasions there was fraternization between French and German soldiers. Exchanges of confectionery, promises of peace, etc.'

Edouard Deverin described an artilleryman who 'grumbled' while taking part in a truce to bury the dead, and who went to complain to his brigade, which then ordered a 75 to be fired. As many soldiers wrote, 'It's only the artillery which is firing' in their descriptions of an accord between the infantry on each side.

Nonetheless it sometimes happened that the artillery took account of intolerable flooding in the trenches, and suspended their firing. Sometimes the tacit agreement brought the artillery into ritualized combat. Relations were not always of the best between officers of the two military branches,[56] but they still thought of each other as their comrades. They met and talked together; it might be the opportunity for the infantry to win a relatively quiet period from the artillery.

Biscay, as officer in command of a section, described a very interesting case when he wrote of a three-way interaction: the cordial relations and exchanges of various items between German and French front-line soldiers; the demand from German infantry to their artillery to lengthen their range, to spare their French comrades; information from the German infantry to the French on what they had just been doing. Through studying a large number of accounts of all kinds, the concrete reality becomes apparent of an extraordinarily complex set of relationships.

## Observing the *poilus*

The unleashing of violence was one of the most characteristic features of the Great War and remains central to any history of its development. To take only the Western Front, it is impossible to disregard the immense number of men killed and wounded, during both the extensive war of movement in 1914 and the substantial offensives of each of the following years. It is also necessary to bring out the distinctive features of this particular war, the long periods spent face to face in the relative shelter of the network of trenches.

While the fighting at Verdun was raging, life in the Vosges was quiet; a sector that was a scene of tragedy in 1915 would be absent from the communiqués of 1916; a quiet sector could flare up. In every case, the soldiers were caught in the dual grip of the hierarchy which gave the orders and the propaganda net which demonized the enemy. Everything promoted aggression but when this pressure was relaxed, other forces came into play. Like many members of the armed forces Captain Rimbault remarked on this: 'A Frenchman and a German cannot live in this way, side by side, without one of the two following hypotheses developing: *either killing one another or living on friendly terms'*.

The soldiers frequently chose the second of these, and put it into practice in various ways. The Christmas Truce of 1914 was striking because it was seen as an exceptional phenomenon. More than any other day in the year, this day was holy – but it was accorded no official recognition from either Church or Army, and the truce was a spontaneous soldier-led movement. Smaller in scale and more fragile in the French-held front line than in the British sector, it was nonetheless preceded by actions which were described as early as October. The understandings appeared at the same time as a new form of warfare emerged. No doubt these earliest forms of camaraderie were limited in number; but they were described in well-developed forms with 'exchanges of confectionery, promises of peace, etc.'

Subsequently, 1915 and 1916 provided frequent occasions for understanding, despite the offensives in Artois, Champagne, Verdun and the Somme. The winter of 1916–17, the year of 1917 and the following winter 1917–18 were the periods most fully documented by the postal censor, with equally favourable conditions apart from the Nivelle offensive on the *Chemin des Dames*. The return to a far more mobile war in the spring of 1918 made matters more difficult but did not mean that incidents of understanding and fraternization ceased.

We can take a tranquil sector in January 1918 as a representation of many of the other sectors and periods. A soldier of the 202nd RI expressed his appreciation: 'The sector is quiet, the Boches leave us alone, they must be like us and fed up with it all.' The postal censor allowed this phrase to pass, but without any further detail. The expression 'they leave us alone' while the war was still continuing is significant, and of course French troops also left the Germans in peace.

In sectors of this kind, there was no rifle fire, which paralysed much of the movement on the two sides. Grenades were not thrown, although in theory the nearness made 'precise' encounters with this well-established weapon possible. Exposed trenches were not machine-gunned. 'If they had wanted to kill us, no sooner said than done,' remarked Lieutenant Morin as he arrived at a new post. 'They can see us, from head to foot, and if they'd wanted, what was preventing them from sending over a few rifle shots?' wrote a soldier in the 118th RI in January 1918.

In certain peaceful sectors the enemy trench was visible, but no one was ever seen. The understanding was tacit; neither camp wished to engage in hostilities. No one took advantage of the excellent targets formed by smoke from fires, which no one bothered to conceal because they were tolerated on both sides. Elsewhere, men came out in the open and each side carried out its work without speaking to the other.

The term 'fraternization' was no longer applicable, even if the situation described was indeed a suspension of warfare. To formalize the truce, a few signals were sufficient, a message, sometimes genuine discussion if the language barrier was not a problem. Then exchanges could begin: items thrown from one forward post to the other (when they fell short of the trench, someone would go out to fetch them); they might be placed halfway across No Man's Land or handed over directly. There might even be a friendly drink together, working together while sharing tools, 'watching' together while smoking and conversing as far as was possible.

If a truce was imposed by flooding in the trenches, a fairly frequent occurrence, the soldiers' attitude was initially a common-sense reaction rather than a matter of taking a pacifist or humanitarian stance. To escape from the water did not imply fraternization, although that was the consequence. Looking at a mud-coated German soldier in front of him, the Frenchman saw himself as in a mirror. They were 'in the same boat', to the extent of using the expression '*poilu-boche*'. After going out in the open, feelings of solidarity developed.

No doubt such feelings already existed, ill-defined, and no doubt an 'obscure sympathy' had developed during the months of suffering during which everyone had understood the similarity of circumstances on each side. Fraternization thus enabled the expression of pacifist and antimilitarist feelings. Despite soldiers' fear of the censor, the anecdotes and comments revealed in their correspondence often made comparison possible with such acts of camaraderie. Those who dared to express their hostility to the war also dared to speak of fraternization.

Excessively fraternal understandings were eventually discovered and forbidden, more or less effectively. Tacit accords sometimes brought about peace for weeks or months; in these cases the customs became accepted and the truce evolved automatically. Relations could continue to improve over time but might also deteriorate. A soldier of the 106th RI wrote in July 1917:

'The Boches are still quite a cheeky lot at the forward post; they let us see a bucket of beer; we told them to bring it halfway across between the barbed wire lines (the posts are thirty metres apart); immediately a great big Fritz appeared, came halfway over and two of us went to collect the drink in return for a packet of tobacco, saying don't fire and they won't fire either. Today the camaraderie is over, we just stick to throwing over newspapers weighted with a stone.'

No reason is given: did an officer arrive? From which side? Here, relations were not broken off, but ruptures occurred which could prove brutal; the officer who arrived to stir up hostility would sometimes take advantage of the men opposite, unless a warning had been possible with signs or in some other way. Interruptions of a truce could sometimes be overlooked after an exchange of explanations. All sorts of language was used, including ritualized aggression, which could be recognized as such rather than as a true act of war.

Sources are insufficient to establish any precise calculation of the number and significance of understandings and fraternizations. Despite continuing publications, many soldiers' notebooks have been lost or remain unnoticed. Fear of the censor made many letters 'of no interest'.

Many officers chose to keep silent and not to refer incidents to their superiors. In June 1917, for example, in a sector on the Aisne–Marne canal, Lieutenant Morin surprised his men in the midst of a bartering session:

'One morning, I don't know why, before going to sleep, I glanced over the parapet, and I was transfixed with astonishment at what I saw: all the men in my section were on their feet on the parapet or on the canal towpath. I saw some of them making wide gestures, as if they were throwing grenades, others bending down to pick up something, and others trying to catch objects, jumping in the air. I rushed along the trench: my soldiers were throwing chunks of bread, even whole loaves, or chocolate, across to the other side of the canal! In exchange the Boches were sending packets of tobacco in hand-grenades, previously defused and emptied of their explosive charge.'

The lieutenant spoke severely to his men, but it went no further:

'No doubt if a superior officer saw such activity there would have been punishments. Although it was my duty to inform my colonel, I did not put in a report; I am afraid that the sanctions would be too severe at this difficult time.'

The same lieutenant expressed his stupefaction: 'I found this un-expected situation exceptional, paradoxical, disconcerting, disarming. Such surprise could be used to defend the theory of the rarity of such episodes.' But Morin also added: 'I had already occupied sectors where, through tacit understanding, no one disturbed the peace, but at least one remained invisible.' Apart from that, he had only discovered the great barter by accident, when he was thought to be asleep in his dug-out after a night on duty.

How many times did this happen without the officers' knowledge? How many cases – apparently isolated incidents – indicated broad complicity and connivance? Even in its incomplete form, the documentation seems to indicate that the formal truces arranged to bring in the dead and wounded were more numerous than formerly believed, even though they implied an agreement at a higher level, a setting in which men did not react in the same way as the men in the front lines.[57]

Truces and fraternizations were described on the Italian front by Bruna Bianchi, and for the British section of the Western Front by the authors already cited.[58] Tony Ashworth estimates that one-third of the reliefs in the British army were affected by the phenomenon of 'live and let live'. As John Keegan remarked:

'Unless harassed by their officers, soldiers have always been ready to understand each other to remain quiet, to chat and exchange essential items, even to conclude local truces.'[59]

In the French army, understandings and fraternization as part of trench warfare cannot be seen as exceptional or marginal. The information derived from even very limited research, from sources with recognized limitations and minimizing tendencies, is impressive. Individual acts may be trivial, but in their accumulation and complexity, and the soldiers' determination, they must be seen as a potentially constitutional element of trench warfare revealing a major capacity for resistance to belligerent attitudes.

Major Henches summarized the situation in April 1916, when he wrote that: 'one no longer sustains oneself for weeks, months or years in a supposed state of anger or exaltation.'

Small groups of soldiers were reluctant to become fully integrated in the confrontation of nations, and showed their capacity to evade constraining rules. In difficult conditions they managed to develop a society in which violence could be more or less regulated by concentrating on deep and long-term cultural traits acquired in civilian life.

## Standards of Civilian Culture

What underlies this tendency towards understanding and fraternization? We may think of Christian sentiments, for the morale of these men had a powerful religious basis. But fraternization in peace time is rarely asserted with reference to dogma or a Church. Moreover, the Churches were engaged in the conflict, speaking belligerently and preaching submission, the virtue beloved of God.

Alternatively, could this be seen as the establishment of a practice of proletarian internationalism? Such a position was a minority approach in pre-1914 France, as was the failure of the Second Internationale to oppose the war. The structures of the Socialist party and the CGT trade union movement rallied to the *Union sacrée* (the sacred union), which was supported by the vast majority of the nation at the outbreak of war. Many workers employed in large factories were not at the front. Fraternization did not arise from internationalism but sprang up from chance opportunities to express individual feelings. Such reflections inevitably remain simplistic: the little man against the great; the extermination of the worker class (urban or peasant) in a war provoked by capitalist appetites.

Where the British army was concerned, cultural values could be advanced that were forged by the enthusiasm and practice of sport, loyalty and fair play. At the time of the Christmas Truce in 1914, some Tommies noted with approval identical feelings on the German side of the front line, reviving the question of the image of 'the Hun'. The French did not have the same sport-related culture but could be considered more generally in terms of very widely shared moral norms. Tony Ashworth evokes the very obvious moral concepts of reciprocity and justice, and consideration of the history of the popular classes rapidly reveals the concept of 'what is just'. Such an approach may appear imprecise but it is strongly anchored in patterns of thought that seek to preserve the worker's dignity. Such a cultural construction became established over the long term, from generation to generation, in civil life.[60]

War created fundamental disturbance. It inflicted unimagined sufferings, broke up families, killed close friends from school or work or the football team,[61] it turned neighbours into enemies. For the most part, the men in the trenches held an ideal of 'the quiet life' (Georges Bonnet); when they manage to 'escape' from the war, they have the impression of 'rejoining society' (Jean Bonnet). Fraternization was one such way. Peace, conversations between good neighbours, camaraderie, family – all these expressions appear over and over again in the descriptions of understandings and episodes of fraternization.

Relieved from Hill 304 at Verdun in June 1916, the private soldier Joseph Bousquet wrote:

'Completely disheartened by everything that we have just seen, which seems impossible well into the twentieth century, supposedly the century of enlightenment and progress in which we should all live like brothers. What disgust at this life of misery and horror . . . Cursed war! Cursed life! And when we will see our family life again?'

Like Marcel Papillon, Delphin Quey and so many others, Elie Vandrand wrote to his parents to ask for more news of home, always more news, of work in the fields and of harvests: 'I am more interested in what you are doing at home than in watching the Boche.' Fraternization was an opportunity to meet men who were also thinking of their families. Photographs were shared. Louis Barthas said of a German captain that he was a 'good family man', evoking not only an actual circumstance but a style of behaviour.

'It often happens that we can chat with them while we smoke an old pipe, almost like family life' (5th RI, January 1917). 'Those who are now opposite us pass over cigarettes every day and we carry on the war as a family.' (29th BCP, October 1917). 'Soldiers are hardly ever knocked out because it's all in the family with the Boches' (2nd Engineers, January 1918).

\* \* \*

In the morning, the neighbours greeted each other and asked if their coffee was hot . . . Following a breach caused by the French, Henri Despeyrières wrote that 'there's a final row with the neighbours'. The story is told in a letter of 25 January 1915 in which one sentence ('it seems that once upon a time people even lived on fairly good terms with them, chatted with them, exchanged newspapers, didn't even fire on them') evokes once again the early appearance of the phenomenon.

On 6 September 1915 Sergeant Roumiguières observed: 'This is not the first time the Boches have asked to live in a state of good friendship with us.' 'We have some good fellows opposite us', wrote a soldier of the 172nd RI in October 1917. And a Parisian in the 143rd:

> 'They are good types . . . Yesterday evening they sent me a card. I am keeping it, I will show it to you when I'm back on leave. It will be a reminder of them.'

As Léon Werth remarked:

> 'Despite the acquired hatred, despite school text books and the newspapers, the workers in the mud, the men digging in the two sets of lines, sometimes feel obscurely that they are from the same system.'

Both sides, it seems, were working in the same site. At such a situation in civilian life, along with forms of respect and solidarity, no one hesitated to challenge or insult one another and throw jibes around. The Germans were treated lightheartedly too, as can be seen in two incidents of enemies who had just been taken prisoner:

> 'The officer observing firing saw a curious incident in the front line which he recounted to me that evening: during the shelling of the German outwork, he saw an enemy soldier come out towards our line, arms up, without weapons "Fire, fire", cried our infantry, "watch out for shells!".
>
> He arrived safe and sound, very out of breath, his arms still

raised. He was surrounded and the men joked with him and gave him some bread and a mug of wine.'

Jean Galtier-Boissière described the capture of a slightly wounded German during the battle of the Marne. The man was about to be sent to the rear:

'We pointed out Villers-aux-Vents, and there was our fellow running towards the village, leaping to right and left to avoid the German shells, and joyfully greeted by the French marksmen scattered in the open!'

*Kamerad/Camarade*! was the Franco-German word uttered when a man was taken prisoner, to the extent that 'to do *camarade*' indicated submission.[62] In civilian life, in peace time, everyone had comrades in class, at work, in the trade union; in fraternizations, camaraderie crossed the barriers of barbed wire.

Men made 'friendly' agreements. Customs developed, and good neighbours respected custom. As in civil life, there were things that were 'not done':

'The other evening, they were ordered to go and reinforce the network of barbed wire in their section and, while they were driving in the stakes, with great blows of the mallet, the Boches began to fire, which was contrary to custom. When one came out of the trench to set up pickets, it was traditional that those opposite did the same. During these times, firing ceased. This violation of the rights of man therefore raised great anger amongst our dragoons, although they did not interrupt their work. You could hear them then, at night, maintaining the rhythm of their hammer blows with loud swearing, sending up terrible insults against the individual Boches and their parentage.'

'It's not playing the game', wrote Pierre Masson when 'some bad-tempered artilleryman' (no nationality specified) broke the calm achieved 'through tacit convention'.

The Savoyard soldier Fernand Lugand had his sights set, one day, on 'a German soldier equipped with a pick, digging a hole at the edge of the wood'. Before pulling the trigger the soldier thought 'that it would be cowardly to kill a man in this way who was perhaps digging the hole to bury a comrade'. And he did not fire. On one occasion a colonel broke a fraternization with an order to fire on unarmed German soldiers. The sergeant did not carry out the order until he had given a signal to take cover: 'It would have been an abuse of confidence to kill them.' A British general, while refusing to encourage situations of 'live and let live', remarked that, among his men, a murder in cold blood was never acceptable.[63]

Understandings and fraternization between adversaries were more than an expression of a small degree of peace at the heart of the war. They were part of the general effort at sociability to avoid descent into a savage state of existence. They advanced the cultural values which had survived what would now be called the 'brutalization' of the common soldier in war.[64] When the truce was broken the soldier, like this one of the 147th RI in October 1917, had the impression that he was returning to an animal state:

'Every day recently we have been working out over the parapet, that is in the open. The Boches were about 200 metres away, they were doing the same as us. Neither side fired, not them or us. But since yesterday evening everything has changed, we have to go to ground again. Hurry on the end of all these miseries.'

# 3

# Brother Boche

## Olaf Mueller

In 1914 Carl Zuckmayer,[1] the future adapter of *The Blue Angel*, was an eighteen-year-old volunteer in the army. In his autobiography in 1966 he described direct contacts between German soldiers and their enemies:

'When a detachment of prisoners crossed the lines to be taken to the rear, the attitude of the front-line soldiers was generally one of friendly sympathy mixed with a slight feeling of envy: for those men, the war was over. From the other point of view, it was impossible to know that one would not be in the same position the next day; then what would happen? Whenever possible, men slipped them cigarettes and sometimes in return they gave us brown 'Caporal' tobacco or an English 'Players' cigarette. Hatred for the enemy in the opposite trench had long since evaporated.

For all of us the real enemy was the war, not the soldier in his steel-blue or khaki uniform who was forced to endure the same challenges as our own men. Fraternizations began very early. Already towards Christmas 1914, to the east of Roye, soldiers in adjacent trenches suspended night-time firing on their own initiative, at a time when firing was standard practice even in quiet front lines. Instead of grenades we threw little packets of *charcuterie* or chocolate across the barbed wire.

One day a German patrol from a Hesse regiment began talking to a French patrol. There were handshakes, and invitations from each side to visit their shelters. The Germans brought beer and schnapps, the French brought wine. Naturally, none of the officers knew what was happening – until one evening when a

young lieutenant on his round of inspection found some
Frenchmen celebrating cheerfully in a German squad's shelter,
belt put aside and rifle in the corner. Stupidly or through a strong
sense of duty, he immediately arrested the men and took them
prisoner. That marked the end of our brief fraternization.'[2]

Signs of non-aggression, in the name of a general feeling of solidarity born out of fellowship in misfortune, included gestures as
simple as the surreptitious gift of cigarettes to prisoners. In a rudi-
mentary version of 'cutlet for cutlet'[3], the cigarette represented a
sort of advance instalment; thanks to their friendly attitude
towards a defenceless enemy, the soldiers could hope to benefit
from similar treatment if they were taken prisoner themselves.
'Friendly compassion' replaced 'hatred' when co-existence in a
particular area lasted beyond a certain time.

Cigarettes were soon replaced by the exchange of food instead
of grenades across the trenches, and finally the clinching element
of fraternization, the encounter between German and French
soldiers during their patrols. In sharing the typical drinks of their
respective countries – wine for the French; beer and schnapps for
the Germans – the soldiers were to some extent enjoying the
'friendly drink' of ordinary neighbours. But more often than not,
military authority would reappear in the form of the particularly
zealous young lieutenant who ordered the arrest of the French
soldiers and brought this 'brief fraternization' to an end.

For Zuckmayer, these scenes occurred almost simultaneously, as
if telescoped together, and, above all, the two scenes seem to hold
equal importance. In reality, open fraternization was only one
element in a broad range of subversive or more or less ordinary
patterns of behaviour. The various degrees of fraternization varied
from the common hope that the war would end to a feeling of
equality with whomever one was obliged to see as an enemy – a
feeling fostered notably by geographical proximity and the knowledge that the soldiers opposite were also struggling for their
survival in appalling conditions. The weather was thus frequently
a decisive element in establishing tacit agreements.

Small gestures of non-aggression did not however automatically
develop into moments of fraternization. Indeed the more discreet

the gesture the greater the likelihood that the relative suspension of hostilities would last. This also meant that the various forms of agreement, more modest than the spectacular Christmas fraternizations, were both possible and probable throughout the war whenever external circumstances allowed. Personal contact with the enemy in No Man's Land, outside the trench or even inside the enemy's trench, was much less frequent and much more difficult to establish. In cases where exchanges reached this stage, it is difficult to imagine that the officers remained in total ignorance.

Such stories immediately arouse sympathy. We think of the *Adventures of Soldier Schweik*, of Arnold Zweig's 'Sergeant Grischa', or the noble attitude of the enemy officers in Jean Renoir's film *La Grande Illusion*. But such attitudes remain marginal even when they can be identified on almost every front and at almost every stage of the conflict. There would not have been millions of dead if the men who were capable of mutual understanding had not also been ready to commit the most terrible massacres when the order reached them.

Perhaps the chance to escape, however briefly, from the horror of static warfare enabled so many men to endure more than four years of conflict and prevented any genuinely effective resistance. Similarly, we cannot be certain that the agreements, often tacitly tolerated by the officers, did not in the end 'help' to extend the war. The historian Christoph Jahr[4] shows convincingly that if the war had been undertaken from start to finish in line with the thinking of the various headquarters – that is, implacably offensive – it would probably not have lasted more than twelve months because by then the armies would have wiped each other out.

Non-aggression agreements therefore existed within the system of delivering orders which were never in fact perfectly executed. Arrangements between soldiers were officially forbidden, and the protagonists were rarely able to mention them openly. Further, German soldiers had no interest in talking about them, for fear of attracting attention from officers.

We must suppose that the officers in direct contact with the front-line troops (that is, non-commissioned officers and officers up to the rank of lieutenant and captain) knew very well what was happening. For them to avoid sanctions too, discretion was in their interests. Above all, as Bruna Bianchi discovered in the Italian military psychiatry files, many officers suffered grievously from being responsible for the deaths of subordinates and for this reason would often seek to avoid offensive actions. They might also simulate such actions and then falsify their reports. In the end, this attitude plunged them into a dilemma which rendered them psychologically sick.[5]

The fact that the officers felt responsible for their soldiers should be clearly understood. It was not simply a paternalistic relationship between a superior protector and subordinate juniors. In many cases it was the inverse age relationship between a very young officer and his more mature subordinate which led to psychological tensions. For the younger man, this produced emotional blocks which prevented him from fully exercising his powers of command.

A twenty-one-year-old Italian sub-lieutenant, in civilian life a student from a poor family, gives a good description of his state of mind in a letter to his fiancée for the New Year 1918 – a letter which earned him three months in prison:

'Just think, Gina, that today we could finally be together in my house, in your house, in our house. Instead, I have to take it on myself yet again to give orders to men more exhausted than me – the same orders which, as usual, will only be half carried out, or not at all. I am obliged to give the usual warnings, the usual threats to fathers of families. These men are worth nothing as soldiers; they deserve to be treated like children yet they are fathers, perhaps even good fathers. This situation represents a permanent oppressive contradiction, which cannot be evaded.'[6]

Already in November 1914, a few weeks before his death, a young German officer wrote to his family about the weight of responsibilities which oppressed him even during his sleep:

'I don't suffer at all from physical fatigue . . . It's the feeling of responsibility which is so undermining. At night, it stops me sleeping. We constantly inspect the different posts so that everyone keeps on the *qui-vive*, which continues even after the relief; so much so that afterwards one dreams of posts and trenches.'[7]

How can a melancholy young man of twenty-one behave when a little group of family men who may be nearly twice his age, wretched soldiers in his view, come to an arrangement with the enemy which enables them not to fire and not be killed in the front line? It is not difficult to imagine that this resigned sub-lieutenant took note of such an incident without taking the appropriate disciplinary measures. We can imagine the problems posed by such behaviour, which was certainly punishable but also tacitly tolerated within certain limits or even openly acknowledged. Accounts are generally coded, due to censorship, or allusive. Judicial sources are almost equally discreet. In general the 'crime' was not named and no appropriate policy for dealing with it existed in 1914.

In addition, it is worth considering this in the light of events at home. In July and August 1914, an international general strike failed to halt the outbreak of hostilities. Many found the failure of proletarian fraternization to achieve peace hard to accept. Clandestine publishing was also affected by this setback, as were the international conferences at Zimmerwalk, Kienthal and Stockholm. In Germany in particular, the concept of universal brotherhood was used against anti-militarists on the left. Foreshadowing the post-war 'stab in the back' assertions which were used to question or deny the German defeat in 1918, international fraternization was evoked in debate to illustrate the dangers of global sympathies. French, English and Italian sources can supply references to proletarian fraternization, revealing its resurgence on all fronts from the time of the Russian Revolution of February 1917. As a further complication, accounts written after 1918 included acts of non-aggression.

Everywhere, the cost of the massacre over more than four years appeared unjustified in relation to the results obtained. It was increasingly apparent that the war had achieved precisely what from the outset it was intended to avoid, notably the collapsed empires of Germany, Russia and Austro-Hungary. International soldierly sympathies focused on the aberrrant nature of the slaughter and not on the requirement that they should kill each other. Veterans, for example, recognized that they had more in common with soldiers in the opposite trenches than with the civilians on their own side.

This international spread of instinct was redirected from 1933 onwards, as German veteran activities became subject to very strict state control in order to serve National-Socialist propaganda. The apparently pacifist rhetoric of fraternization between the front-line veterans was applied to justify German vengeance for 1918.

## Brothers

The Italian poet Guiseppe Ungaretti, a friend of Guillaume Apollinaire, fought on the Austro-Hungarian front from 1915 until he was transferred in 1918 to the Western Front, in time for the final great offensive in Champagne. Most of his many poems on the war were written near the front line, and his first collection was published in 1916. Also from this date comes one of his best-known texts:

> Brothers
> From which regiment
> Brothers?
>
> Brothers
> The word which trembles
> In the night
>
> A leaf barely born
>
> In the spasms of the air
> Involuntary revolution
> Of the man who is present at its
> Fragility
>
> Brothers
>
> Mariano, 15 July 1916[8]

Reading this poem, it is easy to imagine a scene in which a soldier mounts guard through the night and meets other soldiers, whose uniforms and therefore identity are unrecognizable because of the dark. For a moment he does not know whether they are men from his own unit, or enemies.[9] In calling them 'brothers' he locates himself, as well as those whom he encounters, in a broader sphere, as members of a human community beyond uniform or nationality. It is here, in the general meaning frequently attributed to the poem, and in this setting, that the 'involuntary revolution' can be seen as a form of intimate protest against the inhumanity of war.

In this case, however, the four repetitions of the word 'brothers' suggest a revolt that has suddenly acquired a very precise meaning. A sentry addresses a soldier who is possibly an enemy. To call him 'brother' is to express an abstract protest against the war. Above all he is infringing the password, a misdeed which had the minimum potential penalty of imprisonment.

In June 1918, moreover, an Italian military tribunal was a real threat.

In April 1918 the illiterate G. C., aged 25, from Messina, a widower, father of several children and a coachman in civilian life, was approached while on sentry duty by an Austrian:[10] 'Italian, Italian, are you afraid to talk?' he was asked, to which G. C. replied in the negative. The visitor immediately asked the Italian how he was. The Italian, who clearly knew his interlocutor well, responded: 'No, you tell me how you are, because you complained yesterday. How was the night?' The Austrian replied that it had been a bad one and that moreover he was hungry. He asked G. C. if he could give him some bread and whether the Italians had cigarettes. G. C. explained to him that he had just received his tobacco ration. The discussion stopped at that point.

In the judicial file no other charge was recorded against G. C., who apparently gave neither bread nor tobacco to the Austrian. However, the tribunal's considered judgement was to send G. C. to prison for five years. The wording of the judgement certainly indicates acknowledgement that the accused man had neither left his post nor neglected his duty. But the simple fact of having engaged in a *pacifica conversatione* with a soldier from the other camp was a serious matter because the accused had the 'delicate duty of standing guard, at a point where damage caused by the enemy was directly identifiable and where he was supposed to defend his country'.

Having heard of the irreproachable patriotism of G. C., the tribunal produced a long commentary which showed how it saw the potential threat represented by this breach, and the significance attributed at that time to the concept of 'fraternization'.

'This action should be put down to carelessness and the non-observation of constantly repeated orders which legitimately forbade all conversation and fraternization with the enemy. The soldier whose purpose was to protect the country and push back the enemy has no right to discuss ideas with the enemy. This is a particularly obvious principle. This type of exchange inevitably ends in a fraternization which can lead rapidly to dangerous consequences through facilitating destructive enemy attacks.

Experience has shown that the enemy takes advantage of such discussions. Initially harmless, in fact they serve to prepare a state of mind and atmosphere favourable to the diffusion of a poisoned propaganda which helps to weaken the troops who have unwisely fraternized while continuing their duty of loyalty to the army. As we have already indicated, the consequences could prove disastrous. For the nation's genuine defence, it is thus absolutely essential to prevent anything that could enable the enemy to defend himself more easily, to harm us more.'[11]

Military justice thus saw a simple conversation with the enemy as an act of fraternization, an interpretation which the young British officer Charles Sorley seemed to support in a letter addressed to his mother in June 1915. He described how the soldiers avoided the Germans as much as possible, even though they were posted only a few metres from the British lines:

'Last week, we took over some trenches and have been very busy. We are working more like labourers than soldiers. Otherwise, even though he acts in a friendly way towards us, we avoid all relations with our "Brother Bosch" [sic] less than seventy metres away. We do not "fraternize" in any way.'[12]

With his very British ironic reticence, Sorley recognized a brother in the stereotypical and caricatural figure of the 'boche'. He shows clearly, however, the difference between the general concept of 'fraternity' and the fraternization which, as an officer, he was duty-bound to reject. We can understand how, as in the case of the Italian military court, he would define any peaceful contact with the enemy as 'an act of fraternization'. It is true that in the same letter Sorley described an arrangement which seems to have already been in operation with the German enemy for a while, but for him this evidently did not constitute fraternization.

> 'Our chief enemy is nettles and mosquitoes. All patrols – English and German – are much averse to the death and glory principle; so, on running up against one another in the long wet rustling clover, both pretend that they are Levites and the other is a Good Samaritan – and pass by on the other side, no word spoken.
>
> To either side, to bomb the other would be a useless violation of the unwritten laws that govern the relations of combatants permanently within a hundred yards of distance of each other, who have found out that to provide discomfort for the other is but a roundabout way of providing it for themselves.'[13]

Fraternization was not, therefore, the simple avoidance of firing on the enemy, which Sorley appears to see as a relatively straightforward and uncontentious act. It additionally involved talking together, even if only about the weather and the quality of food supplies, a point which also supposes some mastery of a language that both sides could understand. In the case of the convicted Italian the court file was silent as to whether it was the Italian who spoke German or the Austrian who spoke Italian. Charles Sorley certainly spoke German well enough for conversation with the enemy; he had stayed in Schwerin from January to April 1914, then studied German literature and philosphy at the University of Jena until July before being arrested for twenty-four hours as an enemy foreigner on 2 August. On his release he travelled through Belgium and on 6 August reached England and enlisted in the army. On 13 July 1915 he wrote again to his mother from the front line, asking her for his personal copy of Goethe's *Faust*.[14] For him, the British and the Germans were both as guilty as innocent, like boxers who hit out at each other blindly. To designate the German soldiers,

Sorley always softened the pejorative French word 'boche', by adding 'Brother':

> 'A vagueness and dullness everywhere; an unromantic sitting still 100 yards from Brother Bosch. There's something rotten in the state of something. One feels but cannot be definite of what. Not even is there the premonition of something big impending; gathering and ready to burst. None of that feeling of confidence, offensiveness, "personal ascendancy", with which the reports so delight our people at home. Mutual helplessness and lassitude, as when two boxers who have battered each other crouch dancing two paces from each other, waiting for the other to hit.'[15]

Sorley presents the enemy as a brother and protagonist in a combat full of violent incident, dancing from one foot to the other and waiting for something to happen. In this case the brotherhood of the trenches was genuine, although fraternization was wrong. This stands out strongly in contrast to the edifying tone and patriotic prose of war correspondents. In a poem entitled 'To Germany' and sent to his parents in April 1915 – before his arrival in France – Sorley is already showing that he was not ready to interpret the war according to the officially-defined categories:

> You are blind like us. Your hurt no man designed,
> And no man claimed the conquest of your land.
> But gropers both through fields of thought confined
> We stumble and we do not understand.
> You only saw your future bigly planned,
> And we, the tapering paths of our own mind,
> And in each other's dearest ways we stand,
> And hiss and hate. And the blind fight the blind.
>
> When it is peace, then we may view again
> With new-won eyes each other's truer form
> And wonder. Grown more loving-kind and warm
> We'll grasp firm hands and laugh at the old pain,
> When it is peace. But until peace, the storm
> The darkness and the thunder and the rain.[16]

The poem opens by emphasizing the equality between enemy camps; both blind, both ignorant of reality, with a distorted view of the adversary. In this setting, in the spirit of Sorley's poem, moments of fraternization are like lightning and anarchic apparitions in the darkness of war. The slightest sign of fraternization aroused the self-protective instincts of the military hierarchy and required the merest hint to be stamped out. The simple fact of saying out loud that the enemy was also a human being was enough to entail disciplinary measures.

In April 1918 an Italian soldier was condemned to two years in prison and a fine of a hundred *lire* for sending a postcard declaring that he was already sick of the front, that it was in a state of general disorder, that the Austrians were fed up too and that they were not firing at each other because they were all sharing the same fate.[17] What in peace-time would be a mere comment became, for military justice in a nation at war, 'information liable to weaken the national strength of moral resistance.'[18]

In his war memoirs the German playwright Ernst Toller, who volunteered in 1914, described the moment when, as he emerged from combat, his mind recovered its values; the 'truth of the human being'. To underline this awareness he, like Sorley, adapted his vocabulary, and spoke of blindness (linked to the war) in the face of knowledge (peace). The initial shock occurred when Toller, digging the ground, dug his pick into human entrails:

'A – dead – man
And suddenly, as if the light had emerged from the shadows,
        the word of meaning, I grasped
The elementary truth of the human being.
Truth forgotten, buried, smothered; I seized the principle of
        community
Of unity and of unification.
It was not a dead Frenchman.
It was not a dead German.
It was a dead man.'

'All these dead were men, all these dead had breathed like me,
all these dead had a father, a mother, a beloved wife, a little patch

of ground where they belonged; their faces expressed their joys
and their pains, eyes which saw the light and the sky. From that
moment I know that I was blind because I had blinded myself.
From then on I knew finally that all these dead men, these
Frenchmen and these Germans, were brothers, that I am their
brother.'[19]

Acts of non-aggression and fraternization put the authorities in a
very difficult position, which remained a subject for specialized
study even after the end of the war. We have seen the appearance
after 1918 in Germany of many energetic works, offering a supposedly scientific explanation for the defeat and its origins. In 1923
the military lawyer Heinrich Dietz wrote about the legal challenges
of such unprecedented war behaviour. In Germany, no one had
foreseen the problems of trench warfare, and military justice had
difficulty in dealing with crimes committed in unforeseen circumstances; that of living in close proximity to the enemy in a relatively
limited space over a lengthy period.

'The military penal code was conceived for an offensive war. But
the world war introduced a new and specific type of combat of a
hitherto unknown pattern; the war of positions, interrupted from
time to time only by vast attacks directed against precise targets.'[20]

In 1914 German military law was still based on the penal code of
1872, which reflected the classic offensive Franco-Prussian war
of 1870. This code had been extended in 1898, naturally also
without covering the circumstances of virtually static trench war. In
his conclusion Dietz stated, with obvious relief, that the penal code
for 1872 remained applicable in 1914–18. Using a biological image,
he suggested that the relatively normal functioning of military
justice during the First World War proved that the majority of the
population approved the fundamental norms of offensive war. He
then appeared to believe that the functioning of justice was founded
on social consensus and not, as everyone recognized in the specific
case of military justice, on a restrictive or didactic framework:

'The norms of the military penal code have remained unchanged,
while adapting to the new forms of warfare. This proves sig-

nificantly that the code itself, developed from the experience of a victorious military campaign (that of the Franco-Prussian war of 1870) was of a quality higher than its reputation. This also shows that its norms retained an ethical foundation for the majority of our compatriots.'[21]

There remained what Heinrich Dietz called 'a possible exception':

'. . . appreciation of the crime of cowardice (sudden weakness, collapse, psychosis linked to exhaustion, particularly during the war, with its incessant pounding from heavy artillery).'[22]

These words seem to limit the concept of 'cowardice' only to those classic cases with an attempted definition of 'war neurosis', 'shell shock' or 'war hysteria', and which were treated with the most brutal methods.[23] None the less, he then shows that the behaviour created by trench warfare required new legal definitions:

'The definition of the circumstances in which acts of cowardice could occur "during combat" or "while moving forward" (Articles 84–87 of the military penal code) should be adapted to the new demands of the military campaign, above all, to trench warfare.'[24]

The traditional definition in the 1872 penal code envisaged only the case of one or several soldiers taking flight:

'Any soldier fleeing out of cowardice in battle and inciting his comrades by words or gestures to do the same, will be condemned to death.'[25]

A crime of flight in the case of a tacit agreement or even of fraternization could not be defined. Further, the general definition of when the expression 'battle' could be applied to calm sectors where gestures of fraternization became possible had to be reframed. This definition of the penal code was in effect tautological because it asserted that combat occurred 'during the battle against the enemy.'[26] Thus, in declaring somewhat vaguely that it would have been necessary to redefine the meaning of the phrases 'during combat' and 'while moving forward' to adapt them to 'the new conditions of the war', Dietz expresses the dilemma of military justice.

Yet there were attempts to bring the new crimes committed in the trenches into the conceptual framework of Articles 84–87. The courts also had access to other possible forms of action, through Article 92 on 'disobedience to an order in service manifesting itself in its non-execution, by its modification or by its deliberate transgression'. This paragraph provided only for an arrest which could lead to punishment, depending on the gravity of potential consequences, and could theoretically extend to the possibility of life imprisonment. There was also Article 94, which defined the measures taken in cases of disobedience 'in the face of the enemy' – an act necessarily corresponding to examples of non-aggression. None the less, even putting all these together, these legal definitions did not truly cover the behaviour which concerns us here.

Italian justice had to face a similar challenge, but with one difference; its judicial framework was even older. In June 1917, discussing the verdict on a deserter, the military tribunal was reproached with having used the penal code of 1859, the *Codice penale per l'esercito* which was 'old and unsuitable to the modern era'.[27] In this particular case it was still possible to get away with the 1859 definition because it was merely a matter of knowing whether the crime had been committed 'in the presence of the enemy' or 'facing the enemy' – even though the life of the accused depended on it.

The first case envisaged direct contact with the enemy, the probability or possible eventuality of a troop's assault against the enemy. Article 137 provided for severe sanctions such as forced labour or a long period in prison, but did not go so far as the death penalty. On the other hand, in a situation 'facing' the enemy, when the assault had already begun or was in the process of starting, desertion or refusal to carry out orders entailed capital punishment (Article 92). It can be seen, once more that, even taken together, these definitions could not offer a precise definition of the phenomenon of tacit agreements between soldiers, and that the law still had a certain margin of separate understanding.

By definition, arrangements between soldiers always related to the presence of or face-to-face contact with the enemy, and ideally they led to the non-occurrence of combat. Strictly speaking, the death penalty was therefore always applicable but, as will be shown, this did not always happen. In effect, even Italian military justice, so cruelly quick to execute, accorded a statute of exception to the various fraternizations – unlike cases of desertion. Very few soldiers, therefore, were shot for having reached an understanding with their enemies in a moment of forbidden peace, although excessively severe penalties of imprisonment remained the general rule.

The Italian military justice archives for 1918 are instructive. Detailed descriptions of cases with the anticipated verdict reveal the impossibility of administering existing laws appropriately in cases of tacit understanding between soldiers who should by definition be enemies. Here, justice was forced to apply a range of interpretations which might be broadly favourable to the soldiers or could equally well make the death verdict available for most of those concerned.

In January 1918, in the Monte Perizza region on the Austro-Italian front, three Italian soldiers and two non-commissioned officers of the 252nd infantry regiment were charged with a *violata consegna*, an infraction of orders. The legal dossier contains the following passage:

'On 31 January 1918, Major LA and Soldiers BS and PO were accused by the commanders of the 252nd Infantry Regiment. On 21 January, while on guard on the section of the front line near Monte Perizza, the two soldiers did not fire on the enemy emerging from trenches near to them. This failure to act contravened the precise instructions of the regimental command, which were imperative in nature. The enquiry revealed that at the same place and at the same time two other soldiers, FU and non-commissioned officer DTG, threw bread to the enemy. Just after this an enemy soldier came out again and threw three cigarettes into our trenches, wrapped in paper. The two soldiers on sentry duty, BS and PD, again failed to fire on this occasion. Major LA intervened to restore order in this group of soldiers and to ascertain who had thrown the bread. However he did not give the order to open fire on the enemy trenches.

After the separate interrogations on the facts as charged, Major LA sought to defend himself. He declared that he had not seen the enemy soldier when the latter demanded bread because he was at that moment a little distance from the site where the exchange took place. On the other hand, as soon as he was informed of what had happened, he had run to the place and had immediately restored order. Concerning the second appearance of the Austrian soldier, the problem was different; it had been impossible for him to give the order to fire because the soldier had been extremely swift . . . The two sentries, BS and PO, acknowledged that they had seen the Austrian soldier ask for bread and throw the cigarettes. But they stated that they had been too surprised and taken aback by this action to think of opening fire. As for the two other soldiers, FU and the non-commissioned officer DTG, they had admitted throwing the bread, but without reflecting on the action.

The tribunal considered that it could not honestly convict Major LA because it was not fully proven that he had been present at the time of the acts and had failed to take the necessary measures. He said that he had been about 100 metres away from the place where the soldiers had thrown the bread, a distance that the other accused had not been able to judge precisely. On the other hand, the latter have asserted that they saw him a few minutes later giving the soldiers the orders and directions necessary in case the enemy appeared again. In view of this relative uncertainty as to the time and place of the intervention of Major LA, the tribunal cannot be sure that he failed to obey orders received and finds itself obliged in consequence to acquit him for lack of proof.

Concerning the two sentries, BS and PO, they have admitted their fault. The tribunal considers that this relates not to Article 98 but Article 94 of the military penal code and that the accused should threfore be condemned according to the terms provided in the latter case. In effect, they appear here for a fault committed during their period on watch. Their purpose was to open fire on the enemy (whether single or in a group) as soon as the latter was in a position to attack.

However while accepting that the soldiers did not compromise the security of our troops by disregarding orders, the tribunal considers it appropriate to sentence them to seven years in prison.

But soldier FU and non-commissioned officer DTG committed a genuine infraction of their orders by throwing bread to the enemy. The arguments that they have advanced to excuse themselves cannot be accepted. Such disregard, already inexcusable for a soldier ignorant of the regulations, is even less pardonable for those who have been promoted such as FU (who was a corporal at the time of the facts) and the non-commissioned officer DTG. However, the tribunal considers it appropriate to recognise the general attenuating circumstances of the two accused and instead of the death penalty to declare a penalty of imprisonment, for twenty years for the soldier and for twenty years and six months with loss of rank for the non-commissioned officer DTG.'[28]

It is interesting to examine the facts as they really occurred and as they appeared in the legal file. The incident took place on 21 January, less than a month after the two feast days which had given soldiers opportunities for tacit truces in many places. At the end of January this mountain region would still have been under snow, another factor likely to encourage a truce.[29] It is more than likely, therefore, that the soldiers had already been in a pacific state of mind for some weeks and that the agreement reached around Christmas or over the new year had simply remained in operation after the end of the 'festive season'. The trenches from which the Austrians emerged were evidently very near their Italian counterparts – a situation which frequently led to arrangement between soldiers on each side of No Man's Land. The clauses of the verdict also showed that the regiment had given express orders to sentries to fire on the enemy.

It is therefore almost undeniable that the section of the front line in question was more or less quiet and that it had already seen acts of non-aggression, at least since Christmas 1917. The regimental command had reacted to this situation by issuing fresh orders designed to remind soldiers of the formal interdict against treating the enemy in any friendly way.

Originally only the sentries were accused, but the inquiry into their actions interrupted an arrangement that had clearly been established between Italians and Austrians throughout the sector. The investigations brought officers from outside, of high rank but not necessarily with great experience of the front, to examine the situation and pass judgement according to the regulation which made no allowance for peaceful understandings with the enemy. The accused argued persuasively in their defence that they did not wish to fire on the Austrian at the very moment when someone was throwing bread to him from the Italian camp (to which he had responded by giving them cigarettes). These statements turned the attention of the inquiry to others who were active at the scene; the corporal and the non-commissioned officer who defended themselves in their turn, stating that they had thrown the bread without thinking about it.

This, at the latest, was when the inquiry learned of the existence of an established pattern of peaceful co-existence between the enemy camps, raising the question of the duty of surveillance on the part of the officers responsible. The sentries had not fired on the Austrians for an obvious reason; they had become accustomed over a long period to seeing soldiers leave the opposite trenches and come over to the Italian camp to barter – a fact which in the strict sense of the password necessarily threw a fresh and negative light on the authority of the officers present. Manifestly, all the accused attempted to find a version enabling them to explain how the major had more or less carried out his duties, even if no shot had been fired.

The version from the major, who claimed to have been too far away to be able to identify the actions immediately, was not contradicted by the vague statements from the sentries and the two other soldiers. However, the list of 'measures that should be taken' included no reference to the most obvious from the military code point of view; to fire on the enemy. This confirms the long-standing existence of an agreement between the soldiers, and also that the wholly unexpected aggression from one Austrian would necessarily have been interpreted as an act of treason in violation of all the tacit rules in force. The major was reflecting this when he reminded the soldiers of their duty for form's sake, without giving any order to fire.

The case deserves further consideration; the only men to be denounced initially were the two sentries who failed to fire on an Austrian soldier. Who denounced them? The tribunal's description of the situation shows that the information came entirely from the statements of the two soldiers concerned. This tells us that initially only this one incident was observed, perhaps from a neighbouring Italian sector where soldiers could see, and envy, the peaceful dealings between the accused and their Austrian enemies. Thus, if the supplementary information came in effect only from the accused men's statements, if no other person had given evidence, we may suppose that the content of the report on the major's attitude had been agreed in advance. It is possible that he did nothing to halt the bartering and that in exchange his soldiers did their best to excuse him at the tribunal by making their declarations extremely vague.

The major's acquittal shows that the soldiers achieved their aims. But the sentries were also judged relatively generously, to the extent that the tribunal implicity recognized the existence of an arrangement that was acceptable to all parties. This choice in effect enabled the judges to avoid applying Article 98, which provided for the death penalty, and drew their authority instead from Article 94 concerning a breach of the password during sentry duty. These two articles, however, show that in reality neither of the two corresponded exactly to the facts described. Article 98 states clearly that: 'the death penalty is applicable to punish soldiers who, in the presence of the enemy, abandon their post on sentry duty or activity without direct order or authorization, and also soldiers who have infringed a legitimate order!'[30] The 'presence of the enemy' was obligatory in the case cited, and the application of Article 98 would therefore have entailed the death penalty.

As for the text of Article 94 on which the tribunal relied, it authorized several solutions, stating that:

'The guard placed forward of a position or section exposed to enemy attack is to be punished with the death penalty if he compromises the security of the position or of soldiers through failure to execute orders or through abandoning his post.'[31]

The clauses of the judgement insisted that the sentries had acted contrary to all instructions. The tribunal was therefore well aware that, given the tacit agreement in operation between the two trench lines, the Italian soldiers were not in any real danger. Finally, therefore, and without further explanations, it applied the second paragraph of Article 94 which stipulates that '. . . If security has not been compromised, the sentry is subject to a prison sentence of between three and ten years.' This in any case is what can be suspected from the vague justification for the penalty attributed to the two other accused. The reference to 'attenuating circumstances' effectively indicates that the lawyers present in March 1918 had entirely understood the circumstances in which the *violate consegna* had been committed.

## Christmas and Feast Days

Around New Year 1914, the British in Northern France took the initiative of arranging a truce so as to bring in their dead. After three days it was still in operation without anyone seeing an end to the temporary arrangement. A German officer cadet wrote:

'Christmas Eve was very strange here. A British officer approached with a white flag and requested a truce from 11 in the morning until 3 in the afternoon to bury their dead. (Shortly before Christmas our enemy's violent attacks had cost them many men killed or captured.) The truce was agreed. It was pleasant not have the dead men lying out in front of us any more. And then the truce went on. The British came out of their trench and came forward to halfway across No Man's Land. They exchanged cigarettes and tinned meat and even photographs with our men. They declared that they did not want to fire any more. At the moment we are living in a strange calm. We move about freely. We are up on the bank, outside the trench.'[32]

Further information from the same writer shows that in this part of the front line soldiers on the opposing sides came to a mutual understanding, and that this would only be broken by a sudden attack from one side or the other. Yet such an attack was no longer imaginable, at least from the British side; indeed the author adds:

> 'This could not go on in the same way. We sent a message across, telling them to go back into their trench because we were going to fire. The officer responded that he was very sorry, but that his men were no longer obeying him. The soldiers no longer wished to fight. They stated that they could not stay any longer in the waterlogged trench, and that the French were done for. In fact they were a good deal dirtier than we were; they had more water in their trenches, and many men sick. In fact these were mercenaries and they were quite simply on strike. Of course we are not firing because our tunnel trench (from the village to the front line) is also permanently full of water and it's much nicer to be able to leave the shelter without risking our lives.'[33]

What in the Alps could only be imagined is shown here explicitly as a reason to 'go on strike'; the difficult situation endured by the soldiers as a whole in the flooded trenches. If we add to this the first scene in which the English officer requested a truce in order to remove the dead, and we then recall that it all took place close to a major feast day, we see three factors coming together, each of which is frequently sufficient to justify some form of mutual accommodation. From the point of view of the military hierarchy, two forms of temporary truce were blended, of which only the first, negotiated by the officers, could with a moderate amount of good-will be accepted by the disciplinary system. The second, a 'strike' arising out of the initiative of ordinary soldiers in the ranks, could not be tolerated on principle because it threatened the army's military framework. Only an external German observer could understand this concept as legitimate: he could hope to derive a direct advantage from the situation and wondered, for example, 'whether the entire British army was not on strike and whether it was not in the process of obstructing the plans of those gentlemen in London.'[34]

On the British side, since their men refused to break the truce – contrary to orders – the French artillery was called on. But they too turned out to be in an unwarlike frame of mind and sought above all to limit the damage caused:

> 'One day a British officer arrived and told us that his staff officers had given the order to fire on our trenches. He therefore invited us to take shelter. Then the artillery (French!) began very intensive fire, but without inflicting any losses.'[35]

It is clear that the German letter-writer is trying to avoid any reference to the personal German initiative over these arrangements. The inevitable assumption must be that, before the British initiative, the Germans had also indicated their wish to interrupt the attacks. During his description of the Christmas Truce, the author mentions the German participation at the end of the accord:

> 'On New Year's Eve we shouted out the time and agreed to fire artillery salvoes at midnight. It was a cold night. We sang songs which they applauded (we were about sixty to seventy metres away from them.) At one time I asked them whether they had any musical instruments on their side. They brought out a bagpipe and played some fine Scottish airs, and sang them too. At midnight, the guns fired on both sides. Our artillery fired a few times, I don't where they were aiming. Tracer fire, which is usually so dangerous, burst like fireworks. The soldiers waved torches and cheered. We prepared some hot toddy and raised our glasses to the health of Kaiser Wilhelm and the New Year. It really was New Year's Eve, just like peace-time.'

Here, Aldag attempts to show the conditions before the establishment of the truce as a matter of national work ethic. In effect he is showing the men in the British regular army, the professionals, as war-workmen using their right to strike in the same way as civilian workers. The Germans, meanwhile, appear to consist of an army of volunteers who may have lost their enthusiasm but who remained aware of their duty.

It became known later that the feast-days, at Christmas 1914 and at other times, could not have been celebrated together without the agreement and participation of the officers, and that they even appeared occasionally in press accounts.[36] German military papers, for example, give detailed descriptions of the celebrations that united Germans and French on the Western Front. How is it possible to justify the appearance of such accounts in publications designed to sustain troop morale and idealize the reality of war? Why did the members of the military censorship not perceive any risk in these descriptions of celebrations?

It is worth looking more closely at one of these accounts, which comes from an article published on 1 January 1918 in the war journal of the 1st Army, describing Germans and French celebrating New Year's Eve together in Champagne on 31 December 1916. Karl Adam, an infantryman, tells the following anecdote under the title 'Happy New Year! A happy reminder of 31 December 1916':

'We were in a quiet and lovely place in Champagne, in well-constructed trenches fitted out with all modern facilities. From time to time the artillery fired towards the rear lines, but in the afternoon it all fell quiet. No firing, no explosions to disturb the peace – a truce? Darkness fell quickly and it was so cold, brr! Yes, it was winter here too. When it was dark the dinner fatigue party went to the field kitchen. An order had come to fill the pot with hot punch to warm us up, but also to put us in a festive mood . . . At last it was midnight! The New Year had begun. In line with an old German custom we paid farewell to the old year by taking a drink without a word, then we greeted the new year with a resounding "Cheers!" We did not worry that the "enemy" were very close and would hear us. Moreover, they were shouting with joy as well! And that's how a real conversation began between the Germans and the trench. All the soldiers, on duty or not, met in the trench. Just a few men slept, stretched out in the shelters, and missed this magnificent moment.

Hurrah, hurrah, we've got some punch! – What about you? – Monsieur *Camarade*, have you got a cigarette? – Send me over a bit of white bread!'

Cigars, cigarettes, chocolate, bread, and so on, were wrapped up and flew from one trench to the other. Sometimes a packet dropped on to the bank in front of the barbed wire networks. Then two or three soldiers jumped out of the trench where they were sheltering and rushed for the gift. They all wanted to be the first one to get it. Here and there the punch and the few bottles of Cognac available were already having an effect. A soldier in very high spirits climbed up on to the bank and went to shake the barbed wire. The French were amused at this and exploded with laughter. Enemies? On the other side, they must have had something to drink too; an empty bottle landed at my feet. For a moment I thought it was a grenade and jumped away. That set off bursts of laughter in our own camp, and in theirs. After a few minutes our splendid bottle fight was going full tilt. Jugs of Steinläger, bottles of red wine, flasks, white bread and little packets of tobacco flew through the air amongst the mounds of earth and snowballs. "Touché, ha ha!" Everyone was shouting, crying out in every direction, officers and soldiers . . . They were all happy and celebrating the New Year.

After the delights of alcohol and the festivities of the last few hours, nature took over again. The soldiers disappeared one after the other to sleep for a bit. The uproar died down. Finally, the sentries were on their own again in the trenches, buttoning up their coats with a shiver. In the distance, to the east, the dawn was bringing in a new day: 1 January 1917. A shot was heard and a bullet whistled over our heads. That's war!'[37]

How could this text have appeared in a paper written for soldiers in the front line when it contained the detailed description of a spontaneous truce? The carnival atmosphere, with the ritualized reversal of the usual order, is stressed by the exchange of ridiculous projectiles which arouse laughter and not fear. Elsewhere, officers' participation in this exuberance proves that this was a form of controlled anarchy, a feature that ended with the dawn like a ghostly apparition. The ending shows clearly that the interval was over and that on the morning of 1 January 1917 all the soldiers returned without complaint to the activities that were interrupted at midday on 31 December 1916. Everyone followed the popular maxim: 'Work as usual!' Thus the reader understands that these moments of carnival are limited in time and space, that they represent nothing but a brief and ritualized distraction from daily life at war.

No individual soldier is identified here, there is no reference to direct and personal contact. The soldiers of both sides are still cloaked in national anonymity and nothing happened that could draw down irreversible consequences for their ability to fight. It is this, however, which often lay behind such enounters, and the officers of the troops concerned then generally reacted by moving their men in the section affected.

The Italian soldier Alberto Recanatine narrates an incident of this kind which occurred in 1916 after a Christmas Day celebrated between Italians and Hungarians. The first indication here is also the slackening of bombardments on Christmas Day. Then an Italian began to sing without any returning fire from the Hungarians opposite. A small package containing food was sent, and at first taken for a grenade: 'An object landed in our trench. We thought that it was a time-delayed bomb, but it was only a packet of cigarettes. We sent chocolate in return.'[38] Both camps became more confident; the men began to talk to each other, and to shake hands:

'Someone stuck his head above the parapet, but the snipers did not react. The faces of some Hungarians appeared. Cautiously they spoke a few hesitant words in Italian, the first that came into their head. They just wanted to say something. The officers did not intervene; they were themselves surprised and disarmed by the unreal peaceful atmosphere in this second year of warfare in our front line trench. We outdid each other in sending presents: a little wine, dried fruit, biscuits; little things, part of our poor Christmas, of our own poverty like the poverty of the Hungarians in this rich man's war. The truce lasted till the evening. Next day our commanding officers sent up the relief and posted our unit to another sector. We learned that the Austrian command had done exactly the same. They did well, because after this Christmas truce [tregua] we would certainly not have fired on each other again.'[39]

Certain details appear in this unofficial account which, significantly, are absent from the German text. The Italian writer
understood that, in their social circumstances, the Italian and
Austro-Hungarian soldiers had more in common with each other
than they had with their own compatriots who were responsible
for 'this rich man's war'. After the encounter with their enemies,
they saw them as individuals and could no longer open fire on
them.

In using the expression *tregua*, Recanatini referred indirectly to
the mediaeval legal term of the *treuga Dei*, from which was derived
the French word *trêve* and the corresponding English term 'truce'.
The appropriate German word is *Waffenstillstand*, which we find
in the original words of Karl Adam, quoted on page 189. This
expression refers to a military tradition dating back to chivalric
times and gives the term *tregua,* or its equivalents, a precise status
in the soldiers' world.[40] This also explains why accounts of a truce
could appear in official publications designed for the troops; as
shown here, they represent a 'courteous and chivalric style of
behaviour.'[41] On the other hand, Karl Aldag's concept of 'strike'
(page 187) referred to a different social practice which genuinely
threatened military order.[42]

The symbolic significance of Christmas, in relation to feast-days,
is undeniable and recognized by all sides, whether the arrangement
is accepted or rejected. In *Storm of Steel*, Ernst Jünger evokes
Christmas 1915, with the British, like the Germans, demonstrating
their spirit of aggression by sabotaging any attempt to celebrate the
event:

> 'We spent Christmas Eve at the position and as we stood in the
> mud we sang Christmas carols which were lost in the noise of
> the British burst of machine-gun fire. On Christmas Day we lost
> a man in the third section who was shot in the head. Just after
> this the British made an attempt at friendly *rapprochement* by
> hoisting a Christmas tree on to their parapet, which was
> brought down by our men in a fury, with a few rounds of fire.
> The Tommies then responded by firing rifle-grenades. Our
> festive day was thus celebrated in an extremely disagreeable
> atmosphere.'[43]

Jünger's choice of expression shows that all the soldiers clearly considered the obvious respect for the festive day (Christmas carols from the German side, the English side's Christmas tree) as an indirect invitation to set up a peaceful arrangement with their enemy. The deliberate rejection of this kind of relationship shows equally clearly that the rules of communication were familiar to both sides. We know that Jünger belonged to an elite section; and therefore the behaviour that he described confirms Ashworth's comment on the rarity of truces between specialized units.[44] None the less, similar incidents were observed in ordinary infantry regiments, as shown in the following incident which was still remembered at the age of nearly 100 by a German soldier born in 1896:

> 'On Christmas Day 1914 the sentries in the trench sang "Silent Night, Holy Night". As soon as they sang the first words, the French began to fire furiously. They thought that an attack was beginning, even though the carol was not warlike. Soon afterwards they stopped firing because nothing happened. They must have understood that this was connected with Christmas and remained silent. When we had finished our "Silent Night, Holy Night", they sang the "Marseillaise". That's how we spent Christmas 1914.'[45]

Unlike the scene described by Jünger, these Germans did not respond to aggression that was no doubt due to a misunderstanding. The French had possibly confused the opening of the singing with the cheers which the Germans often shouted as they left the trenches to attack. When the Germans kept silent in response to this misunderstanding, the French realized what was happening. Although Christmas Day did not automatically bring a truce, there was none the less more than one truce each year.

Tacit agreements were also reached at other religious celebrations or certain Sundays. In his memoirs the Italian intellectual volunteer Giani Stuparich described a Sunday truce between Austrians and Italians which seems particularly unusual in occurring in an otherwise very active sector. The action was in June 1915 at Monfalcone, some thirty kilometres outside Trieste. In constant danger of major insurgency, the Italian sector witnessed almost incessant fighting throughout the war. Since arriving at Monfalcone Stuparich had experienced continuous Austrian artillery fire, and he therefore expressed great surprise when a truce was called:

> 'It is unprecedented: we have peace in the streets of Monfalcone and absolute calm throughout the sector. Men are looking at the sky in amazement, and it is surprising to hear neither gunfire nor rifle fire. As far as I can recall, this is the first time that the atmosphere here has been so undisturbed. It is Sunday, and everything is really very Sunday-like. I would not be surprised to see our band on parade. Have we come to an agreement with the men opposite to celebrate the day? . . . The evening, the growing dusk, are making us deeply depressed. There is nothing left for us but to lie down and take advantage of the truce [*tregua*] to get some sleep.'[46]

Both camps started to fire again during the night, and Stuparich ended his account of 27 June with the comment:

> 'Everywhere there is fierce firing again. In the end, last night was just like all the other nights.'[47]

## Strangers and Brothers

For obvious commercial reasons, many soldiers had developed regular contact before the war with the nations that were now their official enemies. Workers, salesmen, restaurant waiters or hotel staff had sometimes lived abroad for a long time. A British joke recounted that someone shouted 'Waiter!' from a British trench and that fifty German soldiers in the opposite trench replied 'Coming, Sir!'[48] Many Italian workers also emigrated to the industrial cities of central Europe and in 1924 the writer Carlo Salsa described an Easter fraternization. He portrayed a soldier, Molon, who settled himself on the parapet with a flag to draw attention to his presence. Not only was he not fired on, but from the other side an Austrian soldier stood up and began to make large gestures to him:

'"Molon! Hey, Molon!" Dammit, the two men knew each other, they were friends. They had worked together in a factory in Bohemia and met again, face to face as enemies, on Easter Day. Molon naturally jumped down from the parapet and ran over like a madman to meet him. From both sides, curious soldiers began to peer out. As the two men got on together happily, others were tempted to come out from behind the parapet. That eased the way and soon afterwards Italians and Austrians were all outside, unarmed. They fraternized, like two groups of hikers meeting by chance.

It was hardly a daily occurrence to be able to stay outside the trenches and remain safe and sound. So Easter was celebrated, and no one could be blind to what was happening. Those "over there", on the other side, the scorned enemy, suddenly looked thoroughly threadbare, very much like us. In their poor martyrized bodies we recognized sufferings and a fate that were the same as our own. At first the officers tried to hold us back, but finally they came out too under the pretext of stopping the scandalous event and restoring a bit of order.'[49]

The dramatic conclusion seems to indicate that Salsa had adopted a somewhat romanticized touch in his memoirs. In fact the artillery began to fire on the soldiers who were fraternizing, and Molon and his friend, warmly clasped in each other's arms, were shattered by a shell. Yet the passage proves that the scale of worker emigration was so well recognized everywhere that the story could appear plausible. It is in any case credible in essentials, for similar cases appear in various official documents in military justice files.

This shows what happened in December 1916, when the snow lay so deep between the Austrian and Italian lines in the mountains that they could not fire on each other. The Italians decided to carve out steps in the snow-drifts so that they could look across – and saw Austrians out in the open on the other side, also busy clearing away the snow:

'The Austrians shouted something in German to the Italians, who did not understand but made signs of greeting. Then ME arrived. He had already been punished for having spoken with the enemy and had worked in Germany, where his fiancée was waiting for him. He began a conversation which ended in a sort of mutual agreement, enabling each side to continue with their snow-clearing without disturbance. This ended in a series of friendly exchanges which were mainly about Christmas festivities. Suddenly a big poster was hoisted up from the enemy trench, with "Happy Christmas" written on it. Then we threw cigarettes over. CM collected them and threw back some bread in exchange.'[50]

No exact date is given for this incident; but the events described must certainly have stretched over several days, even several weeks, since the arrangement was clearly well established by Christmas Day. Until then it was more like an extended truce, encouraged by the presence of the Italian soldier ME, the former emigrant worker who spoke German sufficiently well to communicate easily with the Austrians. In reading the statement from an Austrian deserter the Italian inquiry learned, notably, that:

'Corporal ME had told the Austrian Corporal S that he had a fiancée in Germany (in Dresden). He had then asked Corporal S to write a letter for him because he wanted his fiancée to have news of him. The letter was sent and ME received a reply, a letter written in German which was in the dossier and bore the man's address at the front: ME, 129th Infantry Regiment, 6th Company. This file contained another letter in German, sent to an Austrian soldier who was paid by the fiancée to send her news of ME.'[51]

This passage no doubt surprised the military authorities. Peaceful relations between the enemy trenches were so well established that ME and his fiancée in Dresden had been able to exchange at least two letters, and probably more. Further, the letters must have made the return trip between the Italian camp and the Austrian camp. This gives an indication of the length of time that had passed without a shot being fired – and it emerged that before this sequence of events, ME had already been convicted of communicating with the enemy. It is therefore probable that, in this sector, the units (at least the Italians) had remained in the line for a long time without being relieved and that they had taken advantage of this to strike up acquaintance with the men opposite. This supposition is strengthened by the fact that the fiancée in Dresden knew the address of an Austrian to whom she could write in the full hope of obtaining news of ME.

## How to Reach an Arrangement

Signs came first. The soldiers established whether the units opposite were ready to come to an agreement. Then they negotiated its possible terms, in detail. A simplifed form of *rapprochement* consisted of establishing the times and exact level of firing. The enemy could therefore take cover at the time indicated, if the fire happened to be directed towards his position. The French writer Gabriel Chevallier evoked his memory of one of these tacit agreements from his period in the Vosges, at a location known to have witnessed long periods of peaceful co-existence between enemy troops during the First World War:

> 'Very few missiles reached us. Once a week, four German guns sent over about thirty shells in a spray of fire. Once that was over, we could be sure of peace and quiet for a week. Our fire was more variable. From our second lines, winding along the hillside, I could sometimes see bursts of fire from our 75s pounding the German banks or bursting out in the open countryside. But there was little intensity on either side; the artillery made a simple show of what they could do, because it was the custom to fire guns in war-time. As to the infantry, it restrained itself from disturbing such a peaceful sector, such a pleasant rural area. Provocation did not come from us, if orders from the rear did not direct aggression. It was all limited to a careful sentry duty, quite relaxed by day and more strict by night. We developed our own customs in this sector.'[52]

Sign language could be extended by simple words, understandable even by soldiers who did not speak the language in question. Chevallier wrote that:

'One section was living in a state of good understanding with the enemy. Each side carried on with its business in the usual way, without concealment, and sent cordial greetings across to the enemy group. Everyone wandered about freely and missiles consisted of nothing more serious than loaves of bread and packets of tobacco. Once or twice a day a German would shout: "Offizier!" to give warning of an officer's tour of inspection in the ranks. That indicated: *Take care! We may find ourselves obliged to send over a few grenades*. They even gave us advanace warning of raids, and the information always turned out to be accurate.'[53]

The pacifist Chevallier was precise about the reasons for the military command's fear of these truces negotiated at the lowest level of the soldiers' hierarchy:

'Then matters came to a head. The rear prescribed an inquiry. There was talk of treason and court martial, and non-commissioned officers were reduced to the ranks. There seemed to be a fear that the soldiers would reach an agreement to end the war, in the face of the generals. It seemed that such a conclusion would have been monstrous.'

Even if an 'inquiry' was not immediately forthcoming, the command could move units, leading to disagreeable surprises for the enemy camp which had noticed nothing. Ernst Toller remembered a ritualized exchange of fire with the French, so well regulated that the two camps employed it to set their watches, and which once changed abruptly:

'Every day at eleven o'clock, a dozen shells came in on our guns with mechanical punctuality. We were used to it. We knew which guns had been targeted by the enemy and we responded an hour later. At five to eleven, Josef declared: "Here we go, they are about to fire." We responded, "Oh, it's not quite time yet, give it another five minutes." Then we disappeared into our shelters to play tarot. The French shots did not harm our guns and the German shots did no damage to the French guns. We fired to indicate that the war was still going on, that we knew the men

opposite were still there, that we were still here. We were still in
the shelter at eleven o'clock, two minutes past, ten minutes past
... "Good God", cried Josef, "why aren't they firing?" – "Their
watches must be slow," replied Aloïs. We continued to play for
ten minutes without a word. The silence was worrying.

A shell burst twenty metres from our gun. "Ah, at last!"
exclaimed Aloïs. "One all!" Another shell exploded. Aloïs burst
out again, "That's not our Frenchmen," and threw down his
cards.'[54]

There would be shots to send a message, not for an attack: 'We are
firing to signal that the war hasn't stopped, that the men opposite
are still there, that we are still here.' But both sides made efforts
not to inflict losses on their enemy. Each camp knew so precisely
when enemy shells were due to arrive that the two Bavarian soldiers
could continue calmly with their card game, knowing that it was
not yet time for the 'normal' shots to be fired. On the other hand,
they became nervous when they observed that nothing happened
at the usual time. The threat must be dangerously close for the
soldiers to realize that it was no longer a matter of 'their
Frenchmen'. Either their French troops had been relieved, or a
superior officer had made sure that the tacit agreement was broken.

Toller entertainingly describes an event that was often experienced as a psychological shock. The troops had lost a
reassuring sense of security that was a rare experience at the heart
of the madness of war and saw themselves facing an absolute uncertainty that was psychologically unbearable. Decades later,
Giovanni Mecheletti, an Italian peasant from the Brescia region,
would still weep as he recounted the following incident:

'We were posted behind the front lines at Cerovo, near Görz,
where they wanted us to take over as the relief. That's when a
sort of revolt broke out because we did not want to go back into
the front-line trenches. Why? Out of fear; an emotion that has to
be felt before you can understand what it means. This is what
happened next: our trenches were only a few metres from the
Germans (some of them were in fact linked to the Austrian
trenches). Halfway between the positions there was a small

stretch of barbed wire, and nothing else. We could even hear each other talking. When we were engaged at the front our officers, who were generous- minded, asked us not to fire on enemy troops coming out of the trenches for everyday labour. On their side, our enemies behaved in the same way. For example, we had to get out for the latrine because of course there weren't any toilets in the trenches. You just went where you could. So there was a certain degree of mutual respect. As for the regiment which relieved us every week or ten days, it was led by officers determined to kill the enemy. So once they had replaced us, the Germans no longer respected us.'[55]

Micheletti then described, in a tone of rage, the pretence of a trial established against soldiers who were accused of refusing to obey an order. Two of them were shot, eight others condemned to seven or eight years in prison and the remaining soldiers, including Micheletti, were forced to return to the trenches. Their revolt, as Micheletti called it, was indeed an act of protest from a unit who had reached an arrangement with the enemy which was now challenged by the belligerence of the relief. However, the Italian soldiers did not encounter as much aggression from their enemies as they had expected. The trenches were in fact so close that the Austrian artillery would not have been able to fire on the Italians with endangering its own troops:

'Then we went back into the trenches and, to be honest, we were even safer than before. What happened was that over there they avoided firing in order to avoid hitting their own men . . . In the middle there was just some barbed wire. The others were so near that we were swapping our bread for their tobacco and cigarettes . . . It was thanks to the officers of the 57th infantry regiment, they were good and didn't push us into firing: "Don't fire," they said, "unless they attack".'[56]

The attitude described here by Micheletti closely resembles that of the French soldiers on the *Chemin des Dames*, at the beginning of 1917. After the setback in April these troops refused to fire on the enemy if they had not themselves come under attack. What

Micheletti described as a 'revolt', and which was condemned as an act of 'mutiny' in the case of the French soldiers, now appeared as primarily the expression of a demand. The soldiers wanted respect for a long-standing tacit agreement which was threatened by orders to attack.'[57]

During the war the headquarters of all the warring nations knew that these arrangements were common. Once the war was over, however, the recording of such episodes in official history took very different forms, according to each nation. In Germany it acquired a heavyweight terminology, with the engagement of German soldiers along the front acquiring a heroic character which left no room for fraternization in the accounts.[58]

In contrast, the report on the causes of the decisive defeat of the Italian army near Caporetto in November 1917 was remarkable in its open and dispassionate consideration of the question. This text was presented in August 1919 by a governmental commission of inquiry consisting of high-ranking army officers and members of parliament. The commission, presided over by General Carlo Caneva, included Vice-Admiral Alberto De Orestis, the senior military legal officer for the armies, Senator Paolo Emilio Bensa, as well as Deputies Alessandro Stoppato and Orazio Raimondo.[59] The final report recorded:

'The losses which were added to the length of the war, the demoralizing conditions of life in the trenches, the certainty of the uselessness of efforts and sacrifices in terms of human life; and, on the other side, the repressive measures, meticulous but thoroughly unjust: all this helps to explain how the idea of desertion easily took hold in the minds of some discouraged men, how others saw captivity as their liberation and, finally, how a sort of *modus vivendi* came to be established in places where the losses were greater and continual as a result of the proximity of the two enemy camps. In such positions, men avoided killing in order not to be killed themselves, as the result of a tacit agreement that required no advance arrangement.'[60]

From 1922 onwards, we look in vain for declarations of such sincerity in Italy. This also applies to Germany where, soon after

1919, it was only anti-militarist left-leaning circles that expressed themselves so clearly. From 1922 onwards, for example, the pacifist newspaper *Weltbühne* expressed its disquiet at the tendentious attitude of published war narratives. This disquiet was led by the German national archive office which gradually turned into a shelter for retired imperial officers disinclined to sympathize with the new democracy. The *Weltbühne* was all the more concerned because 'the extracts inserted into school books came from minor works from this institution'. According to the newspaper, 'this gave glimpses of what would be retained in the mind of a German boy in the 1940s, and what a fine image a man in 1970 would have of this war, of this ignominy, of this murderous catastrophe with its false survivors.'[61]

## Fraternization and Revolution

The final appeal of the Communist Party's Manifesto: 'Proletarians of all nations, unite together!' did not fundamentally signify anything other than an incitement to international fraternization. European governments arming their nation for war feared to see future soldiers among socialists associating with their comrades on the opposite side. In France, the *Carnet B* affair showed that this fear was still prevalent at the outbreak of the war.[62] The 'Carnet', or notebook, was a secret list of some 2,500 names held by the Ministry of War which included many representative anti-militarist figures in the French working classes and which formed part of the Ministry's preparations for the arrest of spies in the event of mobilization. Detention of suspected anarchists and anti-militarists was a recognized feature of life, but in 1914 a conciliatory approach persuaded French trade union leaders to appeal to their members to co-operate with the government. Similarly, the introduction of the *Union sacrée*, or 'sacred union', led by the majority Socialist party in European parliaments, reassured governments and high commands. A form of mutual war-time tolerance that encompassed the full range of a liberal society, the *Union sacrée* brought social and industrial peace to civilian life for at least part of the war; its only purpose was to defend France. Yet at various critical moments between 1914 and 1918 each of the belligerent nations witnessed debates on the supposedly defeatist propaganda of pacifist groups.[63]

Just after the outbreak of war, for example, tracts were published in Berlin which challenged the patriotic line of social democracy and emphasized the war's effect on international fraternization. Parodying their lighthearted and casual tone, the socialist march entitled: 'Arise, socialists, close your ranks!' appeared with the following second stanza:

> You who in your millions
> Come from mines and fields, from cities and the land
> You are now mere cannon fodder
> Cannon built by proletarian hands!
> From now we fire upon our kin with pleasure
> For this is what our highest masters wish,
> To wipe out the greatest score of human lives
> This is the goal towards which we are led,
> This is what is known as 'holy war'.
> With us, the people! With us the victory is assured![64]

In 1916 the circle around Karl Liebknecht and Rosa Luxemburg, which acquired the significant name of the 'International Group,' began the clandestine publication of the *Spartakist Letters* calling for proletarian resistance to the war machine. The first of the group's twelve directing principles defined the war as 'fratricide':

'The war has destroyed the results of forty years of work in European socialism. It has eliminated the political importance of the revolutionary working class and the moral standing of socialism. It has destroyed the proletarian Internationale, led its sections into fratricidal combat and in the main capitalist countries it has packed the goals and hopes of the popular masses away in the great vessel of imperialism.'[65]

At the General Congress of the German Social Democrat Party, in late September 1916, the representative of the International Group used this statement as the grounds for these following conclusions:

'The proletariat living outside our frontiers are our brothers, our comrades; they are closer to us than the managerial classes in our own lands, and we have more obligations towards them than towards the latter. We are setting the ideology of inter-nationalism in opposition to the ideology of the nationalism to which the party capitulated on 4 August . . . My feelings as a human being and a socialist make me feel as much pain and anger when French, Belgian and Russian soldiers are murdered as when members of the German proletariat are affected. The nation is in distress – these are our brothers whom we are in the process of killing!'

On the Russian front, as the collapse of Tsarist forces began, German officers initially encouraged their men to offer gestures of fraternization in the hope of accelerating the collapse, although the Russians had been employing fraternization to destabilize the enemy in this way since 1917. An account of the ceremonies of 1 May 1917 – the first time that it could legally be celebrated as Labour Day in Russia – emphasised the participation of German prisoners of war. In particular, the local worker representative from Ascha in the Urals expressed his great joy at seeing workers reunited, and his 'deep satisfaction at seeing fraternization with prisoners of war'.[66] After this date, many Russian newspapers carried similar accounts.[67] The German War Ministry became anxious about the ideological reliability of prisoners liberated from Russia, to the extent of setting out measures to be taken in a secret annex to a decree of March 1918:

'It is particularly important to ensure that the prisoners who return from captivity recover their full moral strength and sense of discipline. All positive and strict forms of respect for the hierarchy must be encouraged. This should be achieved by recalling the rules of behaviour to superior officers, the soldier's corresponding duties and infractions of the duty of military subordination which are subject to penalty. Patriotic feeling must also be stimulated through appropriate reading and teaching which use both text and images, in order to counteract ideas which may have been aroused by revolutionary events.'[68]

A general turned historian wrote of his own war after the end of
the war, in the light of the revolutionary events which began in
November 1918:

> 'The Marxist concept of the world which so seduced the modern
> German mind represents an extreme danger. While for other
> states, even the Soviet Union, a strong national engagement is
> dominant, Germany and Austria see dreams of worldwide frat-
> ernization, of world citizenship or the global proletariat.'[69]

In 1928 another official military historian, General Hermann von
Kuhl, thought it definitively proven that during the war, '. . . independent social-democracy had been accomplished within the
army, a work of undermining threatening military discipline to the
highest degree.'[70] According to von Kuhl, propaganda from
Germany to promote revolution and fraternization had had disastrous consequences for troop morale, particularly during the last
year of the war:

> 'According to their own admissions from members of the in-
> dependent social democratic party, the subversion and
> demoralization of soldiers engaged at the front were proposed
> within the heart of the army itself from the beginning of 1918.
> The soldiers were worked at [in their corps] and incited to desert.'

This image of the German soldier fighting courageously to the very
end and encouraged to desert by the dark intrigues of socialist or
communist civilians fed the legend of the stab in the back. In fact
anti-militarist propaganda influenced relatively few front-line
soldiers, apart from those who aligned themselves with the German
workers' political organization. Certain soldiers with left leanings
even thought that 'the country's exterior enemies must be
conquered' before it was possible to engage in interior conflict for
the rights of the people.[71] And yet – even among survivors – the
myth of the brave soldier betrayed was such an immensely powerful
influence that, a few years later, public evocation of fraternizations
or any other form of behaviour that was not heroic had become
impossible in the Weimar Republic.[72]

In the post-war period the French left-wing view of the fraternizations was also not without ambiguity. Already in 1920, just
before an international meeting of war veterans, Henri Barbusse
expressed strong reservations about the fraternizations, although
without specifying exactly what he really understood by the
expression:

> 'There were partial fraternizations in the mechanical and un-
> restrained chaos of the war. But these natural *rapprochements* of
> man to man, or rather between one sufferer, with a purer heart
> and a purer mind, and another – and which, sometimes, nothing
> could prevent – were disorganized and worse than useless. They
> did nothing but add victims to the massacres and intensify the
> war.'[73]

At Geneva Barbusse apparently sought to impose a new model of
institutionalized fraternization, through helping to found an
assembly of national veterans' associations. This new concept
seemed to be the only one of which he could approve, as he tried
rather unconvincingly to explain a retraction of his declarations:

> 'It is not during the war that we must fraternize, it is beforehand.
> We gathered together in solid and definitive fraternization before
> the wars which are likely to break out again.'

In contrast, a communist leaflet protesting against the Moroccan
war was published in 1925 with the title: *Fraternization: a historical sketch of the tradition of the French proletariat*. The author,
Michel Marty, uses it to recount the proud history of significant
fraternizations from the French Revolution onwards, during which
French troops had refused to fire on innocent victims:

> 'At the moment when fraternization seems to be the only way to
> impose immediate peace on a government which, with its high
> command avid for advance and glory at a low cost, is nothing
> but the executing agent for the colonizing banks of Morocco, it
> struck me as interesting to recall here some exampes of frater-
> nization by the French revolutionary proletariat.'

Next came a series of evocations: of the union of royal troops with revolutionaries after 1789; fraternization of a governmental regiment with the National Guards and members of the Paris proletariat during the Commune in 1871; the refusal of troops to obey orders to fire on the wine-growers of the Midi in 1907; mutinies in the French fleet in the Black Sea over their refusal to fire on Russian civilians in 1918;[74] French soldiers who fraternized with the German population during the occupation of the Ruhr in 1923; and, finally, the French sailors who refused to leave for Morocco in July 1925. In this list, the fraternizations of the First World War remain without mention. At best it is possible to guess that they formed part of the mass of naive political fraternizations which occurred before the Ruhr circumstances:

> 'For the first time the system of fraternization was applied, forecast and realized by Lenin during the war. Until then fraternization had been undertaken in the way in which, in Molière's play, the stupid *bourgeois* spoke prose without knowing it! It was the first time that fraternization was undertaken with full understanding of what it was.'[75]

Marty thus considered fraternizations before 1923 as instinctive, spontaneous acts without the class-consciousness essential for any action; clearly, he felt uneasy about them. Similarly, in articles for the *Republican Association of Veterans* the concept of 'fraternization' is only used pejoratively. This communist-directed organ sought to discredit the gathering together of a large number of associations of non-communist veterans, from France, Germany and some other European countries. According to the review the *Conférence Internationale des Associations de Mutilés et Anciens Combattants* (CIAMAC) or International Confederation of Disabled Veterans was nothing more than 'an institution designed to sustain veterans and the working masses in their illusions of a Locarno-esqe and pan-European pacifism so as to hide from the daily expanding preparations for the next imperialist butchery.'[76]

Thus the only grouping of international veterans that was acceptable was restricted to the framework of the Internationale of Veterans (IAC), whose congress in Berlin (30 May–1 June 1930) was also the object of a long account in the same issue. In this general climate, the memory of the mutual accommodations and spontaneous fraternizations in the First World War no longer had any place.

## The Memory of Fraternization

How did the memory of the different forms of non-aggression appear in pacifist veterans' associations? What space was available for tacit truces and peaceful arrangements with the enemy in the official rhetoric of democrats amongst former front-line soldiers? While communist sympathizers saw fraternizations as useless or even harmful, pacifist veterans seemed to think that they were not sufficiently bloodthirsty to become part of their martyrdom-centred ideology (from which they drew their moral authority). An article published in 1932 in the *Reichsbanner*, the organ of German social-democrat veterans, seemed wholly characteristic of the current tone that prevailed on both sides of the Rhine. It evoked the significance of the experience of the war for the democratic state:

> 'The popular masses have not sacrificed so many lives in order to remain, arbitrarily, objects of an authoritarian state after the war. They wanted to become emancipated citizens . . . For the German people, the right of shared management represented genuine proof after the colossal sacrifices that were accepted.'[77]

If soldiers, presented as holding profoundly respectable political aims, were also shown to have suffered without a break for four years, it is understandable that the memory of tacit truces could no longer be invoked. This concept was expressed, for example, by Henri Pichot. He was a director of the CIAMAC which was violently attacked by *Le Feu* at the time of a speech on disarmament in October 1933 in Geneva:[78]

> 'Fellow-combatants, we who have suffered and bled, we who have marched, without a backward glance, on the orders of our

country, we whose hands have held weapons, we will not renounce our ideal of peace, whatever happens, we will defend peace!'[79]

Innumerable similar examples exist. The instructional and political authority that the former soldiers drew from their sufferings needed the image of the soldier as sacrificial victim. Yet this was not compatible with recalling arrangements and fraternizations, at least on solemn occasions of public commemoration. True, this experience was shared by very many soldiers, but it no longer allowed them to appear in their role of heroic victims. It showed them as men acting occasionally in ways that were subtle but always widely representative.

After 1918, in truth, no political group knew what to do with this representation. Scenes of fraternization were even absent from films of pacifist inspiration which, following in the wake of *All Quiet on the Western Front*, showed the horrors of the war from the ordinary soldier's point of view. The only exception was Victor Trivas' film *Niemandsland* (1931), which showed how five soldiers from different enemy nations met after an artillery attack, far from their units, at the centre of a No Man's Land that was temporarily calm, and lived together in wonderful harmony. All this was presented so clearly like an edifying dream-world that it was impossible to see in it any true representation of genuine arrangements.

After 1933 all foreign contact with German veterans was overseen by the National-Socialist (Nazi) party. The German postal service stopped distributing the bulletin of the CIAMAC (as well as a number of other pacifist publications), a move which in effect banned the journal in Germany.[80] In official language, no further mention was made of fraternization but only of mutual military respect between former enemies who were expected to sustain their role of soldiers ready to die for their country. The Nazi policy of remembrance was also expressed in other forms. The Nazis, for example, renamed the 'day of national mourning', turning it into a day of 'commemoration of heroes'. In February 1934, the new chairman of the German aid committee for victims of the war, at the heart of which most veterans' associations were obliged to rally,

expressed its view of how the image of the combatant formed by
belligerent ideology affected German veterans' contacts with other
countries:

> 'Germany, the nation which our enemies, French, British and
> American, came to know during the World War, was the
> Germany of the front line which imposed respect on them and
> which obliged them, in the great decisive moments of the war, to
> deploy all their human energy, while the German representatives,
> who have until now taken part in reunions of the CIAMAC,
> preached international pacifism and submission to all the treaties
> imposed.[81]'

The war was no longer an unhappy event which the soldier had
been forced to endure, but a desirable situation, in line with the
soldier's profession. It gave him the opportunity to prove his
heroism or to die gloriously for the nation. The decision of German
veterans' associations to withdraw from the CIAMAC carried no
implication that '. . . the German soldiers of the front and the
victims of the war rejected all collaboration and all conversation
with former adversaries. On the contrary, this state of affairs indicated that they had abandoned a way of acting which was not
worthy of the exploits of the German front-line soldier.'[82]

The historian Antoine Prost has described the disarray of
French veterans' associations, which were slow to understand that
all official contact with Nazi organizations represented a propaganda success for the Germans and did nothing to calm
international politics or to render the German terror regime less
dangerous.[83] This disarray reached its peak during the Franco-
German ceremonies to commemorate the Battle of Verdun at
Douaumont on 12–13 July 1936. The culmination of the events
was a sermon of mutual peace; but an account of the German
veterans' official journal showed how much this body played
down as much as possible any likelihood of understanding
between the two parties:

> 'It was clear that no antagonism existed between all these men,
> no trace whatsoever of hostility. It was possible to state, clearly

and without equivocation, that *the front line soldiers understood each other perfectly.*'[84]

In this respect, the decisive concept that Ernst Toller and innumerable other ordinary soldiers had expressed during the war was no longer conceivable. And yet it was fundamental to assert, even strongly, that the combatants saw their adversaries not as soldiers but as men enduring the same sufferings as themselves. This was necessary, if one wished to escape the military logic of '*kill or be killed*', and if one wished to confront it with the logic of the arrangement, the tacit truce, the '*live and let live*'.

# 4

# Russia: Fraternization and Revolution

## Marc Ferro

'We send them sausage, white bread and cognac; the Germans give us cigarettes.' The soldiers had not yet developed a specific name for it, but from the end of 1915 their letters home regularly described episodes of fraternization. The actual expression, *Bratanie*, appeared very early in the war but was only used by officers. These letters refer to feelings towards the enemy, but only once they were immobile, face to face in the trenches, with Russians and Germans or Austro-Hungarians, watching each other. Occasional clumsy drawings showed soldiers climbing out of the trenches and exchanging gestures and perhaps biscuits.[1] The men opposite were men like themselves; they were living through the same tragedy. Perhaps they could reach an understanding and delay the return to active operations by extending such breaks. Hopes surged up at important dates, particularly at Easter.

These letters also revealed the soldiers' resentment of 'shirkers' and anyone else evading his duty, whether wearing uniform or at the rear: 'The war? They sit there while we are in the muck, they get 500 or 600 roubles when we have only 75.'[2] They were obsessed by unfairness: 'And then, although it's the soldiers who have to bear the hardest part of the war, it's different for them, they are covered with medals, crosses, rewards; but that lot are a long way from the battlefield.'[3] Another man wrote that:

'Here, every patch of ground is red with blood . . . Pray to God, dear wife, that our tortures are coming to an end. Let this war end, it's been going on for two years.'

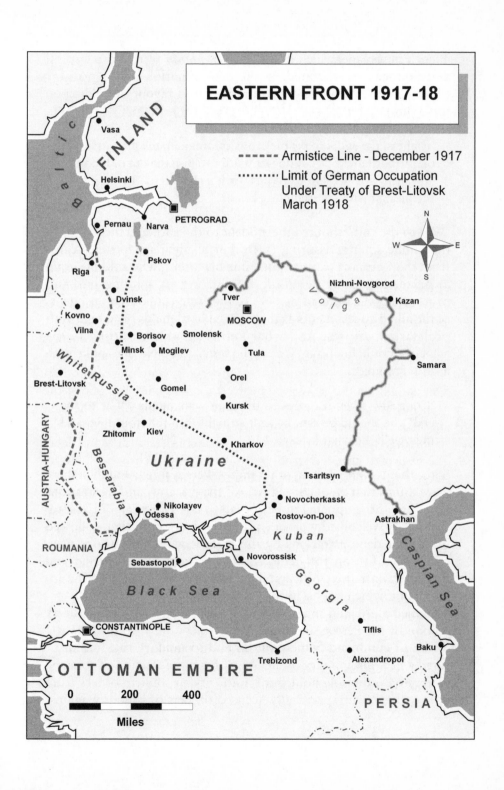

EASTERN FRONT 1917-18

- - - - - - Armistice Line - December 1917

············· Limit of German Occupation
Under Treaty of Brest-Litovsk
March 1918

Baltic

FINLAND

Vasa

Helsinki

Pernau    Narva

PETROGRAD

Pskov

Riga

Dvinsk    Tver    Nizhni-Novgorod    Kazan

MOSCOW    Volga

Kovno

Vilna    Borisov    Smolensk    Samara

White Russia    Minsk    Mogilev    Tula

Brest-Litovsk    Gomel    Orel

AUSTRIA-HUNGARY    Kursk

Bessarabia    Zhitomir    Kiev    Kharkov

Ukraine

Tsaritsyn

ROUMANIA    Nikolayev    Novocherkassk    Astrakhan

Odessa    Rostov-on-Don

Kuban    Caspian Sea

Sebastopol    Novorossisk

Georgia

Black  Sea

CONSTANTINOPLE    Tiflis

Baku

OTTOMAN  EMPIRE    Trebizond    Alexandropol

0    200    400

Miles

PERSIA

N
W    E
S

Trench newspapers such as *Soldier Grajdanin* were more visceral and political, exasperated by the determination of the pro-war contingent which spoke out from the rear in favour of holding on to the bitter end:

> 'Right to the end, croaks the crow, cleaning up the human bones on the battlefield. What does it matter to him that an old mother is waiting for her son to return, or it's the old man who guides the plough with his trembling hand?'

'War to the end,' shouted the student to the gathered thousands in the public square, assuring them that all their misfortunes came from the Germans. At the same time his father, who sold his grain at sixteen roubles per *pud*, was sitting in a noisy bar and proclaiming the same ideas. 'On to the end,' clamoured the agents of the allied governments as they toured battlefields piled high with proletarian corpses. And what about the soldier sitting in the trenches, could he shout 'War to the bitter end'? No. He spoke with a different voice:

> 'Comrade, when it comes to the man who shouts "War to the end", he should be sent be sent straight into the front line, and then we'll see what he says.'[4]

Some things were spoken, other things were written; and then there were things that were concealed. All these secrets and frustrations flared up at the uprising in Petrograd in late February 1917. After the widely welcomed workers' protests – by women first, followed by further demonstrations by the male workforce – troops were ordered to fire on the demonstrators. The soldiers refused and turned against their officers. This ensured the success of the insurrection which led on to the revolution.

Immediately, and more or less in accordance with the military section of the Petrograd Soviet, the soldiers drew up the *Prikaz I* 'order of command' which put an end to military rule and instituted a new disciplinary order. Apart from the election of soldiers' committees, the sole holders of authority to confirm orders from above, the *Prikaz* specifically accused officers of brutality against ordinary soldiers; excessive sanctions, particularly beatings for trivial matters, exceeding regulations, aggressive coarse language, unjust or arbitrary behaviour.[5]

The war archives in Moscow contain millions of texts telegraphed by soldiers to the military section of the Petrograd Soviet. Top of their list of demands was the relaxation of discipline, as well as protests of all kinds against abuse from officers; brutality towards soldiers, making sick men work barefoot, blows and insults, abuse of authority, etc.[6]

On 3 March General Dragomirov recounted that:

'To each order that I gave them, the soldiers replied: "We don't do that now". One of them, every time, referred to a printed text in his hand: "No," he said, "that doesn't happen now." And when I wanted to see this text he refused to give it to me.'

Yet, before the Petrograd Soviet had launched its programme for 'a peace without annexations or contributions', these texts made no reference to peace. The soldiers declared that they would fulfil their duty to the nation, and some added, 'soldiers in the trenches, workers at their labour . . . so that we can defend *your* freedom'. 'There is no conflict between workers and soldiers,' stated others, although they noted that as soldiers they could not themselves go on strike.[7] The fall of the Tsarist regime turned all attention to the Petrograd Soviet, which was seen as an alternative power in opposition to the military command.

When incidents of fraternization appeared again in the spring of 1917, their political significance was unmistakable. Hitherto they had expressed a kind of chatter – expressing, although not in so many words, the very straightforward desire for the fighting to stop or at least for an extension of the truces with the implication of further development. After February 1917, however, these fraternizations became part of a wider and more complex situation. Obstacles to their development included a marked deterioration in relations between ordinary soldiers and a section of the officer corps, questioning the application of operational discipline and orders and challenging the views of commanding officers in relation to the stance of the Petrograd Soviet. All fraternizations, mutinies and desertions were soon treated alike by military order even though the first two were collective acts and desertion was individual.

The way in which the *Prikaz I* was interpreted fundamentally changed the situation at the front. In the soldiers' eyes, the document represented not so much a denial of discipline as a condemnation of any excess or abuse attributable to autocracy. With the exception of violence against officers opposed to the revolution, the soldiers were not concerned to attack their superiors but simply wished to be part of the movement. However, the response of most officers confirmed to the soldiers that the military establishment was one form of the order that had been overthrown. The *Prikaz I* had attacked the officer corps, in a role-reversal which imposed on them a decision restricting their rights as officers; their wish to perpetuate old-style discipline identified them with the *ancien régime*.[8]

The challenge angered the officer corps. Any admission that ordinary soldiers were citizens like themselves, or discussion with them on equal terms in 'committees', struck them as intolerable. Seeing the soldiers as incapable of dealing with problems seen by the officers as part of their responsibilities, they were disturbed to realize that they had never previously considered such matters themselves. They did not know how to approach questions of discipline or of general politics. Their failure in this respect risked exposure of their leaders' incompetence and might cast doubt on the legitimacy of their right to command.[9]

Nonetheless they understood that the military establishment could only survive if it could prove its *raison d'être*, in other words to fight the enemy. In this sense, any military operation set up by the Germans served the interests of those who were hostile to the revolution, since it offered an opportunity to restore control over their troops under the cover of 'military necessity'. The military section of the Petrograd Soviet soon understood that offensive operations undertaken under the pretext of securing their lines of defence were in fact designed to restore calm within the army. All operational orders therefore became suspect.

In the first operations following the fall of Tsarism, at Stockhod, the soldiers had gone on the offensive to 'show their officers that the latter had no monopoly of patriotism'. None the less they feared that the officers might yield positions to the enemy in order to stimulate fresh active operations and could therefore be seen as a more dangerous enemy than the Germans.

By multiplying episodes of fraternization in the period leading up to Easter in April 1917, therefore, the soldiers were expressing more than their wish for peace. Their motives were patriotic since, in their eyes, the officers' 'treason' risked opening the way to the Germans while the absence of active operations could counteract the double threat to Russia, of invasion and counter-revolution.[10]

Communiqués from the Stavka (the General Headquarters of armed forces both in late Imperial Russia and after the Revolution) seem to indicate that, except on one occasion, initiatives towards fraternization came from the Germans. This is how they were announced in the 5th, 10th and 12th armies between 25 March and 29th April:

'In the Kolodina-Stakhovstsy sector, to the south of Lake Naroch, a group of Germans left their trenches twice, waving white flags and making signs with their hands or their caps; on both occasions our machine-gun fire sent them running and forced them back into their trenches. (25 March).'

'All along the 12th Army front, the Germans tried to start conversations with our troops; for this they came out of their trenches with white flags, but our artillery forced them to return to their trenches. (30 March).'

'In the Ushivtsy sector, north-west of Smorgon, the Germans exchanged bread and sausage with our soldiers while in the 16th Regiment sector at Mingrelie the Germans delivered proclamations to two of our soldiers. Anyone who wanted to pick them up was scattered by our artillery. (2 April).'

'In the Antoniny region, facing a sector of the 137th Division, a group of Germans who tried to open conversation with our soldiers was dispersed by our fire. (22 April).'

'In the 21st Corps sector, three of our soldiers in the 129th regiment took advantage of an embarkation to "visit" the Germans – but gave up in the face of the threats and remonstrations of their comrades. (25 April)'.

'In the Shal'duki-Kunava sector, our soldiers and the German soldiers tried to come out [of their trenches] and to meet, but they were dispersed by fire from our light batteries. (29 April).'[11]

After the fall of the Tsar, the Russian high command expected unequivocal disapproval of any attempt at *rapprochement*. If necessary, and for propaganda purposes, it was specified that the artillery was instructed to cut short any such incidents. The Stavka attitude avoided any initiative aimed at encouraging negotiation, still less a peace, even without annexing or giving up territory as demanded by the Petrograd Soviet on 14 March.

On 23 April 1917, General Gurko issued an order against fraternization. Together with General Alekseev, he had been the most determined member of the Russian High Command to decry the Petrograd Soviet and its slogans which had 'disrupted the army by recognizing the rights of soldiers' and to condemn the *Prikaz I* as a charter for the soldier's rights and freedoms. 'Discipline is more necessary to victory than knowledge of the aims of the war', he insisted. He referred to the South African war as an example, in which the regular armies endured better than the volunteer contingents who knew why they were fighting.

General Gurko's order stipulated that:

'Reports concerning losses due to enemy fire prove that in certain sectors of the front, friendly relations have apparently become established between our troops and the enemy; this is wholly unacceptable when the blood of our allied brothers is flowing to liberate the small nations that have been subjugated and ruined ... The Germans are thus able to establish the disposition of our forces, although the men who talk with them are unaware of this fact. Having successfully established calm on our front, the Germans therefore have troops available to move to fight the French and the British ... Having overcome them, they can then turn to us.

Three German divisions have been transferred from our front to the west, others will follow them, as well as artillery and aircraft. A weakened front is no longer a threat to the Germans: either they are suggesting that men surrender, as they have suggested to the 75th Division, like General Yorke who surrendered to the Russians in 1812, or they are threatening us with an offensive if the peace is not signed in time. Above all, they want to divide us from our allies.'

The order concluded:

'Soldiers, for the sake of freedom, and of the nations under enemy control, to avoid our own subjugation, we must fulfil our duty to our allies; let us make a mark on the first pages of liberated Russia. Marked with our blood, they will remain sacred to the generations to come.'[12]

Back in Russia since early April 1917, Lenin had issued a conflicting order: 'Immediate Peace, all power to the Soviets.' Having written about fraternization even before the revolution, he referred to the problem in the 28 April issue of *Pravda*:

'The capitalists ridicule fraternizations, or they attack them furiously with lies and insinuations, insisting on the way in which the Germans are trying to mislead the Russians. Through their generals and officers, they are threatening severe punishment for anyone guilty of fraternization.

If we look at the protection of the sacred rights of property of Capital, and its profits, this is all very well; in fact, for the proletarian socialist revolution to be destroyed at its very foundation, fraternizations must be interpreted in the capitalists' way.

Yet workers who are informed, semi-prolatarians and poor peasants, guided by the accurate instincts of the oppressed classes, are marching in the steps of informed workers, they see fraternizations with the warmest sympathy; it is clear that fraternizations are a route towards peace.

It is clear that this route is not in line with capitalist government thinking, but is pointing in the opposite direction. It develops, strengthens, consolidates the feeling of brotherly confidence which unites the workers of the different nations. It begins to undermine the accursed discipline of this prison-barracks, the discipline that exacts absolute submission to "its" officers and generals, towards their capitalists, for the officers and the generals for the most part either belong to the capitalist cause or defend it. It is clear that fraternization is a revolutionary initiative of the masses, that it signifies the arousing of their awareness, the spirit of courage of the oppressed classes; that it is, in other words, one of the links in the chain which is leading to the people's socialist revolution.

Long live fraternizations. Long live the world-wide people's socialist revolution.

To hasten the effect of the fraternizations, to achieve the goal surely and straightforwardly, we must ensure that they are well organized and that they are based on a clear political programme.'[13]

On 2 May, *Izvestia*, the organ of the Soviet of Deputies, 'voice of the revolutionary defence', presented the third protagonist in the affair, expressing the Menshevik and revolutionary-socialist point of view. The argument denounced the practice of fraternization but ignored the appeal launched by Lenin in *Pravda*.

'Comrades at the front . . .

We address ourselves to you, in this ardent appeal, in the name of the Russian Revolutionary Democracy.

You are bearing a terrible burden: you are paying with your blood for the crimes of the Tsar who has sent you to fight and has left you unarmed, without munitions, without bread.

The workers had no need of war. They did not begin it. It is the work of the Tsars and the capitalists in all nations. Every continuing day of war is a day of mourning for the people. Having dethroned the Tsar, the people of Russia have immediately set about bringing the war to an end as quickly as possible.

The Soviet of workers and officers has launched an appeal to all nations to stop the massacre. It has been addressed to the French as well as to the Germans and the Austrians.

Russia awaits an answer to this appeal . . .

Our own appeals will be nothing but bits of paper if they do not have the support of the power of the revolutionary people, or if William of Hohenzollern is triumphant amid the ruins of Russian freedom. The destruction of free Russia will be a colossal disaster, irreparable not only for us but for the workers of the entire world. Comrade soldiers, defend revolutionary Russia with all your strength. The workers and the peasants of Russia are putting all their heart into fighting for the peace. But this peace must be a universal peace, for all nations, and it must be concluded with a general peace.

What would happen if we wanted peace, a separate peace for ourselves alone? What would happen if the Russian army laid down its arms and declared that it would fight no longer, that it was no longer concerned by what was happening in the rest of the world?

What would happen? Having conquered our allies in the West, German imperialism would fasten on us with all its powers. What would happen is indeed that the German emperor, the German owners and the capitalists would set their heavy yoke on our necks; they would seize our cities, our villages; our lands; and would make the Russian people pay a heavy penalty.

Have we thrown off the yoke of Nicholas in order to fall under that of William? Remember, comrades: at the front, in the trenches, you are the guardians of Russian freedom. It is not the Tsar or the Protopopovs, the Rasputins or the wealthy capitalists who defend you, but your worker brothers, your peasant brothers. They assure the defence of the cause and the sacrifices that you have endured. The front cannot be defended if men decide not to move out of their trenches again, come what might. Sometimes it may happen that an enemy advance can be prevented simply by a preventive attack.

Sometimes, waiting for an attack is the same as waiting for death, as submitting to it. Sometimes it is only by taking part in an offensive that one can be saved, and your brothers in another sector with you. Remember your comrades. You are engaging yourselves to defend freedom, do not refuse to take part in an offensive if the tactical situation demands it.

Freedom and the welfare of Russia are in your hands.

As you defend freedom, be wary of provocation, be wary of traps. The fraternizations that are developing at the front could easy turn into a trap. The revolutionary troops can fraternize – but who with? With an army which is equally revolutionary, which is equally determined to die for peace and for freedom. But the German and Austro-Hungarian armies are not in the same position, even if they can include a certain number of individuals who are fully aware. It is the army which always follows William and Charles, owners and capitalists, which wishes to seize foreign lands, to pillage them. It has its leaders who are counting on your gullibility but also on the blind submission of their own soldiers.

When you go out to fraternize, you are setting out with your heart, and then you meet an officer coming from the enemy trenches disguised as an ordinary soldier. While talking with him, in the fullest good faith, his superiors are busy photographing the site where you are. And when you stop firing to fraternize, the enemy artillery moves its ground, and enemy troops as well.

Comrade soldiers . . . It is not through fraternizations that peace will successfully be achieved, nor through tacit agreements between individual groups, between separate military units. Neither a separate peace, nor a separate truce, will save the revolution or ensure the triumph of peace in the world. Those who tell you that fraternizations constitute a road to peace are leading you to your death and that of Russian freedom. Do not believe them.

The road to peace is different; it has been shown to you by the Soviet of the worker and soldier deputies. Defend it. Sweep away anything that could lead to the disintegration of your army or damage your morale. Your fighting strength is serving the cause of peace. It is on you that the security of the nation rests, thanks to you it will not suffer military devastation, so that the Soviet can accomplish its revolutionary task and apply its power in the service of peace.

Comrade soldiers, in the name of the brotherhood of nations, show yourselves worthy of the confidence that the world has in you; do your military duty with unbending determination.'[14]

But after the celebration of 1 May, when the strength of pacifism was affirmed on the Champ-de-Mars, the organ of the Soviet of

Deputies launched a frontal attack on Lenin's theories on fraternization:

'Scorning the appeal of the worker and soldier deputies' Soviet for fraternizations to cease in the front lines, the newspaper *Pravda* demands that soldiers continue to fraternize. *Pravda* seeks to undermine the soldiers' confidence in the Soviet's appeal. And to this end it decries the motives of the Soviet, motives which the Soviet has never expressed.

The Soviet knows perfectly well that those who go out to fraternize are not traitors [as indicated by the High Command] but soldiers who can no longer bear the hardships of the war. The Soviet knows perfectly well that fraternizations are not the result of Leninist agitation but are indeed the consequence of exhaustion due to the war and the soldiers' hopes of peace.

And *Pravda* is wrong when it puts forward these arguments against the Soviet in defence of fraternizations.

The problem is not one of knowing what is at the origin of fraternizations, but where they are leading. And this is leading to the destruction of the army.

Fraternizations are a separate truce in particular sections of the front. With fraternizations, a powerful army is disintegrating into an assembly of individual regiments and units. Each unit begins to think only of itself. So, brotherly blood flows in a neighbouring sector; a verst away to the left, a verst away to the right, a battle is continuing while between these two peace negotiations are proceeding: is this the way to a universal peace?

No.

We must act with a united army, a united nation; we must not allow workers and peasants in France and England to see us as traitors because small separate groups of soldiers are fraternizing with the enemy . . .

*Pravda* proposes the establishment of an "organization of fraternizations". This proposal is a contradiction in itself. Organized fraternizations are impossible until peace has been concluded, which is what the Soviet aims to achieve. But the achievement of a general peace requires the front to be defended, weapons in hand. Those who fraternize destroy this defence.

Comrade soldiers.

It is a bad army in which each soldier acts according to his own opinion of what he ought to do, whether or nor he should fraternize.

If you have faith in your Soviet, its appeal to stop fraternizations must be sacred to you. The Soviet depends on you, appeals to you to save the army for the survival of the revolution.

Show that on this question, as on all others which arise, you will follow your Soviet unanimously, as one.'[15]

All these events took place on the eve of military operations planned for the first thawing of the Russian winter – but they were in tune with the current and continuing political changes.

In the event, and in parallel with this situation, a crisis had broken out early in the life of the Provisional Government of Prince Lvov. While the Russian Army continued to face the German armies to the west, Milyukov, the Minister for Foreign Affairs, had reaffirmed in March the continuing intention of post-Tsarist Russia to protect its southern border and access to the Mediterranean through the Dardanelles. This proposal, involving the seizure of Constantinople, Armenia and Northern Persia and the division of Austria and Turkey, alarmed the Allies, who saw in it a lack of determination to pursue the war in the west and to defeat the Austro-German empire. It also disturbed the revolutionaries at home, who wished for peace without any annexations or yielding of Russian territory. The continuing debate over Russian foreign policy eroded the Great Powers' confidence in their ally and threatened the Provisional Government with the loss of American war loan funds. To prevent this, Milyukov sent a Note to the Allied governments on 1 May, expressed in terms that were seen by the ambassadors of both Great Britain and France as deliberately vague, designed to secure the loan but not to appear inflammatory to those who wished for peace.

In the days of public demonstration with workers and armed troops on the streets, one manifesto banner read: 'All power to the Soviets, immediate peace.'

With the proposed offensive to be undertaken on both the eastern and the western fronts at stake, the new Provisional

Government under the leadership of Prince Lvov had won the day for the Soviet *fiat*. In return, however, it had promised the anxious Allies that Russia would remain true to its alliances and would continue the conflict as a partner.

The publication of this Note, to which Lenin, Lvov and Kerenski were hostile, triggered mass anti-war demonstrations by soldiers and workers in Petrograd on 2 May, with tens of thousands of marchers taking to the streets with banners reading 'Down with Milyukov'. A week later, Milyukov resigned, as did Guchkov, Minister of War. Both recognized that they could not carry on their foreign policy objectives without interference from Soviet leaders who would soon join the Provisional Government.

Alexander Kerenski, later to become leader of the revolution, became Minister of War while responsibility for Russian foreign affairs was taken over by Tereschensko, who had no political affiliation or background in published statements on foreign policy. He was, however, more sensitive than Milyukov to the anti-war mood in Russia and proposed a reconsideration of the Allies' ultimate war aims. By now both the government and the Soviet had adopted the policy of peace without annexations or yielding territory, and the directors of the so-called 'democracy' undertook to assure the defence of the country and help the regeneration of its military power. Understanding between the two powers born of the February Revolution – the Soviet and the Provisional Government – had never been so close. The government's next significant foreign policy effort was the Russian offensive on both fronts at the same time.

For this policy[16] to become operational, however, it required the socialists of the Second Internationale to impose on their respective governments the policy proposed by Petrograd; it also required these governments to give up their ambitions of conquest or re-conquest – which was not acceptable to any of the belligerent nations.

The Stockholm Peace Conference of April 1917, organized by international socialist groups, failed in its ambition to find a way to end the war. The United States saw the conference as a possible threat to its own war aims and refused passports to Americans who wished to attend; Britain, France and Italy followed suit. Although

Kerenski did not prevent Russian socialists from travelling to Stockholm, only a few 'internationalists' did so, and representatives who attended from neutral nations (including Dutch and Scandinavian socialists) found themselves effectively powerless. This fiasco, which had been foreseen by the Bolsheviks, led Lenin and Trotsky – a 'unitarian' Menchevik in the process of joining the Bolsheviks – to give their encouragement to further 'action', that is, fraternizations.[17]

The Bolshevik activists included Dimitri Petrovic Mikhaïlov, later known as Mikhail Frunze. A Social Democrat activist who had supported the Bolshevik faction from his youth, he escaped from imprisonment in Siberia after arrest in St Petersburg in 1904. In the 1917 February Revolution Frunze led the Bolsheviks in Minsk and became chief of the city's civilian militia before being elected President of the Byelorussian Soviet. Charged by the Bolshevik party to inspect the Russian armies and to stimulate and invigorate fraternization, he encountered opposition; to prepare for his arrival General Tcheglov (Ceglov) organized meetings and then action in the 218th and 220th Regiments and questioned Frunze's mandate: 'The officers' arguments have prevented nothing'.

General Gurko, who was the Provisional Government's Commander-in-Chief following the February Revolution but was soon in conflict with it, felt strongly that Frunze should be stopped:

'He is now leading a campaign to distrust the officers, that they must now be elected. The Petrograd Soviet must have him recalled, to halt the collapse which is developing in certain army corps.'[18]

In a report to his party, Frunze responded:

'On 1 May large numbers of German and Russian soldiers met in the middle of open trenches. The Germans came with their officers and took part directly in developing motions on war or peace, and on international relations. This meeting made a very great impression on everyone. Russian officers and soldiers recognized the value of gatherings of this kind, but the High

Command and staff forbade participation, under threat of being shot. Grave consequences may ensue, for this sows discord between soldiers and officers, and the diffusion of commands from the Soviet is meeting stubborn opposition on the part of the High Command.'[19]

In highlighting the high Command's opposition to the Soviet's orders, Frunze made no reference to soldiers' resistance to Bolshevik orders. They saw the Soviet as the legitimate authority and any fraternizations that had occurred did not affect the attitude to be adopted when the revolutionary power raised the subject.

Reflecting the coalition Provisional Government's wish to respond to the Bolshevik arguments and match their initiative led by Frunze and Krylenko among others, Kerenski planned a tour in the field. He was aware that his reputation had gained considerably in February through his support in creating a revolution from insurrectional days, when he appeared both in the Petrograd Soviet and in the Provisional Government as Minister of Justice. On becoming Minister for War before the April crisis, he restored to the High Command the rights that had been lost three months earlier, but promulgated the rights of the soldier to maintain the *Prikaz I*; his decision to go on campaign would demonstrate his solidarity with the Bolshevik speakers.

At the beginning of his tour Kerenski was confronted by both the High Command, which saw him as the incarnation of the revolution, and the Bolsheviks. He was aware of the difficulties facing him in having to persuade soldiers to go on the offensive while episodes of fraternization represented the opposite attitude:

'Commanding troops when one has lost the faculties of command; preparing them for action when for them action means treason or counter-revolution; tolerating the poisoned propaganda of the bolsheviks, . . . all this after three years of difficult and unhappy combat.'[20]

Fraternization was only one factor in soldier and officer behaviour in the trenches and Kerenski did not condemn it directly. Under the scheming or sceptical eye of senior officers and bolshevized elected representatives of soldiers' committees, he threw himself into the arena where he won the nickname of 'Persuader in chief'. Addressing a mutinous group, he spoke out:

> 'Comrades, for ten years you have suffered and remained silent. You undertook the obligations imposed on you by a hated regime. And what is happening today? Has free Russia become a state of slaves in revolt? [Intense stirrings in the soldiers assembled.] Comrades, I cannot, no, I cannot lie. Oh, my comrades! What grief! Not to have died three months ago! Then I would have died with the finest of dreams; I thought that a new life was about to begin for my country . . . that there would be no further need for whip or cane to achieve self-respect.
>
> Yes. It is necessary to fight because, to fraternize, there must also be fraternization on the French front . . . Oh, my comrades; the fate of nations is in your hands and the nation is in danger. You have tasted the wine of liberty and you are a little drunk . . . What we need is discipline, so that you enter into History and so that on your graves can be written: 'They died but they were never slaves.'[21]

A remarkable and sympathetic orator, Kerenski overcame hostility and brought his audience round – an ability demonstrated in his meeting with Krylenko, an experienced Bolshevik leader from a populist revolutionary background, who by mid-April 1917 was chairman of the 11th Army's committee. At Kamenec-Podolsk, in the Ukraine, Kerenski had the soldiers' meeting well in hand. He expressed the misfortunes of Russia and the need for sacrifice with such fervour that Krylenko himself began to weep. For Kerenski, the day was won: 'I spoke out against the offensive,' replied Krylenko. 'But if Comrade Kerenski gave us the order for it, even if my company did not leave the trench, I would march and would go on the attack, alone if necessary.'[22]

Three weeks after Kerenski's visits, after injunctions from *Isvestia* and similar voices and objurgations from the Soviet and the Provisional Government, Bolshevik propaganda was countered and to some extent the war regained its legitimacy.

On the eve of the offensive planned for the middle of June, Krylenko returned from the front and reported to the national Conference of Bolshevik military organizations:

'The mass of soldiers is still without organization even though they are tending towards bolshevism. Many regiments are declaring that they will not go on the attack. Kerenski enjoys a great reputation even among the bolsheviks who are having to struggle above all against the revolutionary-socialists of March [i.e. of the Right]. *Fraternizations have ceased*, but the fighting has not resumed. There is serious thought of the offensive and shock troops are forming. Desertions have ceased but soldiers are not returning from leave.'[23]

Under no illusions as to the range of his action and under pressure from the Allies and staff headquarters, Kerenski finally gave the order for the offensive on 16 June 1917. It was a flash in the pan that soon turned to disaster – yet Kerenski still retained his popularity in soldiers' eyes. He represented the revolution, and the fact that he gave orders to the generals confirmed the troops' sense of gratitude; his presence in office was a continuing reminder to everyone that they were free men. But with the collapse of the offensive, hostile demonstrations in Petrograd during July and later the *putsch* of General Kornilov, his authority leaked away even while his personal authority was more substantial than that of the rebel general.

The fraternizations which resumed at the end of the summer lacked the spirit of those which had preceded the offensive, but in the meantime the army had partially dissolved and a form of civil war was in progress. Since some regiments had refused to take up their allotted positions, the High Command threw all responsibility for the defeat on to the Bolsheviks. This shocked the soldiers who had taken part in the offensive operations, and found themselves saddled with responsibility for a setback which had in reality been the outcome of several contributory causes. The 506th Infantry Division, for example, which had specifically been accused of failure, had suffered 2,513 dead or wounded out of 3,000 men, while Annex 3 to the report drawn up by

Generals Gavrilov and Gustov showed that the defeat was the result of crushing enemy artillery superiority – 200 guns against sixteen. The High Command, however, held to the terms of its communiqué.

In Moscow, the Bolshevik journal *Spartak* was edited by an experienced Bolshevik revolutionary, Nikolai Bukharin, who had encountered other leading revolutionaries such as Lenin, Zinoviev and Trotsky during a period in exile. By reporting on the clash of opinion between soldiers and their officers, *Spartak* helped to keep readers informed on how statements from the headquarters staff were judged by front-line troops.

Henceforward, officers would be seen in the same light as the main enemy, the Germans – 'traitors to the Revolution'. As a consequence of the offensive and its outcome, discipline was restored and charges brought against mutineers, with the result that soldiers in the Luga garrison demanded the general disarmament of the officers. 'They were traitors to Russia, with allegiance to France and England.'[24]

Since the offensive, non-commissioned officers had recovered their traditional military role and effectiveness without difficulty, and any slow or recalcitrant soldier was defined 'a Bolshevik'; and since this was the party that rejected the operation of command, it won fresh approval and attention after the setback to the offensive. On the combined fronts of the south-west and Romania, the number of recorded Bolshevik groups grew from 74 in July to 173 in September and 280 in November.[25]

In this context, fraternization was no longer a daily occurrence, but there were plenty of desertions and still more episodes of group indiscipline or mutiny. Soldiers' attitudes towards deserters, men on leave who did not return to their unit, evolved through several phases. In March, they had condemned such acts; in May and June, before the offensive, they had threatened such men as shirkers; after July, they defended them, judging that the counter-revolutionary leaders deserved as much as they did themselves to be brought before the courts. Overall there were far fewer desertions than legend asserted; but there were many more mutinies.

Fraternizations, meanwhile, resurfaced in a very different context, during the negotiations for the Treaty of Brest-Litovsk.

Following orders from Lenin and Trotsky, this time it was a matter of acting so that 'from fraternization to fraternization, the Revolution passes from Russia to Germany'. The initiative for managing fraternization, however, had evidently passed to the German officers.

# Chapter Notes

## 1 The Christmas Truce, 1914: The British Story: Malcolm Brown

*[Note: Imperial War Museum sources include Department of Documents collection references and names of copyright holders where known]*

**Captain R J Armes**, 1st Battalion Staffordshire Regiment, Staffordshire Regimental Archive; **Private George Ashurst**, 2nd Battalion Lancashire Fusiliers, [IWM 66/141/1], Mrs E E Ashurst; **Captain (later Brigadier General) E W S Balfour**, 5th Dragoon Guards, [IWM 66/301/1], Mr P E G Balfour; **Captain (later Lieutenant Colonel) J W Barnett**, Regimental Medical Officer, 34th Sikh Pioneers, [IWM Documents ref 90/37/1], Mrs C Robertson; **Lieutenant (later Captain) E E H Bate**, 1/2nd Battalion London Regiment, [IWM 90/37/1], Mr H M Knight; **Major Arthur Bates**, 5th Battalion London Regiment (London Rifle Brigade), personal letter; **Second Lieutenant Sir Edward Beddington-Behrens**, Royal Field Artillery, [IWM 66/142/1], Dr S Kane; **Captain Rudolf Binding**, *A Fatalist at War*, Allen & Unwin, 1929; **Lieutenant Ralph Blewitt DSO**, 39th Brigade Royal Field Artillery, [IWM 99/38/3], Mrs C G Bazeley; **Major General Thompson Capper**, GOC 7th Division, National Archives WO95/154; **Lieutenant Frederick Chandler**, RAMC, [IWM 60/77/1], Sir Geoffrey Chandler; **Captain A D Chater**, 2nd Battalion Gordon Highlanders, [IWM 87/56/1], Mr S D Chater; **Ethel Cooper**, *Behind the Lines: One Woman's War 1914–1918*, Jill Norman & Hobhouse, 1982; **Captain (later Lieutenant Colonel) Sir Morgan Crofton**, 2nd Life Guards (Major Edward Crofton); **Second Lieutenant (later Brigadier General) Cyril Drummond**, 32nd Brigade Royal Field Artillery, taped reminiscence 1976; **Rifleman G Eade**, 3rd Battalion Rifle Brigade, letter *Evening News* 2nd January 1915; **Lieutenant Colonel L R Fisher-Rowe**, Officer Commanding 1st Battalion Grenadier Guards. [IWM 66/110/1], Major D L Greenacre; **Field Marshal Sir John French**, later Viscount French of Ypres, *1914*, Constable, 1919; **Lieutenant (later Major) E H Giffard**, 76th and 61st Brigades Royal Field Artillery, [IWM 05/9/1], Sir Sydney Giffard; **Captain Guy Goodliffe**, 1st Battalion Royal Fusiliers, [IWM 07/26/1], Mrs C. Gwynne-James; **Lieutenant Wyn Griffith**, 15th Battalion Royal Welch Fusiliers, *Up to Mametz*, Faber & Faber, 1931; **Brigadier General Frederic James Heyworth CB DSO**, Officer Commanding 20th Brigade (7th Division), [IWM 66/76/1], Mr R P Heyworth; **Lieutenant Michael Holroyd**, 1st Battalion Hampshire Regiment, [IWM 97/37/1], Miss P Dunn; **Captain (later Brigadier General) H H G Hyslop**, 2nd Battalion Argyll and Sutherland Highlanders [IWM 94/13/1]; **Captain Tom Ingram DSO MC**, RAMC, attached 1st Battalion King's Shropshire Light Infantry [IWM 67/65/1] Professor G I C Ingram; **Captain (later Brigadier General) J L Jack**, 1st Battalion The Cameronians (Scottish Rifles), *General Jack's Diary*, ed. John Terraine, Cassell, 2000; **Rifleman P H Jones**, 1st Battalion Queen's Westminster Rifles, [IWM P246], Mr P P H Jones; **Lieutenant J A Liddell VC MC**, 2nd Battalion Argyll and Sutherland Highlanders [IWM PP/MCR/281], Mrs G M Clayton; **Brevet Lieutenant Colonel (later Major General) Lord Loch**, 2nd Battalion Grenadier Guards [IWM 71/12/15] Lady Loch; **Captain Maurice Mascall**, Royal Garrison Artillery [IWM P121 & PP/MCR/284]; **Rifleman Ernest Morley**, 16th Battalion London Regiment (Queen's Westminster Rifles), [IWM 93/25/1], Mr B P Waite; **Captain (later Brigadier) P Mortimer**, Requisitioning Officer, Meerut Division, [IWM P253], Mr N Mortimer; **Gunner B C Myatt**, 23rd Brigade Royal Field Artillery, [IWM 97/4/1], Mr T R Myatt; **2nd Lieutenant Dennis Neilson-Terry**, 7th Battalion The Queen's (Royal West Surrey Regiment), [IWM 01/38/1], Ms J. Nightingale; **Captain (later Lieutenant Colonel) F E Packe**, 1st Battalion Welch Regiment, [IWM Con Shelf]; **Captain George Paynter**, Officer Commanding 2nd Battalion Scots Guards, quoted in Captain Sir Edward Hulse, *Letters*, privately printed 1916; **2nd Lieutenant Arthur Pelham-Burn**, 6th Battalion Gordon Highlanders, [The Company of Ten, St Albans]; **Lieutenant General Sir Henry Rawlinson**, GOC, IV Corps, Diary: Churchill College, Cambridge; **Frank Richards**, 2nd Battalion Royal Welch Fusiliers, *Old Soldiers Never Die*, Faber & Faber, 1933; **Sergeant A Self**, 2nd Battalion West Yorkshire Regiment, [IWM 74/154/1]; **CQSM R A Scott Macfie**, Liverpool Scottish, [IWM Con Shelf], Mrs P Pehkonen; **2nd Lieutenant A P Sinkinson**, attached 2nd Battalion Lancashire Fusiliers, letter in *Daily Telegraph*, 5th January 1915] ; **Lieutenant General Sir Horace Smith-Dorrien**, GOC, II Corps, National Archives WO95/1560, WO95 157/262; **Captain Charles Inglis Stockwell**, 2nd Battalion Royal Welch Fusiliers, quoted in *The War The Infantry Knew*, edited Captain J C Dunn, Cardinal 1989; **Private William Tapp**, 1st Battalion Royal Warwickshire Regiment [IWM 66/156/1]; **Rifleman Oswald Tilley**, 5th Battalion London Regiment

(London Rifle Brigade) [IWM 67/12/1], Lieutenant Commander P J Martin RN; **Major (later Brigadier General) Herbert Trevor**, 2nd Battalion King's Own Yorkshire Light Infantry, [IWM P229], Mr I S C Parker; **Rifleman (later Major) Leslie Walkinton**, 16th Battalion London Regiment (Queen's Westminster Rifles), personal letter, Mrs J Cadge; **Second Lieutenant (later Brigadier) John Wedderburn-Maxwell**, 45th Brigade Royal Field Artillery, [IWM 99/83/1 & Con Shelf], Mrs R Turner; **Crown Prince Wilhelm of Prussia**, Commander German Fifth Army, *My War Experience*, Hurst & Blackett, 1922; **Rifleman Graham Williams**, 5th Battalion London Regiment (London Rifle Brigade), BBC TV interview 1981; **Lieutenant (later Lieutenant Colonel) T S Wollocombe**, 4th Battalion Middlesex Regiment, [IWM 89/7/1]; **Major Murdock Mackenzie Wood**, 6th Battalion Gordon Highlanders, *Hansard*, 31st March 1930.

**Battalion War Diaries** quoted courtesy of the National Archives.


## 2  Good Neighbours: Rémy Cazals

NOTES
1. Norton Cru, *Du témoignage*, Paris, Gallimard, 1930, pp.117–253. Some re-issues do not include the full anthology, a factor which considerably reduces the scope of the book; André Ducasse, *La Guerre racontée par les combattants. Anthologie des écrivains du front (1914–1918)*, Paris, Flammarion, 1932, 2 vols. 259 and 249 pp.
2. In order to reduce the amount of material given in note form, all references to the notebooks of combatants, whether published or unpublished, are shown together as an appendix on page 240; similarly for the postal census of French army units (page 239).
3. Eckart Birnstiel and Rémy Cazals, eds. *Ennemis fraternels 1914–1915, Hans Rodewald, Antoine Bieisse, Fernand Tailhades. Carnets de guerre et de captivité*, Toulouse, Presses universitaires du Mirail, 2002, 191 pp. Also accounts by Valdo Barbey, Pierre Champion, Henri Charbonnier, Léopold Retailleau (see appendix), etc.
4. Photographs identified by Marie-Pierre Dubois on deposit with the Archives of the Aude. See *Annales du Midi*, no. 232, October–December 2000, '1914–1918', pp. 428–430.
5. See Leonard V Smith, *Between Mutiny and Obedience, The Case of the French Fifth Infantry Division during World War I*, Princeton University Press, 1994, p. 63; Tony Ashworth, *Trench Warfare*

*1914–1918, The Live and Let Live System*, London, Pan Books, 2000 (1st ed. 1980) pp. 103 and 133.

6. Two JMOs (official military diaries) (SHAT 26 N 605 and 26 N 511), quoted by Coralie Vermeulen, *Les Fraternizations pendant la Grande Guerrre,* thesis, University of Picardy, 2000.

7. Quoted in Coralie Vermeulen, *op. cit.*, p. 40.

8. Jean-Pierre Turbergue, *1914–1918: les journaux des tranchées, la Grande Guerre écrite par les poilus*, Paris, Editions Italiques et ministères de la Défense, 1999.

9. *Ibid*, p.82.

10. Quoted by Stéphane Audoin-Rouzeau, *A travers leurs journaux, 14–18, les combattants des tranchées*, Paris, Armand Colin, 1986, p. 191. Tr. *Men at War 1914–1918, national sentiment and trench journalism in France during the First World War*, Berg, 1992.

11. *'Nous crions grâce', 154 lettres de pacifistes, juin–novembre 1916*, presented by Thierry Bonzon and Jean-Louis Robert, Paris, Les Editions Ouvrières, 1989, pp. 76–77.

12. Jean Norton Cru, *Témoins. Essai d'analyse et de critique des souvenirs de combattants édités en francais de 1915 à 1928*, Paris, Les Etincelles, 1929, 728 pp. (reissued: Presses Universitaires de Nancy, 1993).

13. See Antoine Prost and Jay Winter, *Penser la Grande Guerre. Un essai d'historiographie*, Paris, Seuil, 'Points' series, 2004, pp. 133–134. Also: Rémy Cazals and Frédéric Rousseau, *14–18, le cri d'une génération*, Toulouse, Privat, 2001, pp.129–140.

14. Similarly, Fernand Tailhades in *Ennemis fraternels . . . , op. cit.* p. 172. Referring to the Germans who captured him, the Frenchman wrote, 'On the journey they always called me *Camarade*. That's all I understood.'

15. Presentation by André Minet of Louis Birot, *Carnets. Un Pretre républicain dans la Grande Guerre*, Albi, FSIT, 2000.

16. By Abbé Emile Barthès, quoted in Louis Birot, *Carnets , op. cit.* p. 143.

17. Corporal Barthas recorded such cases on several occasions.

18. This relates to our subject. It occupies a few pages in Léon Werth's book; he, like the other combatants, described the horrors and violence of the war at length.

19. Binet-Valmer, *Mémoires d'un engagé volontaire*, Paris, Flammarion, 1918. Censored passages on pp. 109, 122, 123, 124, 129, 153, 165, 177, 179, 180, 195.

20. Jean-Noel Jenneney, 'Les archives des commissions de contrôle

postal aux armées (1916–1918)', *Revue d'histoire moderne et contemporaine,* 1968, pp.209– 233.

21. A theme in many other censorship interceptions and uncensored letters preserved by families.

22. *Nous crions grâce . . . op. cit, p. 13.*

23. The *Chanson du 17e,* by Montéhus, evokes the mutiny of this regiment at Béziers in 1907 during the 'wine-growers' revolution': 'Greetings! Greetings to you, brave soldiers of the 17th . . .' The refrain was very popular, although the episode had revived the tensions between the Nord and the Midi. See Jean Sagnes, Monique and Rémy Pech, *1907 en Languedoc et Roussillon,* Montpellier, Espace Sud Editions, 1997, 283 pp.

24. Frédéric Rousseau, *La Guerre censurée. Une histoire des combattants européens de 14–18.* Paris, Seuil, 1999, pp. 130–135.

25. We need not focus closely here on poorly aimed artillery fire which killed friendly infantry. See General Percin's book, *Le Massacre de notre infanterie en 1914–1918,* Paris, Albin Michel, 1921.

26. The Carcassonne designer Pierre Dantoine, a soldier in 1914–18, illustrated this theme: an impeccable officer, with an arrogantly worn monocle, questions a muddy and bemedalled *poilu* who is waiting for a leave train: 'Well then! No more saluting . . . I'm a staff officer'. Seated, pipe in mouth, the soldier replies, sarcastically: 'You don't need to worry, you've got a fine job!' Dantoine, *La Guerre,* Carcassonne, FAOL, series 'La Mémoire de 14–18 en Languedoc', 1987.

27. This is what Jean Norton Cru set out to demonstrate. See the author references in *Témoins . . . , op. cit.*

28. See in R. Cazals, *Les Mots de 14–18, op. cit.,* 'Bourrage de crâne et censure', 'Consentement et contrainte', 'Déserteur', 'Patrie, Patriotes, Patriotisme', 'Tenir'.

29. *L'Ami Fritz,* published in 1864.

30. A simple comparison of the number of truces with the number accepted would not make sense. The only aim here is to define the state of mind that made the truces possible.

31. Modris Eksteins, *Rites of Spring. The Great War and the Birth of the Modern Age,* London, Transworld, 1989, p. 110, from a letter written by Emile Décobert. (French edition, *Le Sacre du Printemps. La Grande Guerre et la naissance de la modernité,* Paris, Plon, 1991.)

32. *Ibid,* p. 135.

33. Leonard V. Smith, *Between . . . , op. cit.,* p. 93.

34. *La Paix par le droit,* July–August 1919, pp. 353–354.

35. SHAT 16 N 1431 and 1438, postal censorship quoted by Coralie Vermeulen, *Les Fraternizations . . .* , *op. cit.*

36. Extract from *L'Argonaute*, November 1918. Quoted by Stéphane Audoin-Rouzeau, *A travers leurs journaux . . .* , *op. cit.*, p. 193. See a fraternization of 11 November 1918 between a Bavarian regiment, French prisoners and Belgian civilians, reported by Louis Lapeyre, another barrel-maker from Peyriac-Minervois, in *Ennemis fraternels . . .* , *op. cit.*, p. 18.

37. But Dominik Richert, a peasant from Saint-Ulrich, could speak no word of French. He spoke German, and the Alsatian dialect. He wrote in German. See Dominik Richert, *Cahiers d'un survivant. Un soldat dans l'Europe en guerre 1914–1918*, Strasbourg, La Nuée Bleue, 1994 (German edition, 1989), and Rémy Cazals, 'Deux fantassins de la Grande Guerre: Louis Barthas et Dominik Richert' in Jules Maurin and Jean-Charles Jauffret, eds, *La Grande Guerre 1914–1918, 80 ans d'historiographie et de représentations*, Montpellier, ESID, 2002, pp. 339–364.

38. Jacques Bouis notes the discovery of a board, 'set up on display by the enemy on a tree trunk, with this phrase in French: "Long live the Kaiser and homage to the 18th Battalion of French *chasseurs*"'

39. 26 November 1915, in Josette Lavie, *La Guerre de 14–18 vue par les poilus,* Aiguillon, ATA, 1997, information communicated by Antonio Catarino. Modris Eksteins (note 31) evokes a snowball fight between British and Germans.

40. Roger Boutefeu, *Les Camarades, soldats français et allemands au combat 1914–1918*, Paris, Fayard, 1966.

41. Read in manuscript form, dated 2 April 1916. Only part of the notebooks of this farmer were reproduced in '*Je suis mouton comme les autres'*, *Lettres, carnets et mémoires de poilus drômois et de leurs familles*, presented by Jean-Pierre Bernard et al. Valence, Editions Peuple Libres et Notre Temps, 2002.

42. The account may appear in letters which the censor did not open.

43. The sergeant apparently said: 'I do not like the Boches, I am from the Nord, they are pillaging everything at home. But it would have been an abuse of trust to kill them. So, before firing, I signalled to them to hide.' Henry Nadel, *Sous le pressoir*, quoted by André Ducasse in his anthology, *La Guerre racontée . . .* , *op. cit.* pp. 205–208.

44. In Tony Ashworth's book, *Trench Warfare . . .* , *op. cit.*, see Chapter 5.

45. Ernst Jünger, *Orages d'acier,* Paris, Le Livre de poche, 1993 (1920)

46. Jules Maurin, *Armée, guerre, société, soldats languedociens (1889–1919),* Paris, Publications de la Sorbonne, 1982, pp. 654–655;

Rémy Cazals, Claude Marquié, René Pinies, *Années cruelles 1914–1918*, Villelongue d'Aude, Atelier du Gué, 1998 (first published 1983), particularly the contribution of Jean Safon, p. 52.

47. See the collected work, Nicolas Offenstadt, ed., *Le Chemin des Dames, de l'enfer à la mémoire*, Paris, Editions Stock, 2004.

48. On the bayonet, see the works of Jean Norton Cru. Also Rémy Cazals, *Les Mots de 14–18, op. cit.*, pp. 15–16 and Cédric Marty *La Baïonnette en 14–18, mythes et réalités*, unpublished thesis, University of Toulouse-Le Mirail, 2003.

49. See the text in Guy Pendroncini, *Les Mutineries de 1917*, Paris, PUF, 1967, p. 34.

50. SHAT 16 N 1529, dossier no. 4: 'Service du Moral. Fraternization avec l'ennemi'.

51. SHAT 16 N 1405, Troyes postal censorship, 23 July 1916, as a typical example.

52. Jules Maurin, *Armée . . . , op. cit.*, p. 654.

53. SHAT 16 N 1529.

54. The 'negotiation' between leaders and combatants on how to manage the war is considered in Leonard Smith's *Between . . . , op. cit.* Sometimes effective as in the case of tacit or formal truces, this negotiation only bore fruit on the broader scale after the mutinies of 1917, when the high command accepted what the soldiers had been proposing since 1914, the stopping of offensives. (Smith, p. 205). Before that time, obedience had been strong enough to carry the day.

55. Tony Ashworth, *Trench Warfare . . . , op. cit.* p. 31.

56. See General Percin's *Le Massacre de notre infanterie . . . , op. cit.*

57. It is also true that wounded men were left to die and dead bodies abandoned in No Man's Land.

58. Bruna Bianchi, *La Follia e la Fuga. Nevrosi di guerra, diserzione et disobbedienza nell'esercito italiano (1915–1918)*, Rome, Bulzoni, pp.339–381; works by Modris Eksteins, Tony Ashworth, Malcolm Brown and Shirley Seaton.

59 John Keegan, *The First World War*, London, 1998.

60. See Edward P Thompson, *The Making of The English Working Class*, London, 1963 (La *Formation de la classe ouvrière anglais*, Paris, 1988).

61. See E Birnstiel and Rémy Cazals, ed., *Ennemis fraternels . . . , op. cit.*, 2nd photograph in the notebook, the group of Les Quinze Avenir Castelnaudarien, among whom ten performers were killed in the war, and another, Antoine Bieisse, seriously wounded.

62. See Rémy Cazals, *Les Mots de 14–18, op. cit.*, p. 26

63. Quoted by Tony Ashworth, *Trench Warfare . . . , op. cit.*, p. 144.

64. As an extension to the concept proposed by George L. Mosse for the post-war German political field, in his book *Fallen Soldiers, Reshaping the Memory of the World Wars* (1990), title 'translated' into French as *De la Grande Guerre au totalitarisme, la brutalisation des sociétés européennes*, Paris, Hachette, 1999.

## Postal censorship of regiments and other units

At the SHAT – the *Service Historique de l'Armée de Terre,* the French military historical service – systematic searches were undertaken in bundles 16 N 1392, 1393, 1394, 1405, 1425, 1427, 1428 and 1529. Not all examples were retained; further material has been taken from Coralie Vermeulen's *mémoire de maitrise* or was supplied by Nicolas Offenstadt and Denis Rolland, to whom thanks are due.

5th RI – 16 N 1392 (Jan. 1917)
23rd RI – 16 N 1405 (Oct. 1916)
25th RI – 16 N 1393 (Aug. 1917)
38th RI – 16 N 1395 (Jan. 1918)
42nd RI – 16 N 298 (July 1917)
52nd RI – 16 N 1394 (Oct. 1917)
59th RI – 16 N 1529 (Jan. 1917)
65th RI – 16 N 1529 (Dec. 1917)
75th RI – 16 N 254 (June 1917)
80th RI – 16 N 1392 (April 1917)
85th RI – 16 N 1405 (Feb. 1917)
88th RI – 16 N 1393 (July 1917)
92nd RI – 16 N 1405 (Feb. 1918)
95th RI – 16 N 1405 (Feb. 1917)
105th RI – 16 N 1394 (Sept. 1917)
106th RI – 16 N 1427 (July 1917)
107th RI – 16 N 1405 (Feb. 1917)
114th RI – 16 N 1405 (Feb. 1917)
118th RI – 16 N 1421 (Jan. 1918)
120th RI – 16 N 1394 (Oct. 1917)
121st RI – 16 N 1529 (Nov. 1917)
132nd RI – 16 N 1427 (July 1917)
                1428 (Oct. 1917)
139th RI – 16 N 1394 (Oct. 1917)
143rd RI 16 N 1392 (April 1917)
              1393 (May 1917)
147th RI – 16 N 1405 (Jan. 1917)
163rd RI – 16 N 1431 (Nov. 1918)

170th RI – 16 N 1429 (Feb. 1918)
172nd RI – 16 N 1427 (Aug. 1917)
                        1428 (Oct. 1917)
201st RI – 16 N 1405 (Oct. 1916)
202nd RI – 16 N 1405 (Oct. 1916)
                        1395 (Jan. 1918)
217th RI – 16 N 1392 (Jan. 1917)
221st RI – 16 N 1392 (Jan. 1917)
226th RI – 16 N 1392 (Oct. 1917)
247th RI – 16 N 1405 (Oct. 1916)
297th RI – 16 N 1424 (Feb. 1917)
330th RI – 16 N 1436 (March 1917)
344th RI – 16 N 1529 (Jan. 1918)
349th RI – 16 N 1394 (Sept. 1917)
   (see also for 105th RI)
350th RI – 16 N 1427 (Sept. 1917)
360th RI – 16 N 1428 (Oct. 1917)
366th RI – 16 N 1392 (March 1917)
367th RI – 16 N 1427 (Sept. 1917)
401st RI – 16 N 1424 (May 1916)
2nd BCP – 16 N 1395 (Feb., March 1918)
17th BCP – 16 N 1427 (Sept. 1917)
18th BCP – 16 N 1529 (Nov. 1917)
25th BCP – 16 N 1427 (July 1917)
26th BCP – 16 N 1427 (Aug. 1917)
29th BCP – 16 N 1428 (Nov. 1917)
                        1529 (Nov. 1917)
131st Territorial – 16 N 1394 (Oct. 1917)
29th Infanterie coloniale – 16 N 1394 (Oct. 1917)
29th Tirailleurs Sénégalais – 16 N 1427 (July 1917)
2nd Chasseurs d'Afrique – 16 N 1427 (March 1917)
6th Chasseurs d'Afrique – 16 N 1425 (April 1917)
2nd Génie – 16 N 1395 (Jan. 1918)
4th Génie – 16 N 1395 (Jan. 1918)
9th Zouaves – 16 N 1395 (Feb. 1918)
1st Mixte Zouaves et Tirailleurs – 16 N 1395 (Feb. 1918)

### Appendix: French soldiers' letters and publications

Not all regimental numbers are given. This may indicate that the soldier changed units several times. The reference JNC relates to Jean Norton Cru, *Témoins*.

ALAIN, Emile Auguste Chartier, artillery soldier. Quoted in the anthology by André Ducasse.

ARENE, Julien, *Les Carnets d'un soldat en Haute-Alsace et dans les Vosges*, Paris, 1917.

BALLET, Charles, 75th RI, postal censorship, 27th Infantry Division, June 1917, communicated by Denis Rolland.

BARBEY, Valdo (first edition under the pseudonym of Fabrice Dongot), JNC. *Soixante jours de guerre en 1914*, Paris, Giovanangeli, 2004 (1917).

BARRES, Philippe, 31st BCP, sub-lieutenant, JNC; *La Guerre à vingt ans*, Paris, Plon, 1924.

BARTHAS, Louis, 280th then 296th, corporal; *Les Carnets de guerre de Louis Barthas, tonnelier*, Paris, Maspero, 1978 (reissued La Découverte).

BEC, Jean, 96th then 122nd, sergeant, 'Campagne 1914–1918, notes journalières' in *Bulletin des Amis de Montagnac*, Oct. 2000 and Feb. 2001.

BERNIER, Jean, 117th RI, sergeant, JNC, *La Percée*, Paris, Albin Michel, 1920.

BERTHIER, Gustave, letter quoted in *Paroles de poilus*.

BINET-VALMER, Gustave, sub-lieutenant, JNC, *Mémoires d'un engagé volontaire*, Paris, Flammarion, 1918.

BIROT, Louis, chaplain, *Carnets. Un prêtre républicain dans la Grande Guerre*, Albi, FSIT, 2000.

BISCAY, Jean-Pierre, 413rd RI, sergeant, *Témoignage sur la guerre 1914-1918 par un chef de section*, Montpellier, Imp. Causse, 1973.

BONNET, Georges, JNC, *Notes d'un agent de liaison*, Paris, Berger-Levrault, 1922.

BOURGUET, Samuel, major, JNC, *L'aube sanglante*, Paris, Berger-Levrault, 1917.

BOUSQUET, Joseph, 55th RI, *Journal de route 1914–1917*, Bordeaux, editions des Saints Calus, 2000.

BREANT, cavalry major, then 90th RI, JNC, *De l'Alsace à la Somme, souvenirs du front*, Paris, Hachette, 1917.

BRES, Othon, 273rd RI, sergeant. Unpublished notebook.

BUTEAU, Max, 56th then 134th, JNC, *Tenir, récits de la vie de tranchées*, Paris, Plon, 1918.

CALVET, Jean, sub-lieutenant, *A la sueur du front*, Gaillac, Imp. Dugourc, 1920.

CAMPAGNE, major later colonel, 107th then 78th, *Le Chemin des croix*, Paris, Tallandier, 1930.

CAPOT, Valéry, major. Unpublished notebooks, Archives du Lot-et-Garonne.

CARRE, Jean-Marie, interpreter officer, JNC, *Histoire d'une division de couverture*, Paris, La Renaissance du livre, 1919.

CASSAGNAU, Ivan, *Ce que chaque jour fait de veuves. Journal d'un artilleur, 1914–1916*, Paris, Buchet-Chastel, 2003.

CASTEX, Antatole, captain, *Verdun, années infernales. Lettres d'un soldat au front,* Paris, Imago, 1996.

CAZIN, Paul, 29th RI, sergeant, JNC, *L'Humanite à la guerre,* Paris, Plon, 1920.

CENDRARS, Blaise, Foreign Legion, *La Main coupée,* Paris, Denoël, 1946.

CHAILA, Xavier, 'C'est à Craonne, sur le plateau', *Journal de route,* Carcassonne, FAOL, 1997.

CHAINE, Pierre, sub-lieutenant, JNC, *Les Mémoires d'un rat,* Paris, Payot, 1921.

CHAMPION, Pierre, 288th RI, JNC, *Françoise au calvaire*, Paris, Grasset, 1924.

CHARBONNIER, Henri, 229th RI, unpublished notebook.

CHEVALLIER, Gabriel, infantry, *La Peur,* Paris, Stock, 1930.

CHIROSSEL, Louis, 119th Territorial, corporal. Correspondence quoted in '*Je suis mouton commes les autres*'.

CRU, Jean Norton, corporal then sergeant, author of *Temoins* and *Du témoignage*'.

CUZACQ, Germain, 234th RI, *Le Soldat de Lagraulet,* Toulouse, Eché, 1984.

D. Jean de, captain, quoted in *La Plume au fusil* . . .

DANTOINE, Pierre, 272th RI, *La Guerre* (collection of drawings), Carcassonne, FAOL, 1987.

DANTOINE, Roger, 267th RI, quoted in *Années cruelles.*

DERVILLE, Etienne, 33rd RI, sergeant then lieutenant, JNC, *Correspondence et notes,* Tourcoing, Duvivier, 1921.

DESAGNEAUX, Henri, 359th RI, *Journal de guerre 14–18*, Paris, Denoël, 1971.

DESABLIAUX, Robert, 129th, JNC, *La Ruée, Etapes d'un combattant,* Paris, Bloud, 1919.

DESPEYRIERES, Henri, 14th RI, corporal, 'Lettres des tranchées' in *Sous les arcades,* Montflanquin, MJC, 2002.

DEVERIN, Edouard, *R.A.S. 1914–1918, Du Chemin des Dames au GQG,* Paris, Les Etincelles, 1931.

DEVOISE, Emile, 252nd RI, notebook quoted in *Je suis mouton comme les autres.*

DORGELES, Roland, 39th RI, *'Je t'écris de la tranchée'*, Paris, Albin Michel, 2003.

DUBARLE, Robert, captain in the Chasseurs Alpins, JNC, *Lettres de guerre*, Paris, Perrin, 1918.

DUCASSE, André, infantry, author of the anthology, *La Guerre racontée par les combattants*, Paris, Flammarion, 1932.

ESCHOLIER, Raymond, 59th RI, JNC, *Lettres d'un combattant*, Paris, Hachette, 1917.

FAUVEAU, Kléber, 52nd RI, postal censorship, 27th Infantry Division, June 1917, contributed by Denis Rolland.

FOURNET, Victorin, correspondence quoted in *Je suis mouton commes les autres.*

GALTIER-BOISSIERE, Jean, JNC, *La Fleur au fusil* and *Loin de la riflette*, Paris, Baudinière, 1928.

GANDOLPHE, Maurice, JNC, *La March à la victoire*, Paris, Perrin, 1915.

GENEVOIX, Maurice, 106th RI, lieutenant, JNC, *Ceux de 14*, Paris, Flammarion, 1950.

GIBOULET, Justin, 343rd RI, sergeant, unpublished notebooks studied by Solenne Boitreaud (*maîtrise*, Toulouse-II, 2000).

GRANGER, Ladislas, 313rd RI, sergeant, *Carnets de guerre*, Montpellier, ESID, 1997.

GUILDHEM, François, 296th RI, unpublished correspondence.

HENCHES, Jules, major, JNC, *A l'école de la guerre. Lettres d'un artilleur*, Paris, Hachette, 1918.

HOURTICQ, Louis, territorial, lieutenant, JNC, *Récits et réflexions d'un combattant*, Paris, Hachette, 1918.

HUDELLE, Léon, 280th RI, captain, unpublished photographs and articles studied by Marie-Pierre Dubois (*maîtrise*, Toulouse-II, 1997).

ISAAC, Jules, IIIrd Territorials, corporal then sergeant, *Un historien dans la Grande Guerre. Lettres et carnets,* Paris, Armand Colin, 2004.

JOLINON, Joseph, 370th RI, JNC, *Le Valet de gloire*, Paris, Rieder, 1923.

JOUBAIRE, Alfred, sergeant, JNC, *Pour la France. Carnet de route d'un fantassin*, Paris, Perrin, 1917.

LAPEYRE, Louis, 143rd RI, unpublished notebook, partial quotation in *Ennemis fraternels* . . .

LEFEBVRE, Raymond, stretcher-bearer, JNC, *La Guerre des soldats,* Paris, Flammarion, 1919.

LELIEVRE, Pierre, chaplain, 19th Infantry Division, JNC, *Le Fléau de Dieu,* Paris, Ollendorf, 1920.

LEMERCIER, Eugène, 106th RI, corporal then sergeant, JNC, *Lettres d'un soldat*, Paris, Chapelot, 1916.

LIGONNES, Bernard de, 275th RI, major, *Un commandant bleu horizon,* Paris, Les Editions de Paris, 1998.

LINTIER, Paul, artillery, JNC, *Ma pièce* and *Le Tube 1233,* Paris, Plon, 1916 and 1917.

LISSORGES, Marcellin, 287th RI, chaplain, JNC, *Notes d'un aumônier militaire,* Aurillac, Imp. Moderne, 1921.

LUGAND, Fernand, 13th BCA, *Carnets de guerre d'un poilu savoyard,* Montmélian, Fontaine de Siloé, 2000.

MADELINE, André, artillery, JNC, *Nos vingt ans,* Paris, Calmann-Lévy, 1925.

MAIRET, Louis, 127th then 8th RI, sergeant, JNC, *Carnet d'un combattant,* Paris, Crès, 1919.

MASCARAS, Paul, 15th RI, sergeant, unpublished correspondence quoted by Mathieu Fantin (maîtrise Toulouse-II, 2002).

MASSON, Pierre, 261st RI, sergeant then lieutenant, JNC, *Lettres de guerre,* Paris, Hachette, 1917.

MAUROIS, André, interpreter, JNC, *Les Silences du colonel Bramble,* Paris, Grasset, 1918.

MEYER, Jacques, 329th RI, lieutenant, JNC, *La Biffe,* Paris, Albin Michel, 1928.

MORILLON, Gervais, 90th RI. Letter quoted in *Paroles de poilus.*

MORIN, Emile, 60th then 42nd RI, sergeant then lieutenant, *Lieutenant Morin, combattant de la guerre 1914–1918,* Besançon, Cêtre, 2002.

NADEL, Henry, corporal, *Sous le pressoir,* quoted in the anthology by André Ducasse.

NAEGELEN, René, 172nd RI, corporal then sergeant, JNC, *Les Suppliciés,* Paris, Baudinière, 1927.

NOE, Léopold, 28Oth RI, *Nous étions ennemis sans savoir pourqoi ni comment,* Carncassonne, FAOL, 1980.

NUBLAT, Marius, Postes aux Armées, correspondance quoted in *Je suis mouton comme les autres.*

ORMIERES, Louis, stretcher-bearer, eyewitness account quoted in *Années cruelles . . .*

PAPILLON, Lucien, 174th RI and PAPILLON, Marcel, 356th RI, *Si je reviens comme je l'espère,* Paris, Grasset, 2003.

PARAF, Pierre, 92nd RI, JNC, *Sous la terre de France,* Paris, Payot, 1917.

PASTRE, Gaston, artillery, captain, JNC, *Trois ans de front,* Presses universitaires de Nancy, 1990 (1918).

PERGAUD, Louis, quoted by Benoist-Méchin, *Ce qui demeure,* Paris, Albin Michel, 1942.

PIC, Eugène, 75th RI, sergeant, JNC, *Dans la tranchée,* Paris, Perrin, 1916.

POTTECHER, Jean, medical orderly, JNC, *Lettres d'un fils*, Paris, Emile-Paul, 1928.

POUCH, Jean, oral evidence in *La Grande Guerre*, Radio France, 1999.

PUECH, Jules, 258th RI, unpublished correspondence.

QUEY, Delphin, 22nd BCP, correspondence in *Poilus savoyards,* Montmélian, Gens de Savoie, 1981.

REDIER, Antoine, 338th RI, lieutenant, JNC, *Méditations dans la tranchée*, Paris, Payot, 1915.

RETAILLEAU, Léopold, 77th RI, *Musicien-brancardier. Carnets de Léopold Retailleau*, Le Chaufour, Anovi, 2003.

RIMBAULT, Paul, captain, JNC, *Propos d'un marmité*, Paris, Fournier, 1920.

ROBERT, Henri, 123rd RI, sergeant, JNC, *Impression de guerre d'un soldat chrétien*, Paris, Fischbacher, 1920.

ROUJON, Jacques, 352nd RI, JNC, *Carnet de route*, Paris, Plon, 1916.

ROUMIGUIERES, Alfred, 343rd RI, sergeant, quoted in *La Plume au fusil . . .*

SAFON, Jean, infantry, quoted in *Années cruelles . . .*

SOTY, Gaston, 43rd RI, *Dans la mêlée,* Paris, Les Carnets de route célèbres, undated.

TAILHADES, Fernand, 343rd RI, notebook reproduced in *Ennemis fraternels . . .*

TANTY, Etienne, 129th RI, *Les Violettes des tranchées*, Paris, Editions italiques, 2002.

THIVOLLE-CAZAT, Gabriel, 13th battalion of *chasseurs alpins.* Notebook quoted in *'Je suis mouton comme les autres'.*

TIREFORT, Jean, 50th RI, *Roger Gau, Jean, classe 1915*, Toulouse, Amis des Archives de la Haute-Garonne, 1998.

TOP, Gaston, 27th RAC, doctor, JNC, *Un groupe de 75,* Paris, Plon, 1919.

TOUSSAINT, Charles, 74th RI, *Petites histoires d'un glorieux régiment*, Montvilliers, Binesse, 1973.

TUFFRAU, Paul, 246th RI, captain, JNC, *14–18, Quatre années de front*, Paris, Imago, 1998.

VAILLANT-COUTURIER, Paul, sergeant, then sub-lieutenant, JNC, *La Guerre des soldats*, Paris, Flammarion, 1919.

VANDRAND, Elie, 105th RI, *Il fait trop beau pour faire la guerre*, Vertaizon, La Galipote, 2000.

VUILLERMOZ, Léon, 44th RI, *Journal d'un poilu franc-comtois*, Sainte-Croix (CH) Editions du Balcon, 2001.

WERTH, Léon, 252nd RI, JNC, *Clavel soldat*, Paris, Albin Michel, 1919.

## 3 Brother Boche: Olaf Meuller

1.  The famous playwright Carl Zuckmayer (1896–1977) was the son of
    a manufacturer in the Mainz region. Having gained a special
    *baccalauréat* he volunteered for the war. He fought on the Western
    Front until he suffered a nervous collapse in 1917. Decorated several
    times as a lieutenant, he became a member of the Council of Workers
    and Soldiers during the German Revolution. In 1925 he gained his
    first significant success with the play *Le Vignoble joyeux*. Other
    theatrical successes included *Schinderhannes* (1927) and *Katherine
    Knie* (1928). In 1928 he wrote a screen adaptation of Heinrich
    Mann's novel *Le Sujet*. The filmed version, entitled *L'Ange bleu*
    (1929), launched Marlene Dietrich's international career. Zuckmayer
    also expressed his democratic convictions through his collaboration
    in the filmed production of Remarque's novel, *All Quiet on the
    Western Front*; then he was forced into exile from 1933 onwards. He
    reached the United States after travelling through Austria and
    Switzerland.
2.  Carl Zuckmayer, *Als wär's ein Stück von mir. Hören der Freund-
    schaft. Erinnerungen*. Frankfurt am Main, Fischer, 1989 (first
    published in 1966), pp. 195–6.
3.  See Tony Ashworth, *Trench Warfare 1914–1918. The Live and Let
    Live System*, London, Macmillan Press 1980, p. 19.
4.  See Christoph Jahr, *Gewöhnliche Soldaten, Desertion und Deserteure
    im deutschen und britischen Heer 1914–1918*. Göttingen,
    Vandenhoeck und Ruprecht, 1998, pp. 32–4.
5.  See Carl Zuckmayer, *Einmal, wenn alles vorüber ist. Briefe an Kurt
    Grell, Gedichte, Dramen, Prosa aus den Jahren 1914–1920*,
    Frankfurt am Main, Fischer, 1981.
6.  See Bruna Bianchi, *La Follia e la Fuga. Nevrosi di guerra, diserzione
    e disobbedienza nell'esercito (1915–1918)*, Rome, Bulzoni, 2001,
    p. 358.
7.  Karl Josenhans, Letter of 9 November 1914 written in the Hinden-
    burg castle. Quoted here from Philipp Witkop, *Kriegsbriefe gefallener
    Studenten*, Munich, Albert Langen/Georg Müller, 1928, p. 33.
8.  Giuseppe Ungaretti, *Les Cinq Livres*. French text by the author and
    Jean Lescure, Paris, Les Editions de Minuit, 1953, p. 83.
9.  Ungaretti had fought in several sectors of the Isonzo front, where the
    enemy lines were within immediate sight and sound. See a postcard
    sent in May or June 1916 to Giovanni Papini (in Giuseppe Ungaretti,
    *Lettere a Giovanni Papini 1915–1948. Maria Antonietta Terzoli,
    Introduction by Leone Piccioni, Milan, Arnoldo Mondadori, p.331),

in which he wrote, 'At certain points, the enemy forces were three metres away from us. Now they are resting. There is an air of immense calm over everything.'

10. Forcella/Monticone (note 11), pp. 309–10, for all the following extracts.

11. Extract from the judgement of a military tribunal of the 3rd Vestone Italian army corps, dated 18 February 1918, quoted here from Enzo Forcella/Alberto Monticone, *Plotone di esecuzione. I processi della Prima Guerra mondiale* (1968), Bari, Laterzi, 1998, p. 25.

12. Charles Sorley, *The Letters of Charles Sorley*, with a biographical chapter. Cambridge, Cambridge University Press, 1919, Letter of 10 July 1915, p. 283.

13. *Ibid* (see note 12).

14. *Ibid*, p. 275.

15. *Ibid*, p. 274, Letter of 16 June 1915 to his friend Arthur Watts from the Flanders front.

16. First published in *Marlborough and Other Poems* (1916). Taken from *The Collected Poems of Charles Sorley*. Edited by Jean Moorcroft Wilson, London, Cecil Woolf, 1985, p. 70.

17. Forcella/Monticone (note 11), p. 277.

18. *Ibid*.

19. Ernst Toller, *Eine Jugend in Deutschland*, in *Gesammelte Werke*, Hrsg. Von Wolfgang Frühwald und John M Spalek, Bd. 4 Munich, Hanser 1978, p. 66. (First published in Amsterdam, Querido 1933). Toller (1893–1939) enlisted in circumstances similar to those of Sorley. From the beginning of 1914 he was in a university class for foreigners in Grenoble. When the World War broke out he returned to Germany and became a volunteer. In 1916, after thirteen months at the front, he had a nervous collapse at Verdun. He later took part in the pacifist movement and in Republican Councils in Munich. This activity earned him a period of imprisonment, from 1919 until 1924. Toller was one of the most significant writers of the Weimar Republic. After 1933 he emigrated to Britain, then to the United States, where he committed suicide in 1939.

20. Heinrich Dietz, 'Das Militärstrafrechtswesen im Kriege' in Max Schwarte's (Hg), *Der Große Krieg 1914–1918* Bd.10, Die Organisation der Kriegführung, Leipzig et al. Johann Ambrosius Barth et al, 1923, pp. 111–146, here p. 129.

21. Dietz (note 20), p. 129

22. *Ibid*.

23. On German war psychiatry, see Peter Riedesser and Alex Verderber,

'*Maschinengewehre hinter der Front*'. *Zur Geschichte der deutschen Militärpsychiatrie*, Frankfurt am Main, Fischer 1996.

24. Dietz (note 20), p. 30

25. See Militärstrafgesetzbuch für das Deutsche Reich, Article 84 (note 26).

26. See the comments in Article 84 in *Militärstrafgesetzbuch für das Deutsche Reich nebst dem Einführungsgesetze. Handausgabe unter Berücksichtigung der Rechstprechung des Reichgerichts und Reichsmilitärgerichts, sowie der einschlägigen Gesetze*, Verordnungen und Erlasse erläutert von Karl Endres, Kriegs-gerichsrat bei der k. 4 Division, Würzburg, Stahel'sche Verlags-Anstalt 1903, p. 72, with the statement: 'During combat: during confrontation with the enemy (whether against regular troops or snipers etc.). The approach of troops on their way to fight, sections bringing supplies of munitions, etc., are also included in the concept of "combat".'

27. '. . . un codice antiquato e non rispondente più all'epoca moderna'. See Forcella/Monticone (note 11), p. 153.

28. Translated from the original Italian text published by Forcella/Monticone (note 11), pp. 281–283.

29. Tony Ashworth uses the expression 'bad weather truces' when refer-ring to agreements reached in extreme climatic conditions, and gives a whole series of examples taken from the Anglo-German front in Flanders.

30. For the full text: *Codie penale per l'esercito des Regno d'Italia*, Edizione contenante la conferenza del Codico fra loro, con quelli del Codice e Leggi vigenti e del Codice militare abrogato, con molte appendici et un copiosissimo indice analitico-alfabetico. Compliazione dell'Avv Prof G Saredo. Firenze, G Pellas 1870, article 98, p. 43.

31. *Codice penale per l'esercito, op. cit.*, article 94, p. 42.

32. Letter from Karl Aldag written on 3 January 1915 at Fournes, near Lille, quoted according to Witkop, (note 7), p. 30.

33. Witkop (note 7), p. 30

34. *Ibid.*

35. *Ibid*, also for the following quotation.

36. See the illustrations in accounts published in England in January 1915 by *The Illustrated London News,* the *Daily Mirror* and the *Daily Sketch*. These illustrtions are also reproduced in Malcolm Brown/Shirley Seaton, *Christmas Truce. The Western Front 1914*, London, Pan Books 2001; Michael Jürgs, *Der kleine Frieden im Großen Krieg. Westfront 1914, Als Deutsche, Franzosen und Briten*

*gemeinsam Weihnachten feierten.* Munich, Bertelsmann 2003, p. 230, refers to non-illustrated accounts, published in German newspapers, but does not give more detailed references.

37. Kurt Adam, *'Prosit Neujaz! Eine Erinnerung an den 31, Dezember 1916'* in *Kriegzeitung der 1. Armee. Die 'Wacht im Westen' und 'Champagne-Kreigszeitung'*, Nr. 119, 1 January 1918, p. 5.

38. Albert Recanatini, *Di che brigate sei? La mia ha i colori di Camerano' Storia e racconti di soldati cameranesi nella Prima Guerre Mondiale,* Camerano, 1994, pp. 203–204, quoted here from Bianchi, *Follia* (note 6), p. 352.

39. Bianchi, *Follia,* (note 6), p. 352.

40. For a rapid view, see Thomas N Bisson, 'Peace of God, Truce of God' in Joseph R Strayer (Hg), *Dictionary of the Middle Ages,* Bd. 9. New York, Charles Scribner's Sons 1987, pp. 473–475.

41. Guiseppe Garzoni, *Diario della guerra del 1915* in Lucio Fabi (Hg), *La Gente e la Guerra. Documenti,* Udine, Il Camp 1990, p. 74, quoted here from Bianchi, *Follia* (note 6), p. 356. Garzoni here uses the expression *'modi cortesi e cavallereschi'* for the behaviour of the Austrians. The latter helped an Italian unit to evacuate its dead and wounded, after forcing it to surrender under artillery bombardment.

42. Wilhelm Deist has however shown that, during the final year of the war, the practice of 'an enthusiasm strike' had become a mass phenomenon on the German side. See Wilhelm Deist, Verdeckter Militärstreik im Kriegsjahr 1918, in Wolfram Wette (Hg), *Der Krieg des kleinen Mannes. Eine Militärgeschichte von unten,* Munich, Piper 1992, pp. 146–167.

43. Ernst Jünger, *Im Stahlgewittern* (1920). Here from the publication *Sämtliche Werke. Erste Abteilung. Tagebücher, Bd. 1. Der Erste Weltkrieg.* Stuttgart, Klett-Cotta 1978, pp. 64–65.

44. See Ashworth (note 3), p. 21.

45. Account by Dr Bernhard Lehnert, born in 1896, quoted in Wolf-Rüdiger Osburg, *'Und plötzlich bist du mitten im Krieg . . .' Zeutzeugen des Ersten Weltkriegs erinnern sich.* Münster, Aschendorff 2000, pp. 218–219.

46. Giani Stuparich, *Guerra del '15, (Dal taccuino di un volontario)* (1931), Turin, Einaudi 1980, Notes from 27 June 1915, pp.63–64. Stuparich (1891–1961), born in Trieste (then an Austrian city), had already been published before the war in the significant review *La Voce* of articles on the territories occupied by the Austrians. In 1915 he became a war volunteer. For his experience as a soldier, see: Fabio Todero, *Carolo et Giani Stuparich. Itinerari della Grande Guerra sulle tracce di due volontari triestini.* Trieste, Lint 1997.

47. 'Il fuoco è ormai vivo da per tutto e anche questa notte di domenica somiglia alle altre notti', Stuparich, *Guerra*, (Note 53), p. 64.
48. Ashworth (note 3), p. 46, Forcella/Monticone (note 11, pp. 247–249 gives the story of an Italian soldier born in Germany, working as a steward on the Hamburg-America shipping line. In 1915 he joined the Italian army as an officer-cadet, but his defeatist statements discredited him to such an extent with the military authorities that in November 1917 he was convicted for treason under Article 72 of the *Codice penale per l'esercito* and shot.
49. Carlo Salsa, *Trincee. Confidenze di un fante,* (1924) Preface by Luigi Santucci, Milano Mursia, 1995, pp. 157–158.
50. Forcella/Monticone (note 11), pp. 101–102, concerning RD who in May 1917 was condemned to a year in prison for a crime committed in December 1916 ('Refusal to obey commands and conversation with the enemy').
51. Forcella/Monticone (note 11).
52. Gabriel Chevallier, *La Peur* (1930), Nantes, Le Passeur 2002, pp. 161–162.
53. *Ibid*, pp. 256–257 for this quotation and the next one.
54. Toller, *op. cit.* (note 19), p. 59
55. Text developed by Giorgio Sbaraini from an interview by Micheletti. See *La Grande Guerra. Operai e contadini lombardi nel primo conflitto mondiale.* A cura di Sandro Fontana et Maurizio Pieretti, Milan, Regione Lombarda 1980 (Mondo popolare in Lombardia, 9), pp. 361–162.
56. *Ibid.* (note 55), p. 363
57. This is Tony Ashworth's explanation for the French mutinies in 1917. According to the figures, the Italian and Austro-Hungarian soldiers most often demonstrated their refusal to fight and surrendered as prisoners. Of 8,410,000 Frenchmen mobilized, 537,000 became prisoners or registered 'missing', while the Austrian side recorded 2,200,000 prisoners and missing out of 7,800,000 mobilized. See Ashworth (note 3), p. 205 and p. 255, note 4.
58. On this point, see Bernd Ulrich/Benjamin Ziemann (Hg), *Krieg im Frieden. Die umkämpfte Erinnerung an den Ersten Weltkrieg. Quellen und Dokumente,* Frankfurt am Main, Fischer 1997, and also Markus Pöhlmann, *Kriegsgeschichte und Geschichtspolitik, Der Erste Weltkrieg. Die amtliche deutsche Militärgeschichtsschreibung 1914–1956,* Paderborn et al., Ferdinand Schöningh, 2002.
59. In 1915 Bensa, Stoppato and Raimondo formed part of the interventionists who insisted on Italy entering the war. See Giorgio Rochat,

'L'inchiesta su Caporetto' in *L'Esercito italiano da Vittorio Veneto a Mussolini (1919–1925)*, Bari, Laterza, 1967, pp. 67–128, here p. 71.

60. *Dall'Isonzo al Piave, 24 ottobre–9 novembre 1917*, Bd II, *Le cause e le responsabilità degli avvenimenti*, Rome, Poligrafico Ministero della Guera 1919, p. 439.

61. Paulus Bünzly, 'Die Akten' in *Die Weltbühne* 18 February (1922), pp. 126–127, quoted here from Ulrich/Ziemann, *Krieg im Frieden* (note 66), p. 72.

62. See Jean-Jacques Becker, *Le Carnet B. Les pouvoirs publics et l'antimilitarisme avant la guerre de 1914*, Paris, Klincksieck, 1973.

63. See Catherine Slater, *Defeatists and their Enemies. Political Invective in France 1914–1918*, Oxford, Oxford University Press, 1981.

64. Ernst Drahn/Susanne Leonhard, *Unterirdische Literatur im revolutionären Deutschland während des Weltkrieges*, Berlin, Verlag Gesellschaft unde Erziehung 1920, p. 13, attributes the tract to the Berlin Young Socialists Movement, strongly influenced by Karl Liebknecht.

65. *Spartakusbriefe*, Herausgegeben vom Institut für Marxismus-Leninismus beim Zentralkomitee der Sozialistischen Einheitspartei Deutschlands, Berlin, Dietz 1958, p. 27, and also Drahn/Leonhard, (note 72), p. 35.

66. Extract from the journal *Wperjod*, quoted in *Lager, Front oder Heimat. Deutsche Kriegsgefangene in Sowjetrußland 1917 bis 1920*. Hrsg. Von einem deutsch-russischen Redaktionkollegium unter Leitung von Inge Pardon und Waleri W Shurawljow. 2 Bde. Munich et al. K G Saur, 1994, quotation vol. 1, p. 3.

67. See the account on Satka, south of the Urals, in which German prisoners of war wished to take part in the 1 May ceremonies, 'marching under the banner of the Internationale and of Social Democracy. The ceremonies made an impressive sight. The whole parade was accompanied by music, revolutionary singing and speeches. Men from east and west, still until yesterday set one against the other at the word of the capital into a murderous battle, began to fraternize. The distant city of Satka created active links with the front. It understood with all its "being" the absurdity of the killing perpetrated far away. It saw prisoners of war under red banners, felt the enemy's driving power, but at heart felt neither anger nor any desire for vengeance. During all these minutes, it became sharply aware of love and brotherhood between nations.' Quoted from *Lager, Front oder Heimat* (note 66), vol. 1, p. 4.

68. Decree from the Reich's war ministry, relating to the treatment of German-nationality soldiers returning from their Russian captivity

(Berlin, 19 March 1918), quoted from *Lager, Front oder Heimat* (note 66), vol.1, p. 58.

69. Generalleutnant Constantin von Altrock, 'Das deutsche Volksheer' in Max Schwarte (Hg.), *Der Große Krieg 1914–1918. Bd. 10, Die Organisation der Kriegführung.* Leipzig et al., Johann Ambrosius Barth et all., 1923, pp. 511–554, here p. 546.

70. General von Kuhl, 'Entstehung, Durchführung und Zusammenbruch der deutschen Offensive von 1918' in *Die Ursachen des Deutschen Zusammenbruches im Jahre 1918. Erste Abteilung. Der militärische und außenpolitische Zusammenburch,* Dritter Band. Berlin, Deutsche Verlagsgesellschaft für Politik und Geschichte 1928, pp. 211–212; also for the following quotation.

71. On this point see Benjamin Ziemann, 'Enttäuschte Erwartung und kollektive Erschöpfung. Die deutschen Soldaten an der Westfront 1918 auf dem Weg sur Revolution'. In Jörg Duppler/Gerhard P Groß (Hg) *Kriegsende 1918. Ereignis, Wirkung, Nachwirkung.* Munich, R Oldenbourg Verlag 1999, pp. 1965–182, quotation p.171. See also Deist Verdeckter Militärstreik (note 42).

72. See Richard Bessel, 'Die Heimkehr der Soldaten, Das Bild der Frontsoldaten' in der Öffentlichkeit der Weimarer Republik. In Gerhard Hirschfeld/Gerd Krumeich/Irina Renz (Hg): *'Keiner fühlt sich hier mehr als Mensch . . .' Erlebnis under Wirkung des Ersten Weltkriegs.* Frankfurt am Main, Fischer 1996, pp. 260–282.

73. Henri Barbusse, 'Le monde nouveau' in *Paroles d'un combattant,* Paris, Flammarion, 1920, p. 221; also for the following quotation.

74. André, Marty's brother, was one of the initiators of the mutiny and was condemned as a result to twenty years of forced labour. A spectacular campaign of support achieved his release in 1923. In the same year, André and Michel Marty publicly incited the troops occupying the Ruhr to fraternize. In September 1925, Michel was convicted and sentenced, by default, to eight months in prison and fined 1,000 francs for inciting soldiers to disobedience in an article published by *L'Humanité* on 2 February under the title: 'Down with the Moroccan war'; see the entries by Andreu Balent, Jean Maitron and Claude Pennetier on André and Michel Marty in *Dictionnaire biographique du mouvement ouvrier français,* CD-ROM version.

75. M Marty, *Fraternization. Esquisse historique de la tradition du proletariat français,* Paris, Librairie de l'Humanité 1925, pp. 35–36.

76. *Le Feu. Organe de l'Association républicaine des Anciens Combattants,* third year, September 1930, p.1.

77. *Das Reichsbanner. Zeitung des Reichsbanner Schwarts-Rot-Gold. Bund der republikanischen Kriegsteilnehmer,* Nr. 38 vom 17

September 1932, Beilage für die Gaue Berlin und Halle, quoted here from Ulrich/Ziemann, *Krieg im Frieden* (note 58), p. 113.

78. On the history of the foundation of the CIAMAC, see Léon Viala, *Les Relations internationales entre les associations de mutilés de guerre et d'Anciens Combattants*, Paris, Les Cahiers de l'Union fédérale des associations françaises des victimes de la guerre et anciens combattants (c.1930), also Antoine Prost, *Les Anciens Combattants et la société française 1914–1939*, Paris, Presses de la Fondation nationale des sciences politiques, 1977, vol. 1, pp. 103–113.

79. 'CIAMAC. *Conférence Internationale des Association de Mutilés de Guerre et Anciens Combattants/Mitteilungen der Internationalen Arbeitsgemeinschaft der Verbände der Kreigsopfer und Kriegsteilnehmer* 6 (October–November 1933) Cahiers 8–9, p. 196.

80. See in Cahier 6 of the *CIAMAC* (note 79), p. 206, the communiqué dated 25 September 1933 from the Swiss Postal Service, informing the review of the decision of the Minister for the Reich Postal Service in Berlin.

81. Article by Hanns Oberlindober in the Cahier dated February 1934 of the *Deutschen Kriegsopferversorgung*, quoted in Cahier 7 of the *CIAMAC* (January–February 1934), H.1, p. 15.

82. *CIAMAC* (note 79), p.15.

83. See the chapter on 'the Franco-German *rapprochement*, dream and deception', in Prost, *Anciens Combattants* (note 78), pp. 177–187.

84. *Deutsche Kriegsopferversorgung* 4 (1936), Nr. 12, pp. 12–16, here p.13, quoted in Susanne Brandt, *Vom Kreigsschauplatz zum Gedächtnisraum, Die Westfront 1914–1940*, Baden-Baden, Nomos 2000, p. 222.

# 4  Fraternization and Revolution in Russia: Marc Ferro

1. *Carskaja Armija v. period mirovoj voiny i febral'skoj revoljuci,* Kazan, 1922, *passim* also Kal'nickii Ja, *Ot febralja k. Oktjabrja.*

2. *Ibid.* p. 67, and *Vospominauija frontovnika,* Xar'kov, 1964.

3. *Ibid,* p. 75.

4. Quoted in the *Bulletin de Presse de Petrograd* for 25 May 1917.

5. *Revoljucionnoe dvizenie v Rossii posle sverzenija camoderzavija,* Moscow, 1957, p. 617.

6. We have analysed this in 'Le soldat russe en 1917. Indiscipline, pacifisme, patriotisme et révolution', *Annales (ESC)* 1917, 1, p. 14–40.

7. *Cf.* note 5, p. 613.

8. *Cf.* G. Wetting, 'Die Rolle des Russischen Armée im Revolutionaren

Machtkampf 1917', *Forschungen zur Osteuropäishen Geschichte*, 1967, pp. 46–389.

9.   *Cf.* note 6, *passim.*
10. *Cf.* note 5, p. 654.
11. *Razlozhenie Armii, v Rossii v 1917g*, pp. 37–38.
12. Browder R P and Kerensky A F, *The Provisional Government 1917*, Stanford 1961, vol. 2, p. 903.
13. Lenin, 'The signification of fraternizations' *Pravda*, 18 April 1917.
14. *Isvestia*, 2 May 1917.
15. *Isvestia*, 6 May 1917.
16. Refer to *Révolution de 1917*, reissued Albin Michel 1997, pp. 311–336.
17. *Ibid*, pp. 347–372.
18. *Revoljucionnoe Dvizenie v Rossii v aprile*, M. 1958, pp. 481–565.
19. *Revoljuccionoe Dvizenie v Rossii v mae i june 1917g*, pp. 329–389.
20. A Kerenski, *The Catastrophe*, New York, 1927, p. 191.
21. *Cf.* note 12, pp. 913–914.
22. *Cf.* note 20, p. 203.
23. Telegrame NJ in the *Bulletin de presse de Petrograd*, (note 4).
24. *Revoljucionnoe Dvizenie v Rossii v avguste*, 1917g, p. 263.
25. Tkacuk, A G, *Revoljuccionnoe Dvizenie v armijax jugozapadnogo i rumins kogo frontov nakanune i v period velikogo Okjahrja*. L'vov, 1968.

# The Authors

**Marc Ferro:** Co-director of *Annales*, Director of Studies at the Ecole des Hautes Etudes en Sciences Sociales in Paris, specializes in the Great War, the Russian Revolution and the history of the cinema. For ten years he directed and presented the programme *Histoires parallèles* for the Arte television channel. Internationally acknowledged for his expertise, he achieved public recognition for his major biographies (of the Tsar Nicolas II and of Pétain), his work on the Russian Revolution and also his reflections on writing about history and colonialism.

**Malcolm Brown:** Independent historian, attached to the Imperial War Museum, London, since 1989. He contributed five volumes to the Imperial War Museum series of books about the two world wars which was awarded a Duke of Westminster Medal for Military Literature in 2005. He is also the author of *Tommy Goes to War*, *Verdun 1916* (published in French by Editions Perrin in 2006), and co-author, with Shirley Seaton, of *Christmas Truce*, first published by Leo Cooper in 1984 and reprinted three times by Pan Macmillan. In 2002 he became an Honorary Research Fellow of the Centre for First World War Studies at the University of Birmingham.

**Rémy Cazals:** Professor at the University of Toulouse-Le Mirail, he edited the *Carnets de guerre de Louis Barthas, tonneleur,* an essential first-hand account of the trenches, and many other combatant narratives. He has organized several conferences on the history of the First World War, including publication of the proceedings, and wrote *Les Mots de 14–18* (Toulouse, PUM, 2003).

**Olaf Mueller:** A German literary researcher, he has contributed to many books on the Great War and the history of pacifists, in -

particular *Le Chemin des Dames, de l'événement à la mémoire* (Paris, Stock, 2004).

**Helen McPhail:** An independent writer and translator, she specialises in work on literary and social aspects of the First World War. Translations include *Men at War* by Stéphane Audoin-Rouzeau and *In the Wake of War,* by Antoine Prost (both published by Berg in 1992). Her book on French civilian life under the German occupation of Northern France, *The Long Silence*, was published by I.B. Tauris in 1999 and, as Chairman of the Wilfred Owen Association for several years, she has co-authored books on English poets of 1914–1918. She is an Honorary Research Associate at the Centre for First World War Studies at the University of Birmingham.

# Brief Bibliography

## 1. Anthologies, Collections, Books with Substantial Quoted Material

BACONNIER, Gérard, MINET, André, SOLER, Louis, *La Plume au fusil. Les Poilus du Midi à travers leur correspondance*, Toulouse, Privat, 1985.

BERNARD, Jean-Pierre, MAGNAN, Claude, SAUVAGEON, Jean, SERRE, Robert, SEYVE, Claude, SEYVE, Michel, '*Je suis mouton comme les autres*'. *Lettres, carnets et mémoires de poilus, drômois et de leurs familles*, Valence, Editions Peuple Libre et Notre Temps, 2002.

BIRNSTIEL, Eckart and CAZALS, Rémy, ed. *Ennemis fraternels 1914–1915. Hans Rodewald, Antoine Bieisse, Fernand Tailhades. Carnets de guerre et de captivité*, Toulouse, PUM, 2002.

BOUTEFEU, Roger, *Les Camarades. Soldats français et allemands au combat, 1914–1918*. Paris, Fayard, 1966.

CAZALS, Rémy, MARQUIE, Claude, PINIES, René, *Années cruelles 1914–1918*, Villelongue d'Aude, Atelier du Gué, 1998 (1983).

CRU, Jean Norton, *Du témoignage*, Paris, Gallimard, 1930.

DUCASSE, André, *La Guerre racontée par les combattants. Anthologie des écrivains du front (1914–1918)*, Paris, Flammarion, 1932, 2 vols.

DUCASSE, André, MEYER, Jacques, PERREUX, Gabriel, *Vie et mort des Français 1914–1918*, Paris, Hachette, 1959.

GUENO, Jean-Pierre and LAPLUME, Yves, *Paroles de poilus. Lettres et carnets du front, 1914–1918*, Paris, Librio – Radio France 1998.

MEYER, Jacques, *Les Soldats de la Grande Guerre*, Paris, Hachette, 'La Vie quotidienne' series, 1966.

NICOT, Jean, *Les poilus ont la parole. Lettres du front, 1917–1918*, Brussels, Complexe, 1998.

PROST, Antoine, *Les Anciens Combattants et la Sociétié française, 1914–1918*, Paris, Presse de la Fondation nationale des Sciences politques, 1977, 3 vols.

## 2. Reflections on Original Sources

AUDOIN-ROUZEAU, Stéphane, *14–18. A travers leurs journaux, les combattants des tranchées,* Paris, Armand Colin, 1986 (*Men at War 1914–1918: National Sentiment and Trench Journalism in France during the First World War,* tr. Helen McPhail, Oxford, Berg, 1992).

CAZALS, Rémy and ROUSSEAU, Frédéric, *14–18, le cri d'une géneration,* Toulouse, Privat, 2001.

CRU, Jean Norton, *Témoins. Essai d'analyse et de critique des souvenirs de combattants édités en français de 1915 à 1928,* Paris, Les Etincelles, 1929 (reissued Presses universitaires de Nancy, 1993).

JEANNENEY, Jean-Noël, 'Les archives des commissions de contrôle postal aux armées (1916–1918): une source précieuse pour l'histoire contemporaine de l'opinion et des mentalités' in *Revue d'histoire moderne et contemporaine,* 1968, pp. 209–233.

ROUSSEAU, Frédéric, *Le Procès des témoins de la Grande Guerre. L'affaire Norton Cru,* Paris, Seuil, 2003.

TURBERGUE, Jean-Pierre, *1914–1918: les journaux des tranchées, la Grande Guerre écrite par les poilus,* Paris, Editions italiques et Ministère de la Défense, 1999.


## 3. Studies of Fraternization

ASHWORTH, Tony, *Trench Warfare 1914–1918: the Live and Let Live System,* London, Pan Books, 2000 (1980).

BARLUET, Alain, 'Les fraternizations de Noël' in *L'Histoire,* no. 107, January 1988.

BROWN, Malcolm and SEATON, Shirley, *Christmas Truce,* London, Pan Books, 1994 (1984).

GALTIER-BOISSIERE, Jean, 'Fraternizations', *Le Crapouillot,* August 1930, pp. 44–48.

FANTIN, Mathieu, *Les Poilus parlent aux Boches, les Boches parlent aux Poilus,* mémoire de maîtrise, University of Toulouse-II, 2002.

JÜRGS, Michael, *Der Kleine Frieden in Grossen Krieg,* Munich, Bertelsmann, 2003.

VERMEULEN, Coralie, *Les Fraternizations pendant la Grande Guerre,* mémoire de maîtrise, University of Picardy, 2000.

# 4. Some Recent Publications on the First World War and its Combatants

BACH, André, *Fusillés pour l'exemple*, Paris, Tallandier, 2003.

BIANCHI, Bruna, *La Follia e la Fuga. Nevrosi di guerra, diserzione e disobbedienza nell'esercito italiano (1915–1918)*, Rome, Bulzoni, 2001.

BROWN, Malcolm, *The Imperial War Museum Book of the Western Front*, Pan Books, 2001.

BROWN, Malcolm, *The Imperial War Museum Book of 1914: The Men Who Went to War*, Sidgwick & Jackson, 2004.

CAZALS, Rémy, *Les Mots de 14–18*, Toulouse, PUM, 2003.

CAZALS, Rémy, PICARD, Emmanuelle and ROLLAND, Denis, eds, *La Grande Guerre, pratiques et expériences*, Toulouse, Privat, 2005.

COCHET, François, *Survivre au front, 1914–1918, les poilus entre contrainte et consentement*, 14–18 Editions, 2005.

CORNS, CATHRYN & JOHN HUGHES-WILSON, *Bindfold and Alone: British Military Executions in the Great War*, Cassell, 2001.

FULLER, John G, *Troop Morale and Popular Culture in the British and Dominion Armies 1914–1918*, Oxford, Clarendon Press, 1990.

HOLMES, Richard, *Tommy: The British Soldier on the Western Front 1914-1918*, Harper Collins, 2004.

OFFENSTADT, Nicolas, *Les Fusillés de la Grande Guerre et la mémoire collective (1914–1999)*, Paris, Odile Jacob, 2002 (1999).

OFFENSTADT, Nicolas, ed., *Le Chemin des Dames, de l'événement à la mémoire*, Paris, Stock, 2004.

PROST, Antoine, 'Les limites de la brutalisation. Tuer sur le front occidental, 1914–1918', *Vingtième siècle, revue d'histoire*, no. 81, Jan–March 2004, pp. 5–20.

PROST, Antoine and WINTER, Jay, *Penser la Grande Guerre. Un essai d'historiographie*, Paris, Seuil, 2004.

ROUSSEAU, Frédéric, *La Guerre censurée. Une histoire des combattants européens de 14–18*, Paris, Seuil, 2003 (1999).

SHEFFIELD, Gary, *Forgotten Victory, The First World War: Myths and Realities*, Headline, 2001

SHEPHARD, Ben, *A War of Nerves: Soldiers and Psychiatrists 1914–1918*, Jonathan Cape, 2000.

SMITH, Leonard V., *Between Mutiny and Obedience. The Case of the French Fifth Infantry Division during World War I*, Princeton University Press, 1994.

*THE WIPERS TIMES* (reprinted trench magazine), Introduction by Malcolm Brown, Little Books, 2006.

# Index